When Fiction *and* Philosophy Meet

A Conversation with
Flannery O'Connor and Simone Weil

MERCER UNIVERSITY PRESS

Endowed by

TOM WATSON BROWN
and
THE WATSON-BROWN FOUNDATION, INC.

When Fiction *and* Philosophy Meet

A Conversation with
Flannery O'Connor and Simone Weil

E. Jane Doering *&* Ruthann Knechel Johansen

For Connie and Ron,
with sincere appreciation
for your support and
friendship;
Ruthann K Johansen

MERCER UNIVERSITY PRESS
Macon, Georgia
1979–2019
40 Years of Publishing Excellence

MUP/ H971

© 2019 by Mercer University Press
Published by Mercer University Press
1501 Mercer University Drive
Macon, Georgia 31207
All rights reserved

9 8 7 6 5 4 3 2 1

Books published by Mercer University Press are printed on acid-free paper
that meets the requirements of the American National Standard for
Information Sciences—Permanence of Paper for Printed Library Materials.

Printed and bound in the United States.

This book is set in Adobe Caslon.

ISBN   978-0-88146-696-6
Cataloging-in-Publication Data is available from the Library of Congress

Dedicated with gratitude to the memory of
Simone Weil and *Flannery O'Connor*
and to those with aspiration, courage, and wisdom
to love the invisible in all visible forms.

Contents

Preface

"The Red Virgin" and "The Red Clay Virgin"

In 2016, award-winning poet Rita Reese published *The Book of Hulga*, inspired by a letter Flannery O'Connor wrote to Betty Hester on September 24, 1955: "If I were to live long enough and develop as an artist to the proper extent, I would like to write a comic novel about a woman—and what is more comic and terrible than the angular intellectual proud woman approaching God inch by inch with ground teeth?"[1] The woman to whom O'Connor referred was French philosopher Simone Weil about whom she first learned in the 1950s as some of Weil's works were translated into English. Why was a young Catholic fiction writer in the southern United States interested in a European political activist, secular philosopher of Jewish forebears? Her works were attracting extraordinary attention in Europe and the United States on their publication more than half a dozen years after her death. Contrary to the usual notably successful student and intellectual, eligible upon passing the *agrégation* exam for an appointment to the highest teaching post in a *lycée* or one of the faculties of a university, Weil had instead requested that her first teaching assignment be in a workers' region of France. She was assigned to Le Puy, a mining center of the Loire River coal-mining basin. Her empathy for laborers and other socially marginalized groups and an indifference to her appearance inspired a scornful professor to dub her sardonically "the Red Virgin," a label she accepted with equanimity and good humor.

Building her collection of forty-nine poems on the character of Hulga in Flannery O'Connor's "Good Country People," Reese's "The Red Clay Virgin" links O'Connor—with humor, tenderness, and biting precision—to the angular woman with ground teeth described in O'Connor's 1955 letter to Hester. Indeed, Reese's entire collection insinuates the influence of Simone Weil on the creative consciousness of Flannery O'Connor.

---

[1] Flannery O'Connor, *The Habit of Being: Letters of Flannery O'Connor*, ed. Sally Fitzgerald (New York: Vintage Books, 1979), 105–106.

What in Weil's life and thought drew O'Connor's attention, and what was her indebtedness to Weil? Certainly not the first to note the fiction writer's references to the French philosopher, Reese joins scholars such as Robert Coles, Jane Detweiler, Sarah Gordon, Ruthann Knechel Johansen, Lee Sturma, Ralph Wood, and Brad Gooch who have considered particular elements of O'Connor's interest in Weil.

As the first comprehensive examination that juxtaposes the ideas of these two twentieth-century intellectuals, this book delineates the central concerns, both parallel and contradictory, and assesses the overlapping ethical and artistic values expressed in O'Connor's and Weil's work. Since her death in 1964, Flannery O'Connor has had a constant readership among students and scholars who discuss and weigh various interpretations of her finely crafted fictional narratives. We seek in this study to deepen the perceptions of those readers and to refine the skills of anagogical reading, which require the capacity to see beyond literal meanings to a spiritual or mystical sense, that O'Connor herself so desired. Simone Weil has gained an increasing number of readers worldwide who value her prophetic voice that witnesses to injustice and oppression, both social and political, and to a religious vision of the primacy of human dignity. Flannery O'Connor's reaction to the French philosopher's works, as O'Connor herself was composing her early works, illustrates the magnetic attraction of Weil's concepts. These two intellectuals had a dialogical approach to the transmission of their ideas, wanting readers to grapple with the concepts embodied in their writings and to discern the relevance through their own exploration. We intend to further that dialogue by applying specific religious philosophical concepts of Simone Weil to the analyses of selected fictional works of O'Connor.

Goals of O'Connor and Weil

Both women keenly desired to perceive the reality of good and evil impinging on human existence and to make this truth apparent to their contemporaries. They believed that truth is eternal but must be "transposed" and translated, generation after generation, that is, reformulated in language appropriate to each age. The vocation of each woman was to be a vehicle for the truth, while diminishing the role of the ego in transmitting the message. For each writer, this message could be summed up in Christ's two most important commandments: "You shall love the Lord your God with all your heart, and with all your soul, and with all your strength, and with all your mind; and your neighbor as yourself" (Lk 10:27). These commandments are more easily proclaimed than truly embodied as love in every small action.

The personal relationship each of these women had with the supernatural, and their deep concern about the modern world's nihilistic drift, gave them a feeling of being in exile amid their contemporaries who had cut themselves off from a sense of the divine, thus diminishing, if not eliminating, the influence of Christian faith. The secular collectivity had become almost the only source of effective authority. This isolation strengthened both women's sense of mission, as they maintained a clear grasp of the essential balance to be sustained between the individual and the collective, fundamental to nurturing mutual respect and harmony within any social group. Their belief that truth, love, and justice are one, despite wide-ranging differences among people, is reflected throughout their works. In her May 15, 1942 letter to Father Perrin, now called her "Spiritual Autobiography," Weil writes: "The Incarnation of Christianity implies a harmonious solution of the problem of the relations between the individual and the collective. Harmony in the Pythagorean sense; the just balance of contraries." She goes on to explain, "This harmony exists wherever the intelligence, remaining in its place can be exercised without hindrance and can reach the complete fulfillment of its function....The special function of the intelligence requires total liberty, implying the right to deny everything, and allowing of no domination."[2]

The Book Landscape

By placing these two writers side-by-side, our intent is first to demonstrate how reading the two writers together not only illuminates Flannery

---

[2] Simone Weil, *Waiting for God*, trans. Emma Crauford (New York: HarperCollins, 2000), 33-4. (Hereafter cited as *WG*.)

O'Connor's fiction but also makes manifest Simone Weil's religious philosophy, which evolved over her short life. By fulfilling the first objective we propose a second, that the ethical and artistic responses Weil and O'Connor made to their worlds contribute to their continuing relevance for the twenty-first-century postmodern and post-Christian world.

The first chapter considers the worlds and contexts that influenced the intellectual and spiritual formation of Weil and O'Connor, noting particularly the penetrating attention both writers gave to social and political conditions in their separate worlds, to perennial matters of human conscience and behavior, and to the impact their contexts had on their philosophical and artistic vocations.

Chapter 2 discusses the central concerns, both similar and contrasting ones, of Weil and O'Connor and the intellectual mentors who contributed to the development of their thought and art. Applying the Greek concept of *poiesis*, the chapter examines the methods each writer employed to shape distinctly creative and dialogical responses through which to express her concerns. The subsequent four Chapters 3–6 identify six of these concerns found in Weil's writings that were read by Flannery O'Connor, who illustrated similar ones in her fiction.

The three works of Simone Weil that Flannery O'Connor refers to, "Letter to a Priest," *Waiting for God*, and her *Notebooks*, were all written in the last two to three years of Weil's life. Though they may have been composed for a particular purpose, they each hold traces of the many facets of her religious philosophy. Not until after her 1938 major mystical experience, which she described to Father Perrin in the words: "Christ himself came down and took possession of me," (*WG* 27) did she give serious attention to keeping up with her *Notebooks*, which contain the raw data of her thought as it had developed or was intended to be developed in the future. She had had two prior contacts with Catholicism: the first in 1935, listening to the wives of the fishermen in a little Portuguese village singing an ancient lament, praying for their husbands' safety, and the second in 1937 while visiting a Romanesque chapel of Santa Maria degli Angeli in Assisi, Italy, where she felt compelled to go down on her knees. These experiences are all beautifully described in a letter to Father Perrin (*WG* 26-27). So, although the concept featured in any chapter of this book may focus on a particular letter or essay, a full understanding of its context will draw on citations from all the works of Weil, concentrating on those that O'Connor read.

In chapter 3, we highlight the centrality of Weil's concepts of attention and apprenticeship, two prime beacons of thought that run through her philosophy. Drawing upon Weil's "Reflections on the Right Use of School Studies with a View to the Love of God" and "The Love of Our Neighbor," we trace O'Connor's depiction of *attention* and *apprenticeship* found in "The Artificial Nigger" and "The Displaced Person." Using Simone Weil's "Letter to a Priest" and "Love of the Order of the World," chapter 4 outlines Weil's ideas about beauty and charity, juxtaposing them to Flannery O'Connor's embodiment of the presence and absence of those virtues in "Good Country People," "Revelation," and "The Lame Shall Enter First." From the discussion of caritas and its distortions made visible in the characters of Hulga and Ruby Turpin, and of Sheppard in "The Lame Shall Enter First," chapter 5 proceeds to Weil's profound ideas about suffering and affliction in "The Love of God and Affliction." O'Connor turns her sharp irony on Asbury who fears he is suffering on the verge of death in "The Enduring Chill." In *The Violent Bear It Away*, O'Connor's prophetic powers superbly depict the agonizing and disturbing realities of affliction and the high cost of a prophetic vocation in a nihilistic age. Chapter 6 takes up the central issues of grace, which both authors found essential for human beings, and Weil's enigmatic notion of decreation, explicating these ideas through O'Connor's frequently anthologized "A Good Man Is Hard to Find" and "A View of the Woods," and a composite of Weil's works in *Waiting for God* and her *Notebooks*. The book concludes with a consideration of the contemporary relevance of the ideas of Simone Weil and Flannery O'Connor for the social, political, and religious challenges facing our twenty-first-century world.

Notes from the Authors and Interpretive Strategy

The pleasure of reading and writing seriously about Simone Weil began when I (Jane) was a very mature graduate student; I had waited for my four children to finish their graduate education before returning to complete my PhD. At Northwestern University, a presentation I gave on Simone Weil attracted the notice of one of the professors, who offered to be my thesis director. Writing on such a lofty intellect intrigued me then and has never stopped challenging me to rise to new heights in my thinking. Because my first love is literature, the fine literary works, both classic and contemporary, this extraordinary young professor of philosophy brought into her teaching and then later into her religious writings resonated with my own reflections. I have been applying her religious and philosophical concepts ever since to my reading, writing, and publishing, finding that they open new depths of understanding for me.

I (Ruthann) first read Flannery O'Connor and Simone Weil in the 1970s. I read them separately; one I regarded initially as a gifted, though bizarre, fiction writer, the other as a profound spiritual thinker who expanded my own thinking. As a teacher and literary scholar, I published first on Flannery O'Connor. During the 1990s when I read Simone Weil more intently and began to teach several of her essays, I discerned striking resonances of religious outlook between the two writers, which significantly enlarged my understanding and interpretation of each writer. Closer examination of these resonances as Jane and I both taught courses that included works by Simone Weil and Flannery O'Connor, among many other fine writers, led us to want to put our thoughts together more systematically. We began with great pleasure the manuscript: "When Fiction and Philosophy Meet."

In deciding to coauthor this book, our challenge has been to represent each writer as accurately as possible. The purpose of our efforts is to acquaint O'Connor readers with the significance of Simone Weil's religious philosophy in Flannery O'Connor's stories and to illustrate how Weil's philosophy, when embodied in fiction, reveals the lived realities of the human condition. Our intention to honor the integrity of both writers requires the readers' willingness to cross disciplinary boundaries as both these writers did during their lifetimes. Recognizing the marked differences between philosophy and fiction, we did not want to privilege either writer. Rather we hoped to bring these two remarkable women, philosopher and artist, into a four-voiced dialogue: Simone Weil and Flannery O'Connor with Doering and Johansen. Our decision to write in two styles—one in the style of philosophical exposition and the other applying the methods of literary criticism—reflects our desire to engage each writer in the forms of her own genre and to encourage readers, who may know neither author, one, or both of these writers, to enter the dialogue with Simone Weil and Flannery O'Connor as we also project their continuing relevance for our own time.

Chapter 1

Two Twentieth-Century Women and the World

SIMONE WEIL

Simone Weil's continuing relevance arises from her penetrating intelligence and her determination to disseminate in written form her thinking on what became her religious philosophy. Her dedication to alleviate affliction and to have others accept the reality behind human existence makes her a visionary seeker of the wisdom that issues from suffering. Her uncompromising moral absoluteness in the belief that God advocates love of one's fellow man[1] and repudiates aggression in any form that gratuitously harms others affected her decision to refuse baptism in the Catholic Church[2] and to reject the militancy in the Hebrew Bible. Despite her refusal to join the church, the Incarnation, the Passion, and her love of the Eucharist became, after her mystical experience, the principal focus of her writings on humankind's teleological purpose. She undauntedly entered domains previously reserved for males only and advocated strict vigilance over all those who assume positions of authority.

Poet Czesaw Miłosz lauded her intelligence and the precision of her style as a result of giving "a very high degree of attention ... to the sufferings of mankind." In his Nobel laureate acceptance speech, he cited her writings as influential on his own thought and writing style. For her impact on both believers and nonbelievers, he considered her "France's rare gift to the contemporary world."[3]

---

[1] Use of the masculine noun and pronoun was the style of Simone Weil; we will keep it where appropriate.

[2] For further insights into the complexity of her decision not to be baptized see Eric O. Springsted's excellent reflection "Simone Weil and Baptism,"

http://www.laici.va/content/dam/laici/documenti/donna/culturasocieta/en glish/simone-weil-and-baptism.pdf.

[3] Czesław Miłosz, *Emperor of the Earth: Modes of Eccentric Vision* (Berkeley: University of California Press, 1960), 85, 98.

Suffering of Humankind

The carnage of war and the oppression in the workplace from France's industrialization between the two wars made an intense impact on Simone Weil's thinking. As a young girl, she saw suffering up close. She was just six when the massacre began on the deadly battlefields of the "Great War," decimating France's male population, both civilian and military. The French hospitals were overflowing with wounded servicemen; hardly a family was spared from grievous sorrow.[4] Doctor Bernard Weil, assigned to serve in several military hospitals, was accompanied, contrary to military rules, by Mme Weil and their two children. Consequently, young Simone observed at close hand horrendous combat-related traumatic suffering.

Attentive to the distress of others, she and her brother André each adopted a soldier who had no caring family; they wrote to them and sent gifts of candy, chocolate, and small funds they had earned. As a sensitive child, Simone acquired a deep sense of human tragedy and the futility of trying to solve problems by using force, which feeds mindlessly on itself.

Her Education

In France where the best schools are reserved for the most erudite, she easily gained entry to prestigious educational institutions. Later, as a student, she sought a philosophical understanding of, as well as a resolution to, the pain mankind imposes on others. This goal directed the course of Simone Weil's philosophical formation as a young intellectual, first in a secular context and then in the framework of her evolving religious consciousness. Anguish over mankind's aggressively destructive behavior compelled her to confront with dogged determination the incongruity between the uplifting human desire for good and the downward drag of self-serving evil. Everything she wrote had an experiential

---

[4] According to the online *The New Encyclopedia Britannica* (Chicago: Encyclopedia Britannica, 2005) 73.3 percent of the eight and a half million Frenchmen mobilized were killed, wounded, missing, or made prisoner in during the hostilities, which translates into the loss or suffering of seven out of every ten men. https://www.britannica.com/event/World-War-I/Killed-wounded-and-missing.

component; her observations taught her that humankind rarely employs its gift of rationality to strive toward its own common good.

At first, her reliance on an Enlightenment type of rationality, which affirms the value and perfectibility of human beings, individually and collectively, made her increasingly confident in achieving an ultimate good through logical actions. In this mode of thought, determination in achieving the desired goal would counter irrationality in the human psyche; human beings could, through their own striving, realize a society dedicated to the common good. At age fifteen, in 1924, she entered the Lycée Victor-Duruy for her introductory philosophical training under the metaphysician and psychologist René Le Senne. Then, under the direction of humanist philosopher Émile Chartier (a.k.a. Alain), she continued her studies on human perception and the process of knowing. Independently, she pursued her own reflections on the importance of encountering obstacles in work and then overcoming them by reflection. To this end, she greatly lamented the separation of manual work from intellectual work.

Simone made her final preparation for the *agrégation* diploma at the select École Normale Supérieure (ENS)[5] where her concluding thesis was "Science et Perception dans Descartes," a theme directly inspired by the ideas and methods of Alain.[6]

Contradictions and Values

Early on, she was viewed as a very bright, sensitive, and philosophic young person. Much later she recounts to Father Joseph-Marie Perrin her grief at age fourteen from feeling that her intelligence was insufficient for her to be included in the transcendent realm wherein truth abides. She preferred to die rather than live without that truth.[7] Her work with Le Senne, whose research was on the mental process of deal-

---

[5] A French higher education establishment, with the goal of training professors, researchers, and public administrators.

[6] Gilbert Kahn, "Simone Weil et Alain," *Cahiers Simone Weil*, 14.3 (September 1991): 209.

[7] Simone Weil, *Waiting for God*, trans. Emma Crauford (New York: HarperCollins, 2000), 23. (Hereafter cited as *WG*.)

ing with two contradictory truths and of prioritizing values as the criteria of obligations, was very valuable to her. His emphasis on the challenge of coping with contradictions in the process of thinking and identifying assumed values behind interpretations remained essential pillars of Weil's philosophy.

Weil developed her own thinking on these concepts in two late companion essays, "A Few Reflections on the Notion of Value"[8] and "Essay on the Notion of Reading."[9] Her formative thinking on these "Notions" is evident in her *Notebooks*. She varied from Le Senne on the use of contradiction, for he emphasized the obligation to invent a resolution to contradiction, while she believed that the task before the mind is to conceive of a relationship that transforms contradiction into correlation, by which the soul is pulled upward.[10] She gives an example in her *Notebooks*: "The supreme contradiction is the creator-creature contradiction, and it is Christ who represents the union of these contradictories."[11]

After Weil's death, Professor Le Senne, reading her extensive writings published posthumously, praised her originality as a philosopher, adding: "The problems that she brings to light by her life and her example have an obsessive reality that will continue for a long time to haunt honest souls."[12] His prescient prediction of the durability of Simone Weil's insights has indeed become a reality.

Alain

In 1925, Simone, at sixteen years old, began three years of study with humanist philosopher Alain in the Lycée Henri IV, where she was to prepare for the formidable ENS entry exams. Alain, who influenced

---

[8] *Cahiers Simone Weil*, 34.4 (December 2011): 455–462.

[9] *Philosophical Investigations*, 13.4 (October 1990): 297–303.

[10] André Devaux, "On the Right Use of Contradiction according to Simone Weil," trans. J. P. Little, in *Simone Weil's Philosophy of Culture: Readings toward a Divine Humanity*, ed. Richard H. Bell, (Cambridge: Cambridge University Press, 1993), 153.

[11] Simone Weil, *Notebooks* 2, trans. Arthur Wills (New York: G. P. Putnam's Sons, 1956), 386.

[12] René Le Senne, *Introduction à la Philosophie* (Paris: Presses Universitaires de France, 1970), 507. (All translations are mine unless otherwise noted. EJD)

several generations of French scholars, had a seminal approach to philosophy: he rejected the idea of having a "doctrine." His thought was always tied to a particular situation, and he inspired his students to think through difficult problems for themselves. He taught that writing clarified one's thoughts; to this end, he habitually assigned challenging topics (or topoi, Alain's preferred word) for voluntary essays. Simone regularly wrote topoi for him and continued to write them for his critical evaluation after she had left Henri IV. Her professional teaching modeled his: she encouraged her students to reflect on complex problems according to their own lights. They read the great thinkers' own words, limiting their recourse to secondary sources. Rigor and discipline underlay this type of learning. In addition, Alain had proposed that estimable thoughts should look beautiful on paper. Consequently, Simone often recopied her own essays several times,[13] trying to control her hands, weakened from an illness in infancy. Discipline of body and mind remained a constant preoccupation of hers.

Alain's innovative style of inquiry into the human condition resonated with Simone's emergent views of the world. She took his ideas seriously, honed them through her writings, and then incorporated them into her own understanding of the world. Nonetheless, from her first introduction to his lectures, she never hesitated to challenge his arguments where she considered them vulnerable or inadequate. As she became more assured in her ideas, she pushed Alain to be more absolute in his political stances. He later expressed regret at not achieving her style of direct statements striking effectively several times on the main point.

In light of the predominant mode of rational skepticism reigning at that time, Alain's exceptionalism in teaching morality made an impact on Weil's thinking; for him, worthy actions are defined by not compromising moral principles to achieve a goal. He believed that moral decisions entail sacrifice, with no immediate gain besides one's humanity, and their biggest obstacle is the social pressure imposed on individuals by political, social, and religious organizations. Simone Weil thoroughly assimilated this criterion, which then guided all her actions. Taking courageous mor-

---

[13] The multiple copies of each of her essays that she made are in the Fonds Simone Weil in the Bibliothèque nationale, Paris.

al stances that further human dignity—one's own and that of others—is difficult, given the push toward conformity within civic and religious institutions.

Following her mystical experience, her religious understanding of the significance behind the sacrifice of one's self-interest for love of God and one's fellow human beings exemplifies her distancing from Alain's humanist perspective. He never wavered from keeping human will at the center of his morality. Philosopher Robert Chenavier sums up the ultimate distinction of Simone Weil's philosophical divergence from Alain, suggesting that if one can perceive Alain's philosophy as based on the human spirit, that is, a philosophy of man, Simone Weil's is "a philosophy of the human condition viewed from varying levels of reality, up to contact with an Absolute, or a supreme condition."[14]

Alain's early scholarly judgment of Simone's perception noted: "She has cogency, lucidity, and often wit and distinction in her powers of analysis…. [S]hows an inventive mind; much may be expected of her." After three years of assessing her essays, he wrote: "Brilliant in her reflections, great force…. Excellent student."[15] Alain's advice on daily writing as an aid to thinking became first a habit then an obsession for Simone, during the final years of her life, when she spent close to sixteen hours a day writing. The pressure to share with others the "deposit of pure gold"[16] within her had become an imperious obligation.

Much later, Simone confided to Gilbert Kahn, a friend from Henri IV, who was planning a biography of Alain, that she could not write objectively about Alain: "There is one part of the thought of Alain that I assimilated to the point of not being able to distinguish it from my own thought, and another that I rejected."[17] At times Alain's political stances

---

[14] Robert Chenavier, *Simone Weil: Une philosophie du travail* (Paris: Les Éditions du Cerf, 2001), 38.

[15] Simone Pétrement, *Simone Weil: A Life*, trans. Raymond Rosenthal (New York: Pantheon, 1977), 41.

[16] Simone had written to her mother in July 1943, "There is within me a deposit of pure gold which must be handed on…. The mine of gold is inexhaustible." Simone Weil, *Seventy Letters*, trans. Richard Rhees, (London: Oxford University Press, 1965), 196.

[17] Kahn, "Simone Weil et Alain," 212.

drew her ire, but his moral commitments never did. She readily accepted her debt to him; in 1941, when he was quite ill, she felt compelled to tell him, "The break in the course of time, that tossed my own youth into a historic backwater, gives me an extremely clear awareness of all that I owe you."[18]

Achieving the academic rank of *agrégé* is an eminent distinction; nevertheless the French government ultimately decides where each professor will teach. Contrary to her fellow intellectuals, Simone had requested a teaching position in Le Puy, a mining region of France. Because of her empathy with the workers and her indifference to pleasing male colleagues, the ENS professor who had given her the moniker "The Red Virgin," as well as those who had participated in the mocking, were not sorry to see Simone dispatched to a less desirable working-class region. Shortly after arriving in Le Puy, however, a city famous for its iron statue of Our Lady posed on an ancient megalithic dolmen crowning a hill, she resiliently sent that professor a postcard signed "The Red Virgin of Le Puy."

Her initial goal was to encourage French workers to consolidate their efforts in order to show strength in unity when posing their demands for more humane working conditions. At that time, there were two major competing unions: a traditional union and a second formed from communist leanings to counter the first. She joined both, which was unprecedented, and worked tirelessly, but unsuccessfully, to convince them that their best hope for success was in working together toward a unified goal. Her several dozen articles addressed to the workers and published in their bulletins and periodicals reveal masterful rhetorical skills of persuasiveness, irony, sarcasm, and effective argumentation. Nothing intimidated her, nor did any situation or person.

Her philosophy of work, combining thought and action, has its source in thinking inspired by Alain's classes. Purposeful work that contributes positively to society adds to the dignity of the worker. She urged the workers to push for conditions that allow for reflection, with quiet time to think creatively about the task at hand: in other words, to philosophize, to be specific about the values that underpin one's actions.

---

[18] Ibid., 206.

Weil adamantly opposed the installation of Taylorism in the workplace, that is, using time and motion studies to break every action into small and simple segments, thereby achieving maximum job fragmentation, reduction of skill requirements, and the separation of the execution of work from the planning of work. She was convinced that such scientific management applied to work devalues the worker as a thinking individual.

She felt the same antipathy toward the oppressive system of tenant farming and sharecropping, which entails working someone else's land under the landowner's often capricious and self-serving control. In her last full work, *The Need for Roots*, she classifies private property as a vital need of the soul. All persons need to appropriate as their own what they use habitually for their work, pleasure, or the necessities of life, rather than be continually "exposed to painful spiritual wrenches.... The principle of private property is violated where the land is worked by agricultural laborers and farm hands under the orders of an estate manager, and owned by townsmen who receive the profits."[19] She felt strongly that what is wasted is the psychological and spiritual benefit that working the land could procure for the individual.

From her early efforts in the 1930s with the workers, she began to reflect seriously on the causes of social oppression. As an admirer of the thought of Enlightenment philosopher Jean-Jacques Rousseau, she wanted to understand the ways that man, having freed himself from the control of nature, then became subject to his fellow man. Her observations bore out the opening sentence of book I, chapter I, in *The Social Contract*: "Man is born free and everywhere he is in chains." Her revised version is "It would seem that man is born a slave, and that servitude is his natural condition. And yet nothing on earth can stop man from feeling himself born for liberty."[20] Her many reflections in her *Notebooks* on the true conditions of freedom, which she ultimately proclaims can only be realized by complete obedience to God's will, continue this thought.

---

[19] Simone Weil, *Need for Roots: Prelude to a Declaration of Duties toward Mankind*, trans. Arthur Wills (Boston: Beacon Press, 1952), 34–35.

[20] Simone Weil, *Oppression and Liberty*, trans. Arthur Wills and John Petrie (Amherst: University of Massachusetts Press, 1973), 82.

In a long, concentrated, and arduous effort, she composed an essay, which stretched to the length of a small book, analyzing the permanent causes, mechanisms, and contemporary forms of political and social oppression. Her innovative perspective, that of the relation between the worker and his work, rather than the relation between worker and productivity, makes this piece—eventually entitled "Reflections Concerning the Causes of Liberty and Social Oppression"[21]—a major contribution to political theory. Alain wrote her saying: "Your work is of the highest quality; you must pursue it, by further developing all the concepts and social analyses. Your example will give courage to the present generation deceived by ontology."[22]

As always, her actions echoed her polemics, both of which centered on the need for French workers to achieve the social recognition they merited. Though she had theorized about this concept, she felt the need to experience the actual workplace in order to write accurately about it. In 1934-1935, she held positions successively in three different metallurgy factories, joining the workers who put in long hours every day, six days a week, with no paid vacation and scarce time to go to the restroom. Getting hired and then keeping the job, particularly for women, was a humiliating exploitative process.

She saw that industrialization of the workplace was reducing the worker to being a slave to the machine. All the thinking becomes crystallized in the machinery, which the human being then must serve. Her experience in these metallurgy factories, producing the heavy metal parts of the new Parisian transportation systems—trains, streetcars, and subways—showed her that the increasing subjugation of workers to machines diminished their human capacity to reflect both on and off the job. She foresaw that social oppression on a massive scale in the workplace would increasingly enslave human beings—mind and body—to

---

[21] Ibid., 37-124.

[22] Kahn, "Simone Weil et Alain," 206. Alain is encouraging Simone Weil in her wish to elaborate a Critique, that is, a social critique of the workers' situation. By the use of "ontology," he alludes to the position of Kant, who felt pushed to elaborate his Critique. He commends Weil for her new approach to the use of reason. (Thank you to philosopher Robert Chenavier for this clarifying note.)

machinery; inventive minds had fixed all the creativity in the mechanization, reducing the machine operators to automatons. Mind-numbing repetitive and often dangerous actions all day long inhibit any ability to seriously reflect on pressing issues during or after an arduous day's work.

In a letter to Father Joseph-Marie Perrin, she wrote that the prolonged and firsthand contact with affliction during her factory experience had entered her flesh and soul and killed her youth. This experience had left the mark of a slave on her (*WG* 25). She had not expected that she would succumb to being reduced to a passive object in such a situation. Simone Weil's attentive and experiential study of the effects of the modern workplace on human psychology made her one of the earliest philosophers of work and, in particular, of women in the industrial workplace.[23] She widened her experiential study of work and its potential value for humankind by laboring as an agricultural field hand outside Marseille.

Pacifism and the Spanish Civil War

The havoc wreaked on the French population by World War I confirmed Simone Weil as an integral pacifist. Pacifism remained ingrained in her rationalist thinking until Adolf Hitler invaded Prague, at which point she realized that evil forces once aroused must be stopped, but the question of how to block them without polluting oneself tormented her until the end of her life. Her admired Alain had been a lifelong pacifist who, nevertheless, entered military service as an aide in 1914 when the war began. He wanted to share the common misfortune of his countrymen, who were defending their country. Alain considered his participation as the required sacrifice for remaining a free human being.

His example and her honest belief that the Spanish Civil War was a war between simple good people fighting for the right to live peaceably and Franco's evil intention to dominate them persuaded her to follow Alain's lead. When Spain erupted into war, her drive to share in the affliction of oppressed workers led her to join the Buenaventura Durutti International Anarchist Brigade in Spain. She saw the Republican side as

---

[23] Her observations were published as *La Condition ouvrière* by Gallimard in 1951. There is a well-chosen excerpt, "Factory Work," trans. Felix Giovanelli, reprinted in *Cross Currents*, 25.4 (Winter 1976): 367–382.

representing exploited workers—Durutti himself was a trade unionist. Due to an unfortunate but potentially very serious accident, she participated in the ill-fated hostilities for only about six months.

In the anarchy of the hostilities, despite her brief presence, her horror at the senseless killings taking place on both sides, with no remorse or distaste for the humiliation and destruction of human beings, taught her a bitter lesson: No matter how fine-sounding certain principles might seem, once a person gets unlimited power over another, he will use it ruthlessly. She also perceived the reality that this conflict in Spain was not a war of starving peasants against rich landowners abetted by a complicit clergy, but preparation for a much larger war between Russia, Germany, and Italy.[24] History bears proof that international forces were indeed using the Spanish conflict as a pretext for experimenting with devastating new techniques of aerial warfare. In truth, her concept that unlimited power wielded by individuals becomes callous if unchecked had become experientially evident on a worldwide scale.

Hitler's invasion of Prague in 1939 brought another cruel reckoning. Up until then, her rational thinking had concluded that the toll of lives and the destruction generated by war made all striving for a peaceful reconciliation worth humankind's most dedicated and clear-sighted efforts. Hitler's breach of the Munich Pact brought the acute realization that in some situations only equivalent force can halt massive evil. The painful awareness, however, that the pacifists had, in effect, given the Nazis ample time to build up their armed forces caused her a profound and long-lasting sense of culpability.

Knowing that force defiles both perpetrator and victim, she persistently sought some resolution to the enigma of how to resist force without self-contamination. This seemingly intractable problem took on immediacy after the Nazis rolled into France in June 1940. How were her countrymen to eject the occupiers without corrupting themselves? Here the morality of choosing just means toward desired ends shows its complexity. She reiterates her conviction that what matters more than the end goal is the intrinsic consequences involved in the means employed.

---

[24] Pétrement, *A Life*, 282.

How one "reads"[25] or interprets the relationships in any situation is crucial for reaching optimum outcomes. She further developed this concept in her essay "Reflections on the Notion of Reading," published posthumously over half a century after her death.

Thus, how to block evil forces from destroying that which is good without being contaminated by force oneself was the conundrum with which she wrestled ceaselessly. As she witnessed Hitler's psychological prowess over those he wanted to control by fear, she sought to enact a project that would have an equal psychological effect, but as an example of doing good, not evil. To this end, she conceived the "Front Line Nurses Project," which would place carefully selected and trained women as nurses directly on the battlefields to tend the wounded, give them first aid and solace, and offer to deliver personal messages to families and loved ones. The indifference to her proposal on the part of the men who were running the Free French Forces in London and Charles de Gaulle's refusal to even consider the project broke her heart and lingered as a painful failure to the end of her life. General de Gaulle's reported reaction to her innovative ideas was "But she is mad."[26] One of the last entries in her *Notebooks* during her increasing debility of the final days was the isolated word "Nurses."[27]

As for a philosophical resolution to the problem of confronting evil forces, she came closest to finding an answer in the Bhagavad Gita in Krishna's counsel to Arjuna, who does not want to take arms against those family members who would, nevertheless, usurp his lands and enslave his people. Arjuna, however, must follow his inner sacred duty (his dharma) and prevent the evil from spreading to others. The use of force has imperative restraints: one must renounce the fruits of the action, abandon all personal goals, offer the action in devotion to God, ask that all evil consequences fall back on one's self, and vow total obedience to a

---

[25] "Reading" is a term Simone Weil used for interpreting situations and discerning other people's perspectives. We will be developing this concept further.

[26] Pétrement, *A Life*, 514.

[27] Simone Weil, *Simone Weil: Oeuvres complètes*, vol. 6, no. 4, ed. André Devaux and Florence de Lussy (Paris: Gallimard, 2006), 394.

higher law. This concept of detachment or *"action non-agissante"* (action in inaction) became a prime principle underlying her concept of justice in actions.[28] A religious underpinning appears in all her writings subsequent to her mystical contact with Christ in 1938 after spending Holy Week in the Benedictine Abbey of Solesmes. Her prose poem, "The Prologue" describing this experience was found with her papers after her death.[29]

Not being given official support for her nurses project, Simone Weil took on her assigned task of imagining postwar France as a unique opportunity to start with a clean slate on which to create innovative institutions in a society that is based on the principles of justice, goodness, and truth. She devoted all her energies to this manuscript, which became her final oeuvre: *L'Enracinement* (*The Need for Roots*). It was her version of Plato's dialogue *Timaeus*,[30] imagining a new and ideal society. Albert Camus, who began publishing Weil's works for Gallimard under the imprint *Espoir* (hope) in 1950, wrote that it seemed to him impossible to imagine the rebirth of Europe without taking into consideration the suggestions outlined in it by Simone Weil. At age thirty-four, in 1943, Simone Weil died of tuberculosis in a sanatorium in Ashford, England, refusing to eat more than what she imagined the least favored of her French compatriots defending their country had to eat.

FLANNERY O'CONNOR

At the time of Simone Weil's death, Flannery O'Connor was eighteen years old and barely launched on her own short career. What in O'Connor's world and context has contributed to her work's popular reception and its unabated critical attention since her early death? And what inspires this study of O'Connor and Weil? During the half century

---

[28] For a more complete discussion of this concept, see E. Jane Doering, *Simone Weil and the Specter of Self-Perpetuating Force* (Notre Dame, IN: University of Notre Dame Press, 2010), 154–182.

[29] Simone Weil, *The Notebooks of Simone Weil*, vol. 2, trans. Arthur Wills (New York: G. P. Putnam's Sons, 1956), 638-39.

[30] Robert Chenavier elaborates this point in his introduction to Simone Weil's *l'Enracinement* in Simone Weil, *Simone Weil: Oeuvres complètes*, vol. 5, no. 2, ed. Robert Chenavier and Patrice Rolland (Paris: Gallimard, 2013), 46–86.

since her prolific production of fiction ended, literary critics have chased the enigmas of her stories—variously described as grotesque, prophetic, regional, apocalyptic, startlingly violent, Catholic Christian, and mysterious—through the lenses of theology, aesthetics, literary craft, philosophy, history, sociology, and biography, finding justification for all such critical approaches in O'Connor's stories, essays, and letters themselves. In 1997, Laurel Nesbitt observed that critics and readers alike have been trying to locate Flannery O'Connor's vision, to tie it to place, or to place her into some larger historical-religious-literary narrative.[31] Such prolonged investigation of place and meaning in O'Connor's texts suggests depths of resonance that transcend physical geography, even within stories firmly rooted in the U.S. South, and time confined to the mid-twentieth century. Flannery O'Connor's ear and eye, mind and imagination were attuned to ancient saints, biblical prophets, and Catholic doctrine, as well as Protestant fundamentalists of her region who inspired her creative work. In this examination of O'Connor's attraction to the religious philosophy of Simone Weil, we investigate the sense of place to which each writer invites us as twenty-first-century readers and pilgrims.

Immigrant History

We begin this examination of Flannery O'Connor's world, her context, and her interest in Simone Weil with two significant cautions. The first was written by O'Connor herself to Betty Hester thanking her for the *Notebooks* of Simone Weil: "The Lord knows I never expected to own the *Notebooks* of Simone Weil. This is almost something to live up to; anyway, reading them is one way to try to understand the age…. I am more than a little obliged to you. These are books that I cant [*sic*] begin to exhaust, and Simone Weil is a mystery that should keep us all humble…."[32] The second reminder comes from James Baldwin's 1965 essay "Unnameable Objects, Unspeakable Crimes": "The great force of history

---

[31] Laurel Nesbitt, "Reading Place in and around Flannery O'Connor's Texts," *Post Identity*, 1.1 (1997): 145–177.

[32] Flannery O'Connor to "A," December 28, 1956, *The Habit of Being: Letters of Flannery O'Connor*, ed. Sally Fitzgerald (New York: Vintage Books, 1979), 189.

comes from the fact that we carry it within us, are unconsciously controlled by it in many ways, and history is literally present in all that we do."[33] What are the elements of history that O'Connor carried in her bones, lived in her imagination, and transmuted into art, and what of the world was O'Connor trying to understand as she read Weil?

Born one hundred years after her maternal great-grandfather Hugh Donnelly Treanor emigrated in 1824 from Ireland to Savannah, Georgia, the city of her birth, Mary Flannery O'Connor lived an immigrant history in a divided land. During the nineteenth century, most of the Irish Catholic emigrants to the United States settled in the northeastern cities of Boston, New York, and Philadelphia, but some gravitated to southern medium-sized cities such as Charleston, Savannah, and New Orleans. Prior to the Civil War, these immigrants were generally accepted partly because of their willingness to work as unskilled laborers. They did not openly advocate the abolition of slavery out of self-interest to secure their own meager positions, nor did they initially challenge the slave system or threaten the social order.

Differences of views on the position of African Americans in society, however, were sharply apparent. For example, John England, the first Irish Catholic bishop to arrive in Charleston in 1820 recognized the need for communication among Catholics and for education. In 1822 he began publishing the *United States Catholic Miscellany*, the first Catholic newspaper in the United States, which defended the faith against attacks and explained Catholic doctrine. England's interest in education led him to establish a Philosophical and Classical Academy for boys and an academy for girls. His attempt to found free schools for free African American children was blocked by citizens inflamed by the American Anti-Slavery Society in 1835, and a mob attacked England's school. England led a group of Irish volunteers to defend the school, but soon all schools for "free blacks" were closed.[34]

---

[33] James Baldwin, "Unnameable Objects, Unspeakable Crimes," in *The White Problem in America*, ed. Ebony editors (Chicago: Johnson, 1966).

[34] Peter Guilday, *The Life and Times of John England*, vol. 1 (New York: American Press, 1927), 485; vol. 2, 151, 152, 154–155.

The Shaping of War and Division

By the last half of the nineteenth century, growing abolitionist sentiment in the North, strong commitments to the benefits of the slave system for the South's agricultural enterprise, and increasing fears of slave insurrections inspired a secessionist movement among many southern states. Between December 1860 and June 1861, eleven states voted to secede; Kentucky and Missouri passed ordinances for secession but never presented them to the people. The uncompromising differences between free and slave states over the political power of the national government to prohibit slavery, the secessionist movements, and President Abraham Lincoln's overriding desire to preserve the Union led to the Civil War in which white and black Americans fought alike as Union and Confederate soldiers.

Economic devastation followed the Civil War. Much agricultural land was ruined and buildings destroyed where battles had been fought. Remains of Union and Confederate soldiers were strewn across the land. Whites of the South were bitter toward the North, which retained control of the U.S. government, and many opposed Reconstruction efforts to reorganize the southern states to once again become part of the Union.[35] "At stake in Reconstruction," one historian observes, "were fundamentally different conceptions of the war's results, and especially of the place of the freedmen in the new polity."[36] The Radical Republicans who opposed slavery before the war distrusted ex-Confederates after the war; challenged Lincoln's Reconstruction plans, which they regarded as too accommodating to Confederates; and demanded civil rights for all free men, including suffrage.[37] Former slaves now free were displaced, and their displacement resulted in starvation for many and increased crime. Freed slaves desired sharecropping and tenant farming opportunities for

---

[35] See James McPherson, *Battle Cry of Freedom: The Civil War Era* (New York: Oxford University Press, 1988), 689–717. See also Bruce Levine, *Half Slave and Half Free: The Roots of Civil War* (New York: Hill and Wang, 1992).

[36] David W. Blight, *Race and Reunion: The Civil War in American Memory* (Cambridge: Belknap Press of Harvard University Press), 2001, 54.

[37] See Eric Foner, *The Fiery Trial: Abraham Lincoln and American Slavery* (New York: W.W. Norton, 2010), 295–298.

survival. Carpetbaggers from the North who opposed Reconstruction efforts went south simply to acquire political power or to get rich by victimizing former property owners. Though the gradual expansion of roads and railroads, the upgrading of ports, and expanding industrialization opened the South to a larger world, these changes also increased outside influences and undermined the agrarian familial culture on which the South had depended for a century.

Tensions during postwar Reconstruction; increasing struggles between African Americans, the Irish, and other immigrant groups that emerged in the North before the war as well as the South following the war; and the transition from a rural agricultural economy to an increasingly urbanized industrial economy affected the landscape of the South, relations between North and South, and the consciousness of citizens well into the twentieth century. Such postwar social and political upheavals exacerbated racial tensions that had previously erupted, for example, in resentment among the Irish community in Milwaukee of the disdain expressed toward Irish Catholic culture, the social and political marginalization of the Irish, and the elevation of African Americans' status. When an African American murdered Irishman Darby Carney in 1861, an outraged group of Irishmen lynched the African American murderer, Marshall Clarke.[38] The rise of lynch mobs throughout the South was formalized in the Ku Klux Klan on December 24, 1865, by ex-Confederate veterans in Pulaski, Tennessee. During the same period, amendments to the Constitution were adopted and shortly thereafter challenged. In 1865 the Thirteenth Amendment to the U.S. Constitution abolished slavery, in 1868 the Fourteenth Amendment granted African American citizenship and equal protection under the law, in 1870 the Fifteenth Amendment gave blacks the right to vote, and in 1875 the Civil Rights Act afforded full and equal enjoyment of public accommodations to all citizens. By 1883, however, the Supreme Court declared unconstitutional the Civil Rights Act of 1875 and the Enforcement Act of 1871, which forbade meetings of the Ku Klux Klan. Such reversals

---

[38] Michael J. Pfeifer, "The Northern United States and the Genesis of Racial Lynching: The Lynching of African Americans in the Civil War Era," *Journal of American History*, 97.3 (December 2010): 621–635.

opened the door for Jim Crow laws to be passed across the South, further oppressing African Americans and challenging the fragile postwar Union.

The era from the end of Reconstruction to the decade of the 1920s, often considered a gilded and progressive period of U.S. history, brought rapid industrialization, rising wealth and hopes for prosperity, waves of new immigrants, and changing population patterns as people moved from rural to urban areas, trends that altered the nation's landscape. Changing mores about what was morally acceptable or unacceptable; liberalization of views on alcohol, sex, and the place of women and minorities; resistance to the formation of labor unions; and shifting though tenacious prejudices against African Americans reflected geographic locations. For example, during this period of expansion and growing confidence for the North, the aspirations and freedom of former slaves were turned back by southern states and local Jim Crow laws. Following his election in 1912, President Woodrow Wilson sanctioned segregation in federal government offices in an effort to ease racial tensions but, in fact, his decision institutionalized and enforced racial segregation in the South until 1965. During Wilson's presidency, the United States entered the "war to end war" in April 1917, further stressing the social fabric. Flannery O'Connor's father served as an infantry lieutenant in Mexico and France during the war. The horrors of World War I, the immigration challenges at home, including a rising xenophobia, and communist movements in Europe turned the United States toward isolationism for a brief period until World War II.

Although the outer Civil War ended in 1865, the lingering inner work of untangling healing and justice continued. In *Race and Reunion*, David Blight argues that "three overall visions of Civil War memory collided and combined over time": the reconciliationist, the white supremacist, and the emancipationist.[39] The semicentennial commemoration of the war at Gettysburg presented a vision of reconciliation, depicting the war "primarily as a tragedy that forged greater unity, as a soldier's call to sacrifice in order to save a troubled, but essentially good, Union...." The noble impulse for reconciliation, however, did not acknowledge that the

---

[39] Blight, *Race and Reunion*, 2.

nation in 1913 remained "still deeply divided over slavery, race, competing definitions of labor, liberty, political economy, and the future of the West."[40] Hence, by 1913–1915, "Civil War memory was both settled and unsettled; it rested in a core master narrative that led inexorably to reunion of the sections while whites and blacks divided and struggled mightily even to know one another across separate societies and an anguished history. Reconciliation joined arms with white supremacy in Civil War memory … in an unsteady triumph."[41]

An Irish Catholic in the Protestant South

Against the backdrop of the Civil War heritage and profound ambivalence about national union and human community, Flannery O'Connor was born on March 25, 1925. That same year F. Scott Fitzgerald published *The Great Gatsby*, heralding the lure of wealth, beauty, fun, and reckless abandon associated with the Roaring Twenties. During this same year, John Scopes, a substitute high school teacher, was charged with violating the Tennessee Butler Act by teaching evolution instead of divine creation in his classroom. This famous trial with William Jennings Bryan arguing for the prosecution and Clarence Darrow providing defense opened in July 1925 and riveted public attention on the contest between evolutionary theory and religious fundamentalists who believed that the Bible should receive priority over modern science. The Brotherhood of Sleeping Car Porters, the first labor union formed in the United States, advanced the rights of African American railroad porters. Not until after the Great Depression of 1929 and Franklin Roosevelt's New Deal did labor unions garner increased support. On the other side of the Atlantic in 1925 Adolf Hitler released volume 1 of *Mein Kampf.* Also in Europe, Benito Mussolini, leader of the Nationalist Fascist Party and prime minister of Italy, abandoned constitutional rule in 1925 and established a legal one-party dictatorship. Simone Weil experienced these European developments directly as a young adult.

Spreading industrialization and the developing ascendancy of science spurred doctrines of progress; averted attention from historically

---

[40] Ibid., 386.
[41] Ibid., 397.

Christian values and spiritual reality; elevated human imagination and Ralph Waldo Emerson's conception of the Self over the historical figure of Christ, which Emerson regarded as an obstruction to spiritual growth; led toward humanism, philosophical Pragmatism, and efficiency; increased material prosperity; and heightened faith in the developing social sciences, which promised to control social, economic, and political life. Such cultural shifts, the expanding secularization of American society, and the legacy of division and injustice would in later years consume the penetrating intellect of Flannery O'Connor, the writer shaped by the landscape of the defeated South.

In her essay "The Catholic Novelist in the Protestant South," O'Connor acknowledges that "the things we see, hear, smell, and touch affect us long before we believe anything at all, and the South impresses its image on us from the moment we are able to distinguish one sound from another." [42] Subsequent chapters examine how Flannery O'Connor illustrates this influence of sense experience imbided from a troubled landscape and history in her fiction and through strategies of dialogic discourse within stories. For example, she embodies experiences of displacements in such stories as "The Geranium," "A Good Man Is Hard to Find," "The Displaced Person," and "Judgment Day"; she suggests shifting, confusing racial attitudes and African American self-regard in "Everything That Rises Must Converge" and "The Artificial Nigger."

Being an Irish Catholic in the Protestant South between the two world wars and on the eve of the civil rights movement and Vatican II's ecclesial changes marked Flannery O'Connor's life. Many additional factors made her distinctive and unusual in her time and context and prefigured what would develop as she matured. As an only child, throughout her childhood and adolescence O'Connor was protected by her parents, relatively wealthy nearby relatives, the Catholic Church, and Catholic education. In the late 1930s when her father developed disseminated lupus, the family moved to Milledgeville, the home of the Cline family since before the Civil War. Tending to be reclusive and introverted,

---

[42] Flannery O'Connor, "The Catholic Novelist in the Protestant South," in *Mystery and Manners,* ed. Sally and Robert Fitzgerald (New York: Farrar, Straus & Giroux, 1979), 197.

O'Connor spent time alone drawing, reading, and writing. From an early age she possessed a gift for cartooning and satire. Although both parents doted on her, her mother encouraged her appropriate behavior and attentiveness to collective social expectations, whereas her father Edward's own writerly interests and humor affirmed her individuality, her drawings, her short written sketches, and the review notes she inserted on the inside covers of her books.

O'Connor's capacity for keen observation and gift for satire, combined with an ironic eye, ear, and imagination, fueled her fascination with contradictions. From her experience of the differences between her mother's and father's attitudes to her delight in a chicken that could walk backward, Flannery O'Connor discerned subtler and more significant contradictions. She noted social class differences between landowners and tenants, blacks and whites, owners and laborers. When young relatives from the North visited the family in the South, she observed that northerners knew only facts and didn't appreciate or know how to tell stories. In cartoons while a student at Georgia State College for Women she frequently depicted a recluse observing gala social events or athletic contests from the sidelines. She lampooned the Women Accepted for Volunteer Emergency Service (WAVES) not to belittle the goodwill of the female volunteers but because Georgia College for Women was selected as a training site for the women volunteers, their numbers overwhelmed the campus. After the war, the G.I. Bill, which made educational opportunities available to male and female veterans, produced additional contradictions. The influx of veterans filling the colleges to capacity left little room for non-veteran students, particularly women. More weighty contradictions between faith and reason, truth and power, nature and grace, courage and silent or cliché-ridden accommodation to evil, conservatism and liberalism, art informed by Catholic faith or sentimental religiosity, illusion and reality, sociological realism characteristic of mid-twentieth-century literature and "deeper kinds of realism"[43] became central aspects of her creative life. O'Connor did not merely witness such contradictions and embody them in her early and mature fiction; she lived them in Georgia and Iowa, at Yaddo, and in her enduring

---

[43] Ibid., 39.

friendships with politically liberal activists like Maryat Lee or a wrestling atheist correspondent struggling toward the cross.

Education and a Writer's Vocation

Such distinctive personal characteristics of Flannery O'Connor and the influences of her southern history and environment on her, both apparent in her early life, were refined throughout her life by her commitment to her artistic vocation. Flannery O'Connor arrived at the University of Iowa intending to study journalism with lingering hope that she might find a career in cartooning. Early in her first semester in 1945 she concluded that her courses in Magazine Writing, Principles of Advertising, and American Political Ideas were not nurturing her interests or developing her story-writing abilities. As Brad Gooch's biography[44] details, the timid and homesick Flannery assertively made her way to Paul Engle, the director of the Writers' Workshop, to inquire about admission to the Workshop. Upon seeing some writing samples and recognizing unusual talent, Engle immediately admitted her to his seminar and Workshop.

O'Connor's commitment to writing as her vocation becomes visible in the journal she kept from January 1946 until September 1947, published in 2015. Reflecting on O'Connor's transition from the South to Iowa City, William A. Sessions notes in his introduction:

> She consecrated herself to a force that had surrounded her, so she believed, since her birth, in Savannah, Georgia.... Iowa City, in the American heartland, seemed the polar opposite of the racially mixed but segregated port city, which in her time was exotic (the last great port southward, before Cuba and the Caribbean). For her, Savannah had opened up more than the diversity of human existence. There a series of Catholic rituals and teachings had offered her young life a coherent universe. By 1946, Savannah had ceded to the university world of Iowa, where new influences, including intellectual joys, brought with them questions and skepticism.[45]

---

[44] Brad Gooch, *Flannery: A Life of Flannery O'Connor* (New York: Little, Brown, 2009).

[45] William A. Sessions, *A Prayer Journal: Flannery O'Connor* (New York:

At Iowa O'Connor entered one of the early creative writing programs that emerged in the late 1930s and influenced postwar American literary production. She became "the first major figure to emerge from an MFA program,"[46] just as Simone Weil had become a modern female philosopher of distinction over a decade earlier. In what Mark McGurl calls the Program Era of professional writing, such new programs teaching creative writing coincided with the rise of modernism and Anglo-American literary critical theory that appeared following World War I. Associated with writers such as I. A. Richards, William Empson, and T. S. Eliot, both modernism and what became known as New Criticism, after John Crowe Ransom's 1941 book titled *The New Criticism,* arose from the perception that following the war Enlightenment values had been discredited, the world was deeply fractured, and art and literature were marginalized. To regain some footing in the face of these conditions, the New Criticism emphasized the intrinsic value of the text in itself and fostered its careful analysis, much earlier advanced by Aristotle's *Poetics,* in preference to historical or biographical interpretations. O'Connor questioned the New Criticism, which Roger Lundin has described as ushering in a "culture of interpretation," because commitments to "tradition, community, and the notion of authority had been completely supplanted by individual, internal conviction."[47]

The institutionalization of creative writing programs and the vision of New Criticism were supported by the publication of textbooks on writing and interpretation of literature. Cleanth Brooks and Robert Penn Warren's *Understanding Fiction* published in 1943 became a standard, which Flannery O'Connor called her "bible" while at Iowa and beyond. Caroline Gordon, who became a longtime mentor of O'Connor's, explained in *How to Read a Novel* that becoming good readers depends on "a 'self abasement' before the authority of the author and as a humble

---

Farrar, Straus & Giroux, 2015), vii–viii.

[46] Mark McGurl, "Understanding Iowa: Flannery O'Connor, B.S., M.F.A.," *American Literary History,* 19.2 (Summer 2007), 529.

[47] See Roger Lundin, *The Culture of Interpretation: Christian Faith and the Postmodern World* (Grand Rapids, MI: W.B. Eerdmans, 1993), cited in Christiana Bieber Lake, *The Incarnational Art of Flannery O'Connor* (Macon, GA: Mercer University Press, 2005), 6.

'kind of collaboration' with that author."[48] As O'Connor vastly widened
her own reading during her time at Iowa, she received reinforcement for
two guiding principles of narrative form that she instinctively practiced
and that would guide her writing career: "the Jamesian imperative, *show
don't tell*, ... along with the perennial call to *write what you know*."[49] These principles were embodied in three values that O'Connor applied
throughout her life in her writing: impersonality, technique, and discipline. For O'Connor, the surest way to achieve impersonality was
through Henry James's "third person limited" form of narration. She also
acknowledged her kinship with Nathaniel Hawthorne in whose works
she found a "'fastidious, sceptical' re-evaluation of American individual
and communal self-fashioning"[50] with which she sympathized. As
O'Connor revised, assiduously accepting, experimenting, and going beyond instructions and examples, she refined some of the assumptions of
New Criticism with her commitment to the centrality of the Incarnation
for her art.

In addition to exposing her to the tutelage, respect, and admiration
of Iowa faculty like Engle, Paul Horgan, Austin Warren, and Fugitive-
Agrarian Andrew Lytle, Flannery O'Connor was buoyed by affirmations
from visiting writers such as John Crowe Ransom, Allen Tate, and Robert Penn Warren and by publication of her first story, "The Geranium,"
in 1946 by *Accent*. O'Connor confessed to Harvey Breit in a 1955 televi-
sion interview that after her first story was published, she "[began] to
write stories, publicly."[51] Although there were few women students in the
Workshop, the G.I. Bill permitted an influx of military veterans to en-
roll. O'Connor's student peers recognized her literary gifts and her extraordinary dedication to her craft and sense of vocation. She preferred
solitude, an unadorned environment, and ample time for writing to so-
cializing. Her daily routine, developed at Iowa and continued throughout

---

[48] McGurl, "Understanding Iowa," 534.

[49] Ibid., 530.

[50] Hedd Ben-Bassat, "Flannery O'Connor's Double Vision," *Literature and
Theology*, 11.2 (June 1997): 193.

[51] For more extended discussion of Flannery O'Connor's Iowa years, see
Brad Gooch, *Flannery*, 118–147.

her life, included daily Mass followed by several hours of writing.

Living beyond the South in her new northern home revealed a more progressive attitude toward race than Flannery O'Connor expressed in Georgia, and traveling by train and bus from Iowa to Georgia provided material for "The Train," a story she began around Christmas in 1946. In a letter to Betty Hester in 1957, O'Connor reflects on her public transportation travel between graduate school in Iowa and Milledgeville. "I see I should ride the bus more often. I used to when I went to school in Iowa.... Once I heard the driver say to the rear occupants, 'All right, all you stove pipe blonds, git on back there.' At which moment I became an integrationist."[52] O'Connor's inspiration for "The Train" also occurred on a train coming from Chicago. On that train "was a Tennessee boy...in uniform who was much taken up worrying the porter about how the berths were made up; the porter was so regal he just barely tolerated the boy."[53] By drawing upon stories of her war-torn veteran classmates that filled her imagination, she brought to life Hazel Motes, the comic anti-hero of "The Train" and subsequently the church without Christ protagonist in *Wise Blood*.[54] With the backing of Paul Engle she obtained a small fellowship that allowed her to work on her collection of stories that she submitted as her thesis for the MFA.

Following receipt of the MFA degree from the University of Iowa in June 1947, O'Connor began work on her novel under the tutelage of her Workshop teacher Andrew Lytle, a novelist. She accepted an invitation from the Yaddo Foundation to spend the summer postgraduation at the Yaddo writers' colony outside Saratoga Springs, New York. Her invitation to remain at Yaddo was renewed several times lasting until March 1949. The Joseph McCarthy era fears of communism and political radicals reached Yaddo and prompted an FBI investigation of the artists' colony when Robert Lowell charged Yaddo director Elizabeth Ames with supporting the radical journalist Agnes Smedley. While at Yaddo O'Connor engaged Elizabeth McKee as her literary agent, met musicians and artists, and became friends with writers Edward Maisel, Elizabeth

---

[52] Ibid., 132.
[53] Ibid., 134.
[54] Ibid., 134–135.

Hardwick, Robert Lowell who offered her advice on her novel, and critic Malcolm Cowley. After leaving Yaddo, she went to New York with Hardwick and Lowell. There she took a room in the YWCA for a short time until she found a small apartment, and Lowell introduced her to Robert Giroux at Harcourt, Brace and to the poet and translator Robert Fitzgerald and his wife Sally, who became lifelong friends.

The heady benefits of interacting with contemporary literary figures stimulated Flannery O'Connor's natural intellectual curiosity and further widened her reading. Her habit of attending daily Mass established from her youth in Georgia continued at Yaddo where she went to Mass with the colony's domestic staff, and in Connecticut as a paying guest with the Fitzgeralds. As she makes amply clear in essays, lectures, and letters, Catholic doctrine and faith provided the standpoint from which she viewed the world and human actions "at the ultimate level," religious interests that she also discovered in the later works of Simone Weil.[55]

A Widened World Reversed

The literary trajectory on which O'Connor's life seemed set in 1950 was radically interrupted by the onset of disseminated lupus, a diagnosis briefly held from her by her mother, and which required her return to Georgia and the move to Andalusia, the dairy farm to be operated by her mother Regina and a small group of farmhands. Whereas those of weaker intellect and spirit might have greeted such a reversal with resentment and despair, Flannery O'Connor instead continued a regular daily writing discipline from 1952 onward. The publication of *Wise Blood* initially received mixed critical reviews, though it won the praise of John Crowe Ransom and his invitation to apply for a *Kenyon Review* Fellowship, which she received in 1953 and which was renewed in 1954. She sold "A

---

[55] In a July 20, 1955, letter to Betty Hester (called "A"), O'Connor confesses "I write the way I do because (not though) I am a Catholic. This is a fact and nothing covers it like the bald statement. However, I am a Catholic peculiarly possessed of the modern consciousness, that thing that Jung describes as unhistorical, solitary, and guilty. To possess this within the Church is to bear a burden, the necessary burden for the conscious Catholic. It's to feel the contemporary situation at the ultimate level." *Habit of Being*, 90.

Late Encounter with the Enemy" to *Harper's Bazaar* and wrote "The Life You Save May Be Your Own" and "The River" as she began planning her second novel.

The constricted context imposed by disease and suffering O'Connor turned into opportunity for a vigorous correspondence with old and new friends, inquiring readers, aspiring writers, and literary luminaries. When her health permitted she accepted lecture invitations, some of which became essays collected in *Mystery and Manners*, and enjoyed visits with friends. With humor rather than self-pity, she cast her ironic gaze now on her own physical limitations and circumscribed mobility. During the last decade of her life and consuming dedication to her fiction, her reading coalesced increasingly around matters of ultimate concern expressed in works of theology, philosophy, science, history, and psychology. She turned the wide range of her reading into book or journal reviews published in the local diocesan press. Between 1956 and 1963 her reviews of works by authors such as Mircea Eliade, Eric Voegelin, Romano Guardini, Pierre Teilhard de Chardin, Jacques Maritain, Edith Stein, Etienne Gilson, and Daistaz Suzuki appeared in the *Bulletin*, and from 1963 in the *Southern Cross* until her death.

Flannery O'Connor and Simone Weil

In an August 2, 1955, letter to Betty Hester, O'Connor first mentioned Simone Weil as she reflected on her Christian faith and views of reality:

> I believe too that there is only one Reality and that that is the end of it, but the term, "Christian Realism," has become necessary for me, perhaps in a purely academic way, because I find myself in a world where everybody has his compartment, puts you in yours, shuts the door and departs. One of the awful things about writing when you are a Christian is that for you the ultimate reality is the Incarnation, the present reality is the Incarnation, the whole reality is the Incarnation, and nobody believes in the Incarnation; that is, nobody in your audience. My audience are the people who think God is dead. At least these are the people I am conscious of writing for.... I am wondering if you have read Simone Weil. I never have and doubt if I would understand her if I did; but from

what I have read about her, I think she must have been a very great person. She and Edith Stein are the two 20th century women who interest me.[56]

In a subsequent letter on August 28, 1955, O'Connor reports that the piece she read on Simone Weil appeared in the *Third Hour*, a magazine published sporadically by Helen Iswolsky, a professor at Fordham University.[57]

It is significant that O'Connor singled out Simone Weil and Edith Stein as the two twentieth-century women who interested her the most, confessing that her interest in both of them "comes only from what they have done, which overshadows anything they may have written."[58] During the last year of her life, O'Connor added Hannah Arendt to her list of admired women. To Betty Hester on September 14: "I am reading *Eichmann in Jerusalem....* Anything is credible after such a period of history. I've always been haunted by the boxcars, but they were actually the least of it. And old Hannah [Arendt] is as sharp as they come." Two days later to Cecil Dawkins she reports that she is reading *Eichmann in Jerusalem* and concludes "My what a book. I admire that old lady extremely...."[59] All three of these women of Jewish ancestry—Simone Weil, Edith Stein, and Hannah Arendt—espoused the need for careful thought and embodied thought in action; all confronted the problem of evil, and Arendt developed the concept of the banality of evil; all defied easy categorization; all experienced and reflected on suffering; each in her own way understood the past as a story for the present, not a series of principles or lessons.

O'Connor likely formed her early opinions of Weil from discussions in Catholic circles centered on this unusual young intellectual who lived only thirty-four years, yet left voluminous writings as her heritage. In the English-speaking world, when the translations were published,

---

[56] Flannery O'Connor to "A," August 2, 1955, *Habit of Being*, 92–93.

[57] The essay to which O'Connor refers was written by Gerda Blumenthal, "The Cross of Dividedness," *Third Hour*, 5 (1951): 17–24.

[58] Letter to "A," August 28, 1955, *Habit of Being*, 98.

[59] Letters to "A" and Cecil Dawkins, September 14 and 16, 1963, *Habit of Being*, 539, 540.

the reactions to Weil's life and writings varied widely. With just the three critiques of Weil specifically mentioned in *Habits*, O'Connor would have been introduced to a wide spectrum of responses to Weil's life and religious philosophy. The three authors, John Oesterreicher, George Tavard, and Gerda Blumenthal, knew of Weil's works, and each had felt compelled to give a serious and lengthy public response to her.

Monsignor John M. Oesterreicher (1904-1993) was born in Moravia into a family of the Jewish faith, converted to Catholicism after moving to Vienna, and founded an institute to denounce the Nazi persecution of the Jews and the anti-Christian heresy in Hitlerite racism. Having fled to the United States, he became a parish priest as he had been earlier in Austria. Simone Weil met personally with Oesterreicher to discuss whether her ideas were compatible with her belonging to the church. Their lengthy discussion apparently was heated and vehement. In "The Enigma of Simone Weil,"[60] Oesterreicher speaks disdainfully of the ideas he had received from their discussion; according to him, Weil believed that the mysteries of Christianity had been better expressed by the Greek philosophers and poets than in the New Testament. (Simone Pétrement, Weil's close friend and biographer, writes that Oesterreicher's impression differs from what Weil has written.)[61] Granting that her philosophy is consistent and reveals sparks of genius, Oesterreicher accentuates her "rebellious" ideas that are at odds with church teachings, whether on suffering or on the exclusion of non-Christians from the Truth of Christ. He was particularly indignant about her claim that certain past mythological figures are earlier incarnations of Christ, and he angrily counters her criticisms of the Hebrews in the Hebrew Scriptures.

He moves to ad hominem arguments in claiming that her desire for suffering is a residue of her religious identity crisis at age fourteen, and suggests that she who refused to compromise in any argument wanted the church to "relax the role of truth." He states flatly that her message is not part of the Christian message for she rejects the magisterium of the church. Despite the negativity of Oesterreicher's polemics, Flannery

---

[60] John M. Oesterreicher, "The Enigma of Simone Weil," *The Bridge: A Yearbook of Judaeo Christian Studies,"* I (1955): 118–158.
[61] Pétrement, *A Life,* 479.

O'Connor would have appreciated the many citations of Simone Weil's words in the article. They are sufficient for her to decide for herself whether Simone was truly devoid of "real pity for man" or whether, as George Tavard claimed, "Faith is a way, ... a series of personal commitments, each of which has meaning only in connection with the others."[62] Tavard focuses on Weil's belief that contradictions, rightly apprehended and contemplated, lead to God.

George H. Tavard (1922-2007), an ordained member of the order of the Augustinians of the Assumption, specialized in historical theology, ecumenism, and spirituality. In his "Transfigurations of Thought: Simone Weil's Dialectic," he counters Oesterreicher's severity and others' hostility by emphasizing her primary message of love, saying that "Love neither affirms nor denies; it gives."[63] His comments reveal that he had read her works closely, and in particular, her *Notebooks*, which had just been published in English. He concedes that she misunderstood the church, but responds with a question from her *Notebooks:* "How do you know that such an error is not necessary to such a mind as a phase (of its development)?"[64] He advises that to understand the content of Weil's thought, one needs to study it within a dialectic pattern of thinking. His essay focuses on her use of reasoned arguments that juxtapose opposing ideas or contradictions to carry out a critical investigation of truth.

The third author is the previously mentioned Gerda Blumenthal (1923-2004), who was born in Berlin to a Jewish family, converted to Catholicism after her arrival in the United States on the eve of World War II, and became professor of French and comparative literature at the Catholic University, Washington, D. C. Blumenthal sees Weil as a mystic on an anguished spiritual quest and credits her with creating a wider perspective on faith by relating anew the Christian revelation to our own apparently God-forsaken time, to pre-Christian and non-Christian civilizations and to the cosmos at large. Blumenthal perceives a clash of mystic vision and dialectical thought in Weil's reflection on the Incarnation,

---

[62] George, H. Tavard, "The Transfigurations of Thought: Simone Weil's Dialectic," *The Third Hour*, (1956), 52.

[63] Ibid., 54.

[64] Ibid., 55.

but she appreciates Weil's conception of love, consisting of attention[65] and consent, and brings forth in a penetrating manner the mysterious drama being enacted between Weil's personal faith and her sacrifice in refusing the joy of baptism.

These three reviewers of Simone Weil's thought were captivated by the nobility of her quest for God and her drive to live as Christian a life as possible. They did not deny the sincerity of this French philosopher, but her intent way of pursuing the truth, of questioning long-accepted Christian precepts, and of asserting her perception of mankind's role in the universe upset traditional Catholic views. Weil believed that salvation existed for all people from the beginning of time, and that her vocation was to "show the public the possibility of a truly incarnated Christianity," which is catholic in the true sense of accepting all vocations without exception (*WG* 31–32).

Her lack of hesitancy in criticizing the church for its worldly spirituality brought out the ire of the established clergy; her dedication to an austere lifestyle was an implied critique of those who preached one message but lived another. The reviewers' reactions to the ambiguity of her thought would have given O'Connor much to reflect on. O'Connor would have also greatly admired Weil's carefully honed writing skills and the way she used metaphors, analogies, and images to express her message. Weil, by her life and writing illustrates a way to live a life that is harmonious with the teachings of the Gospel; O'Connor in her fiction illustrates the *via negativa* by revealing the unharmonious relationships and the friction between her characters when these qualities are absent.

Weil's *Notebooks* that O'Connor admired are a compilation of her mature thought, full of material in preparation for being refined into essay form. Consequently, through the *Notebooks*, O'Connor would have been introduced to the essential elements of Weil's thinking, about the sacred nature of relationships with others, the world, and God, and would have also attained a fuller appreciation of the controversies swirling around Weil as a person and a thinker.

That Flannery O'Connor understood the past as a story for the pre-

---

[65] Weil's particular interpretation of the concept of attention will be discussed in chapter 3.

sent is visible in the central role the historical event of the Incarnation plays in her fiction—as it did in Weil's mature thought as well—and across time and space, including the torturous legacy of slavery in the American South and in the destruction wreaked by totalitarianism in Europe. O'Connor agreed with Walker Percy's statement that the South had so many good writers because it lost the war. However, she was quick to add that the effect of the Civil War on the South, dark though it was, was salutary to the entire world of letters: "[Percy] didn't mean ... simply that a lost war makes good subject matter. What he was saying was that we have had our Fall. We have gone into the modern world with an inburnt knowledge of human limitations and with a sense of mystery which could not have developed in our first state of innocence— as it has not sufficiently developed in the rest of our country."[66] Resembling a biblical prophet and using the humblest materials of fiction, Flannery O'Connor offers the mysteries of redemption lived out in the mid-twentieth century following the devastations of the Civil War and two world wars.

---

[66] Flannery O'Connor, "The Regional Writer," *Mystery and Manners*, 59.

Chapter 2

The Poetics of Philosophy and Fiction

CENTRAL CONCERNS: SIMONE WEIL

The need for redemption, particularly in times of severe conflict, also preoccupied Simone Weil. She wanted all human beings to understand and to accept the essential truth of their relationship with God, his creation, and their fellow human beings. After a mystical encounter with Christ, her transition from working within secular humanist parameters to being guided by profound religious convictions was interior, none of her close confidants detected her new Christian orientation. Due to the chaos in time of war, few of her writings that express this transformation came to any public notice until the 1950s when Albert Camus began to publish her works; English translations followed immediately after.

Weil's former rational belief that human beings could solve most of their problems by collaborating and working together toward an acceptable solution was subsequently subsumed under a recognition of the need for grace, humbly desired, in order to accept and submit to the painful realities of human moral gravity. In the last years of her life, the motivation behind her work involved seeking ways to convey to others the vital message of the abundance of God's love and mercy in response to obedient consent. This force driving her actions corresponds to a similar impetus behind Flannery O'Connor's fiction writing. In this chapter, we first delineate the central concerns of both writers, then trace more deeply the influence of mentors on the thinking of each woman, and, finally, in the last section of the chapter, we examine the ways, the poetics, they each used to express their central concerns.

Simone Weil's Theology

Christ's revelation to Simone Weil by means of mystical contact introduced new religious dimensions to her thinking. She revealed this supernatural experience to Father Perrin because she wanted him to understand that, despite her refusal to accept baptism within the Roman Catholic Church, she lived according to the Christian inspiration and always had. She did not want her decision against joining the church to cause him pain or weaken their bonds of friendship, which were so precious to her. She informed him that in regard to the problems of the world, she had always shared "the Christian conception in an explicit and rigorous manner," but that her vocation was to be a Christian outside the church. In her January 19, 1942 letter to Father Perrin, explaining her hesitations concerning baptism she writes:

> I cannot help wondering whether in these days when so large a proportion of humanity is submerged in materialism, [perhaps] God ... wants there to be some men and women who have given themselves to him and to Christ and who yet remain outside the church.... Nothing gives me more pain than the idea of separating myself from the immense and unfortunate multitude of unbelievers. I have ... the vocation to move among men of every class and complexion, mixing with them and sharing their life and outlook.[1]

The essays and letters in *Waiting for God* engage the many aspects of Weil's perception of God as pure love: he is the perfect being. She states that God is good before being powerful,[2] and he has made only that which is good. In Weil's conception of the creation of the universe, through kenosis,[3] God abdicated his power by withdrawing in order that the cosmos might exist. He divested himself of his divine omnipotence, endowing the material world with the gift of love and free will. Human beings, consequently, have the freedom to choose between accepting or rejecting his gift of love. The former entails giving complete obedience to God's will, with the acceptance of total dependence on him; the latter gives rise to nurturing the specious illusion of being the center of the universe, thus having the right to exercise power capriciously over others.

---

[1] Simone Weil, *Waiting for God*, trans. Emma Crauford, (New York: HarperCollins, 2000), 6. (Hereafter cited as *WG*.)

[2] Simone Weil, *Letter to a Priest*, trans. Arthur F. Wills (New York: G. P. Putnam's Sons, 1954), 14.

[3] The concept of *kenosis* is the process of the "emptying out" of God, who negates himself to create the universe and give his creatures free will.

Weil explains: "The only choice given to men, as intelligent and free creatures, is to desire obedience or not to desire it" (*WG* 76). For her, freedom is found only in obedience.

Illusions of one's self-worth are a stumbling block to obedience; they can lead the supposed faithful to worship an idol, as an image of the source of the good or of power, rather than the true source found in the power of love. She believes that at the center of the human heart is the longing for an absolute good; this longing is always there and can never be appeased by any object in this world. Although mankind always seeks some good, too often one is satisfied with a false good, such as money or social prestige, rather than persisting in seeking the true good, which is supernatural.

She notes in her *Notebooks*: "I am quite sure that there is not a God in the sense that I am quite sure nothing real can be anything like what I am able to conceive when I pronounce this word. But that which I cannot conceive is not an illusion." Compared to illusions nurtured by the ostentatiously "pious"—the majority of whom she calls "idolaters"—Weil finds that atheism can be a source of purification, whereas, finding consolation in one's religion can be a hindrance to true faith. She makes the strong point that the love of Christ is different from a social enthusiasm. "Of two men who have no experience of God, he who denies him is perhaps nearer to him than the other."[4] She suggests that the atheist who has not accepted false, obscuring, and misleading notions about the true nature of God might be "worshipping the true God in his impersonal aspect."[5]

In Weil's theology, when God withdrew in his act of creation, he relegated the operation of the cosmos to a network of immutable, impersonal laws, which she calls "Necessity": "God causes this universe to exist, but he consents not to command it, although he has the power to do so.

---

[4] Simone Weil, *Gravity and Grace*, trans. Emma Crauford and Mario von der Ruhr (New York: Routledge, 1999), 115. http://www.mercaba.org/SANLUIS/Filosofia/autores/Contemporánea/Weil%20%28Simone%29/Gravity%20and%20Grace.pdf?hc_location=ufi)

[5] Simone Weil, *First and Last Notebooks* (New York: Oxford University Press, 1970), 308.

Instead he leaves two other forces to rule in his place. On the one hand, there is blind necessity attached to matter, including the psychic matter of the soul, and, on the other, the autonomy essential to thinking persons" (*WG* 99). Loving God means loving the blind mechanism of necessity and its effects, no matter what suffering or joy this physical world produces, due to nature or to mankind. Accepting God as pure goodness and as having created only goodness means continuing to love God and his creation even while suffering to the extreme point of affliction. Weil saw Christ's Passion as the epitome of loving obedience to God even as he endured the full affliction of human existence.

For her the simultaneous existence of necessity and of human liberty is a contradiction that must be meditated upon in the fullness of its actuality, without illusions. Weil believed that contemplation of contradictions was a means of arriving at a higher truth. God's withdrawal so that the cosmos, with all its creatures, might exist means that all created things are mixed with good and evil. The contradiction of God's goodness and the existence of evil is a painful mystery that must be acknowledged in humble obedience. Since evil wreaks havoc, all individuals have an inherent obligation to mitigate the effects of evil actions perpetrated on fellow human beings and to eliminate wherever possible all hindrances to any individual's free consent to God's love. This responsibility is an unending challenge that requires profound compassion for others, for "men have the same carnal nature as animals. If a hen is hurt, the others rush upon it, attacking it with their beaks. This phenomenon is as automatic as gravitation" (*WG* 71).

Weil's voice is prophetic in her willingness to confront the rawer elements of human nature and to unveil how they damage the individual's ability to consent freely to God's love. She, like the biblical prophets, carried the message of God's need for man. Political, economic, and social decisions that foster injustice and oppression are products of good and evil mixed within human nature. It is for mankind to correct these transgressions. Although she takes on a religious vision of human dignity, she had always transferred her compassion for those who suffer, particularly the workers, into an advocacy for the oppressed, so that they, conscious of their plight, would willingly struggle for greater respect and better working conditions. Her conviction at this point stems less from reason than from faith.

Her compassion is rare among human beings, since having true compassion for those who are afflicted is an impossibility without grace: our human nature is repulsed by seeing the suffering of others. She explains that when compassion is really present, "we have a more astounding miracle than walking on water, healing the sick, or even raising the dead" (*WG* 69). Only the action of grace makes such miracles possible. Although grace is accessible to all, it must be desired, and when it comes, it nestles hidden in one's heart. God "owes it to his own infinite goodness to give to every creature good in all its fullness. We ought rather to believe that he showers continually on each one the fullness of his grace, but that we consent to receive it to a greater or lesser extent. In purely spiritual matters, God grants all desires. Those that have less have asked for less."[6]

Attention given to our neighbor in dire need is justice. This neighbor in distress has no other claims on our attention than the respect due to him because of his sacred nature: that part of his soul that can consent to God's love. On the supernatural plane, caring for the afflicted is Christ acting within us; on a social plane, this is justice. Weil writes: "The Gospel makes no distinction between the love of our neighbor and justice" (*WG* 85). Attention given to the anonymous mass of flesh lying in the ditch by the side of the road or to the socially marginalized and mocked person is creative in that it re-creates the dignity humiliation had destroyed. This act of attentive care is an illustration of the need God and man have for each other. She writes in her essay on "Love of Our Neighbor": "Only God present in us, can really think the human quality into the victims of affliction, can really look at them with a look different than that we give to things, can listen to their voice as we listen to spoken words. Then they become aware that they have a voice, otherwise they would not have occasion to notice it" (*WG* 93). Weil tells us that, at such times, we do not have to be thinking explicitly of God, for his presence in us is a secret so deep that even we are not aware of it.

The training to be able to give selfless attention requires time and effort, which translates into the need for an apprenticeship since the

---

[6] Weil, *Letter to a Priest*, 69–70.

downward drag of the individual ego and the self-centered mind-set of the collectivity most often prevails. When apprenticeship is undertaken in earnest, one can reach the point of conforming oneself to God's will completely. The fruits of an apprenticeship in attention open new possibilities for appreciating "the reality and presence of God through all external things, without exception, as clearly as our hand feels the substance of paper through the penholder and the nib" (*WG* 3-4).

Giving full attention to others in need involves renunciation on the part of the benefactor, who must abandon all aspirations of personal aggrandizement and wish solely to share the others' pain. "The divine and absolute model of that renunciation," Weil adds, "which is obedience in us—such is the creative and ruling principle of the universe—such is the fullness of being" (*WG* 115). Caring attention given to the socially disenherited can provoke the wrath of the collectivity, whose agenda is to maintain the status quo. Social pressure quickly becomes oppression, whose tools are opprobrium, disparagement, and threats of bodily and financial harm. Consequently, one can expect to be ostracized, punished, even physically attacked for offering dignity, equality, and hope to the marginalized and disadvantaged. Simone Weil believed, as did her admired Alain, that a wary eye needed to be kept relentlessly on authoritative voices, which are motivated by a implaccable momentum toward assuming more and more power.

Standing up for justice requires first "reading" others' point of view, juxtaposing it with one's own, but then trying to discern a third nonsubjective perspective, in view of God's equal love for all his creation. Christ said precisely "wheresoever two or three have gathered together in My name, I am there in their midst" (Mt 18:20). Christ, she says, is the third person in such gatherings. In formidable situations, keeping in mind justice as Christ would see it rather than considering one's personal gain is beyond difficult because all human beings have a natural tendency to see themselves as the center of the universe. To effect the transformation of redirecting our attention toward others' needs, we must recognize that the true center of the universe is outside man's mental universe or anything that is accessible to human faculties. She writes:

> To empty ourselves of our false divinity, to deny ourselves, to give up being the center of the world in imagination, to discern that all points in the world are equally centers and that the true center is outside the world, this is to consent to the rule of mechanical necessity in matter and of free choice at the center of each soul. Such consent is love. The face of this love, which is turned toward thinking persons, is the love of our neighbor; the face turned toward matter is love of the order of the world, or love of the beauty of the world, which is the same thing. (*WG* 100)

To solicit others' free consent, one must be attentive to considering them as inherent equals, despite their deprivations being more consequential than one's own. Coexistent subordination and equality form a contradiction that, if seriously respected, can lead to just behavior.

Mutual consent is the very essence of justice; "supernatural and sacramental virtue is contained in every pure act of justice" (*WG* 85). Justice occurs naturally between two persons on an equal playing field, for their very equality demands that both parties must concur. Assuming equality when exterior conditions might be very unequal becomes a sacramental fulfillment of the second greatest commandment: love of our neighbor. Such an assumption is "the image of that love which in God unites the father and son, and which is the common thought of separate thinkers." Otherwise the strong commands and the weak obey (*WG* 87).

When the gift of the restoration of one's wounded dignity, through an intentional assumption of equality on the part of another, is "rightly given and rightly received, the passing of a morsel of bread from one man to another is something like a real communion" (*WG* 84): a spiritual nourishment. "The just must be thanked for being just because justice is so beautiful" (*WG* 85). Treating our suffering neighbor with love is similar to baptizing him, for generosity and compassion are combined in this action, whose model is in God's act of creation, in the Incarnation and in the Passion. For Weil, these all exist from the beginning of time; to support this conviction, she refers to St. John and the "Lamb who was slain from the creation of the world" (Rev 13:8).

Rightly receiving the gift of dignity, by the inferior being treated as an equal, means recognizing that the treatment is due solely to the generosity of the other party. Supernatural virtue in this case issues from not believing that there really is equality of strength. With this understanding, gratitude becomes a sacramental virtue. She writes in her *Notebook* of the "dignity it gives to the afflicted man who is succored, to know that he can give Christ's thanks to his benefactor."[7]

The above concepts essential to the religious philosophy of Simone Weil all stem from a fundamental precept: the love of God and the desire to embody the teachings of Christ in society. She wrote Father Perrin of their strict obligation, particularly for the next two or three years of wartime chaos, to show the public the possibility of a truly incarnate Christianity. Subsequently, in London, Weil described such a society in her final work, *The Need for Roots*. Throughout her later works, Simone Weil, in her expository style, developed in her *Notebooks* and essays distinguishing concepts of Christianity incarnate. Such dedication to Christ's teachings would have resonated with the faith commitment of Flannery O'Connor, whose fiction holds a mirror up to contemporary society, revealing the effects that stem from a woeful lack of Christian harmony.

CENTRAL CONCERNS: FLANNERY O'CONNOR

Flannery O'Connor read Simone Weil's "Letter to a Priest" written to the Dominican father Marie-Alain Couturier and her correspondence with Father Joseph-Marie Perrin, also a Dominican, as collected in *Waiting for God*. From these sources O'Connor gained insight into the deep religious concerns of Simone Weil, following her mystical experience, and valued Weil's own search for truth as it related to the salvation of humankind. Weil's interest in the Catholic Church, her questions about faith, and her thoughts on joining or not joining the church initially bemused the devout Catholic O'Connor. Although O'Connor did not review any works by Weil or discuss her in a formal essay, as she read more of Weil's religious philosophy, she likely recognized points of similarity between her own ideas largely embodied in fiction and Weil's central spiritual concerns. Evidence for this assertion is best found in the collection of lectures and essays edited by Sally and Robert Fitzgerald, in the book reviews O'Connor published between 1956 and 1963, in her

---

[7] Weil, *First and Last Notebooks*, 84.

correspondence, and in the stories themselves, as will be clear in subsequent chapters.

Flannery O'Connor made amply clear that she did not pretend or aspire to be a theologian or philosopher. She believed that writing stories was her primary vocation. Discourse on her ideas separate from the stories was of lesser interest, although she recognized that commentary on the contexts—literary, regional, religious—that gave rise to the fiction could be helpful.[8] When combined with a survey of her book review subjects and her correspondence, the organization of O'Connor's talks and essays in *Mystery and Manners* provides a rudimentary map, that guides readers toward O'Connor's central concerns and the resonances O'Connor found between her own concerns and Simone Weil's.

Mystery and Manners begins and ends with carefully crafted discursive pieces shaped by O'Connor's narrative gifts. Both "The King of the Birds," which opens the collection, and the closing "Introduction to *A Memoir of Mary Ann*" bear marks of the memoir, indicating O'Connor's religious and metaphysical leanings. They are grounded in concrete, material realities: the first in O'Connor's home place and her peafowl avocation; the second in the cancerous deformity of Mary Ann enlarged by O'Connor's reflections and interpretation of the life works of Nathaniel and Rose Hawthorne. Between these opening and closing discursive pieces, the Fitzgeralds placed O'Connor's essays and lectures on literature, the Catholic influences on her writing, the relationship between belief and writing novels, characteristics of the southern grotesque, and the artist's vocation.

In "The King of the Birds," O'Connor describes her birds with exacting and biographically suggestive detail, confessing initially that "instinct, not knowledge, led me to them," and that she "favored those with one green eye and one orange or with overlong necks and crooked combs." She reports the peacock's association with Greek divinity as the bird of Hera, wife of Zeus, noting that it "starts life with an inauspicious

---

[8] Flannery O'Connor, eds. Sally Fitzgerald and Robert Fitzgerald, *Mystery and Manners* (New York: Farrar, Straus & Giroux, 1957, 1979). See the foreword about the selection and editing of O'Connor's unorganized typescripts of lectures, papers, and talks to a variety of groups.

appearance...,[that] the cock's plumage requires two years to attain its pattern, and [that] for the rest of his life this chicken will act as though he designed it himself." Describing the sound of the cock's tail combined with raising his voice, O'Connor says "he appears to receive through his feet some shock from the center of the earth, which travels upward through him and is released: *Eee—ooo-ii! Eee-ooo-ii!* To the melancholy this sound is melancholy and to the hysterical it is hysterical. To me it has always sounded like a cheer for an invisible parade."[9] Through her muster of peafowl and the peacock in particular, a "careful and dignified investigator," O'Connor, herself a careful and dignified investigator, discloses her predilections for the mysterious invisible that pervades nature and the material world.

In her 1961 "Introduction to *A Memoir of Mary Ann*," on which O'Connor worked initially reluctantly with the Sisters of the Dominican Congregation who took care of Mary Ann at Our Lady of Perpetual Help Free Cancer Home in Atlanta, she wrestled with matters of narrative honesty and talent, caregivers' motivations for lauding a child's piety, respect for individual privacy and suffering, and the work of charity. For example, how could she with clear conscience employ her gifts for narrative in ways that might violate the private suffering of a child? She also wondered if the works of charity themselves could be exploitative. O'Connor expressed such personal misgivings about the request from Sister Evangelista to write Mary Ann's biography by recalling insights gleaned from Hawthorne's "The Birthmark" and her knowledge of the charitable work Hawthorne's daughter Mary Rose, who was Mother Alphonsa and founder of the Dominican Congregation, did with incurable patients in a New York tenement. From her encounter with Mary Ann and her disfiguring disease through the sisters who cared for her, learned from her, and accompanied her toward death, O'Connor revised her perspective on the grotesque. She concluded that not merely is the face of evil grotesque; the face of good, like Mary Ann's, may also be grotesque: "There is a direct line between the incident in the Liverpool workhouse,

---

[9] Flannery O'Connor, "The King of the Birds," *Mystery and Manners*, 4, 5, 7, 8, 15. Miles Orvell took the title for his fine early study (1972) of O'Connor's fiction from O'Connor's reference here to "an invisible parade."

the work of Hawthorne's daughter, and Mary Ann—who stands not only for herself but for all the other examples of human imperfection and grotesquerie which the Sisters of Rose Hawthorne's order spend their lives caring for. Their work is the tree sprung from Hawthorne's small act of Christlikeness and Mary Ann is its flower."[10] For O'Connor, "this action by which charity grows invisibly among us, entwining the living and the dead, is called by the Church the Communion of Saints. It is a communion created upon human imperfection, created from what we make of our grotesque state."[11]

Between 1956 and 1963 Flannery O'Connor published reviews of 143 titles in 120 separate reviews in *American Scholar*, the *Catholic Week*, the *Bulletin*, and *Southern Cross*.[12]

To questions about why she chose to publish book reviews particularly in a local diocesan paper, she gave two answers, which echo Simone Weil's life choices to write for ordinary citizens and to live among all manner of people. First, O'Connor wanted to make people aware of what was going on in the church, and second, she wrote for laypeople more than theologians or the clergy in order to contribute to Catholic intellectual life.[13] In addition to demonstrating the breadth and depth of O'Connor's intellectual interests, her critical acumen in evaluating others' work, and the precision of her own thought and language, the reviews reveal recurring themes that provide further evidence of her central concerns.

Most of her reviews treated works on Catholic thought and some pieces of fiction, even those that she considered mediocre. She favored freedom of thought and the liberalization of "repressive Church policies and practices which impede art and the study of the Bible," even as she is

---

[10] Flannery O'Connor, "Introduction to *A Memoir of Mary Ann*," *Mystery and Manners*, 227–228. In *Our Old Home*, Nathaniel Hawthorne describes the incident in the Liverpool workhouse where a wretched, ugly child mutely requests to be picked up by a reserved gentleman, who is Hawthorne himself.

[11] O'Connor, "Introduction to *A Memoir for Mary Ann*," 228.

[12] Leo J. Zuber and Carter W. Martin, eds., *The Presence of Grace and Other Book Reviews by Flannery O'Connor* (Athens: University of Georgia Press, 1983), 3.

[13] Ibid., 4.

also careful about orthodoxy.[14] Though most of the reviews coalesce around religious subjects, they range widely from works of Catholic and Protestant theology to history, the biblical prophets, science and theology, and art and literary criticism, and they include one of Daisetz Teitaro Suzuki's *Zen and Japanese Culture*. Her reviews reveal an ecumenical spirit and her acerbic wit when she suggests that there should be a reverse Index for the Catholic Church listing books that should be required reading.[15]

Flannery O'Connor's letters personally express many of her central concerns being worked out in her stories or discussed in her reviews of books she gratefully received from journal editors. Her most sustained correspondence collected in *The Habit of Being* is with Betty Hester or "A." Even reading only O'Connor's letters, generally written to Hester every two weeks, one feels encircled in a continuous dialogue that may range from intellectually searching questions about the nature of faith or grace to discussion of thorny problems in a current story on which she was at work, references to ideas from Thomas Aquinas or Romano Guardini, to lighthearted asides about the latest escapades on the farm. Collectively, the letters reveal O'Connor's kindness toward others combined with impatience at clichés and shallow abstractions; her self-deprecating humor as she takes seriously her prophetic mission; her acceptance of tradition and orthodoxy, yet without eschewing risky challenges of these in her accurate presentations of her society; her belief in formality as the preservation of individual privacy and the way for the races to live together with mutual forbearance;[16] and her lack of self-pity.

The above sources disclose at least six key themes that guided O'Connor's life and work and resonate with Simone Weil's concerns. First, for O'Connor divine Reality suffuses all creation. She repeatedly refers to the mystery that exists within the world of matter and toward which she expects her stories to open. She presents signs of an invisible, ineffable presence, discernible to those with eyes that see, in the sun, the

---

[14] Ibid., 5.

[15] Ibid.

[16] Flannery O'Connor, interview with C. Ross Mullins, *Jubilee*, June 1963, collected in the appendix of *Mystery and Manners*, 233.

sky, the woods, dancing hooligan prophets in a burning field, or an opened peacock tail. Pierre Teilhard de Chardin's *The Divine Milieu* and *The Phenomenon of Man* provided confirmation for her view of divine activity in creation. In a February 4, 1961, review for the *Bulletin* she states that *The Phenomenon of Man* and *The Divine Milieu* should be read together, "for the first volume [*The Phenomenon of Man*] is liable to seem heretical without the second and the second insubstantial without the first." And then she continues, "It is doubtful if any Christian of this century can be fully aware of his religion until he has reseen it in the cosmic light which Teilhard has cast upon it."[17]

Second, for O'Connor, divine Reality was illumined by the cosmic light of which Teilhard writes, imprinted in the foundations of the earth, and further revealed in the Incarnation of Jesus Christ. She makes the centrality of the Incarnation clear for her art, reminding us, as we have seen, that "when you are a Christian ... the ultimate reality is the Incarnation, the present reality is the Incarnation,... and nobody believes in the Incarnation; that is, nobody in your audience. My audience are the people who think God is dead."[18] Joining other critics, Christina Bieber Lake points out that O'Connor wrote against the spreading influence of nihilism arising from Friedrich Nietzsche's pronouncement of the death of God, and against the Manichean and Gnostic tendencies found in culture and in churches wherever Cartesian dualisms prevail and the Incarnation is spiritualized. According to Brian Ingraffia, the God that Nietzsche killed in the name of "reality" is founded on the presupposition that God is a construction or projection of the human imagination.[19] Lake asserts, "When O'Connor says the 'whole reality is the Incarnation,' she stands on an event she viewed both as a historical fact with metaphysical implications and as spiritual news that demands personal an-

---

[17] Zuber and Carter, *The Presence of Grace*, 108.

[18] Flannery O'Connor, *The Habit of Being: Letters of Flannery O'Connor*, ed. Sally Fitzgerald (New York: Vintage Books, 1979), 92.

[19] Brian D. Ingraffia, *Postmodern Theory and Biblical Theology: Vanquishing God's Shadow* (New York: Cambridge University Press, 1995). Cited in Christina Bieber Lake, *The Incarnational Art of Flannery O'Connor* (Macon, GA: Mercer University Press, 2005), 7.

swerability."[20] Although O'Connor confesses that some parts of Eric Voegelin's six-volume study *Order and History* were technical and over her head, she found confirmation for her view of the Incarnation as historical fact in Voegelin's *Israel and Revelation*: "This monumental study...has been compared in importance to the work of Vico, Hegel, Spengler, and Toynbee. However, unlike Spengler and Toynbee, Voegelin does not see history as civilizational cycles, but as a Journey away from civilizations by a people which has taken the 'leap in being,' and has accepted existence under God,"[21] a leap and a Journey to which O'Connor wished to awaken her readers.

John Desmond and Susan Srigley confirm the centrality of the Incarnation for O'Connor's fiction as "incarnational art." Desmond explains that incarnational art for O'Connor "implies a whole way of seeing reality, from the immediate concrete to the farthest reaches of human history and beyond. More importantly, it implies an intrinsic relationship between the historical event of Christ's Incarnation, present-day reality, and the creative act of fiction writing."[22] As O'Connor writes, "the meaning of life is centered in our Redemption by Christ and what I see in the world I see in its relation to that."[23] Linking O'Connor's incarnational art to her sacramental theology, Srigley explains that "spiritual reality is experienced in concrete human existence, and God relates to human beings in the flesh. Christ represents the joining of the visible and the invisible: this is the central Christian mystery for O'Connor, and it is a reality that human beings experience themselves as spiritually embodied beings."[24] O'Connor's understanding of the Incarnation was "the perfect expression of spiritually embodied existence ordered by love."[25]

Third, believing that divine Reality suffuses all creation, Flannery

---

[20] Lake, *The Incarnational Art*, 7.

[21] Zuber and Carter, *The Presence of Grace*, 61.

[22] John Desmond, *Risen Sons: Flannery O'Connor's Vision of History* (Athens: University of Georgia Press, 1987), 15.

[23] Flannery O'Connor, "The Fiction Writer and His Country," *Mystery and Manners*, 32.

[24] Susan Srigley, *Flannery O'Connor's Sacramental Art* (Notre Dame, IN: University of Notre Dame Press, 2004), 18.

[25] Ibid., 17.

THE POETICS OF PHILOSOPHY AND FICTION

O'Connor considered the operations of divine and natural grace in relation to good and evil in human life. She asserted that "only when the natural world is seen as good does evil become intelligible as a destructive force and a necessary result of our freedom."[26] The denial or lack of awareness of the interaction between the divine and the human offers an easy opening for evil, a denial she concluded gradually eclipsed evil from view. The rise of nihilism, which rejects religious and moral principles, undermined the relevance of the Hebrew-Christian tradition as a guide for moral choice and, by separating good and evil, led to what O'Connor called the "domestication" of evil. In her understanding of the operation of good and evil, she "follows scripture and Thomistic philosophy...that the essence of moral and spiritual life is the grace of God, both as it is naturally present in all creation as the residual character of the Maker, and as it operates more supernaturally through purposeful Divine activity. O'Connor illustrates that this grace is often prompted by the pressure of malevolent [even violent] events and circumstances and consequently leads men and women to that which they need most, redemption."[27]

Fourth, Flannery O'Connor was concerned about the loss of awareness of the sacred and consequent distortions that replace a sense of the sacred, a concern that resonated with Simone Weil's search for truth about the salvation of humankind. Arising from human limitations, blindness, egocentric pride, and ignorance, the inability to recognize divine Reality produces illusions and contradictions between illusion and reality. In "The Grotesque in Southern Fiction," O'Connor asserts that

> if the writer believes that our life is and will remain essentially mysterious, if he looks upon us as beings existing in a created order to whose laws we freely respond, then what he sees on the surface will be of interest to him only as he can go through it into an experience of mystery itself.... For this kind of writer, the meaning of a story does not begin except at a depth where adequate motivation and adequate psychology and the various determina-

---

[26] Flannery O'Connor, "Novelist and Believer," *Mystery and Manners*, 157.

[27] Henry T. Edmondson III, *Return to Good and Evil: Flannery O'Connor's Response to Nihilism* (New York: Lexington Books, 2002), 4.

47

tions have been exhausted.[28]

In this passage, O'Connor not simply acknowledges her own conviction about the sacred dimension of reality. She signals that her stories arise from the conditions created by familiar behaviors she observed in and beyond her region. With her sacral vision, she depicts the grotesqueness of common human illusions that manifest in greed, merciless pride, self-righteous prejudices, and cruelty. Through her artful presentation of grotesqueries that maim individuals and human community, she points toward that which lies beneath and beyond distorted perceptions.

Displaced from or distorting the ground of the sacred, O'Connor's characters and narrators reveal outlandish and familiar forms of grotesquerie. Although they can be comic, they are not primarily so: "They seem to carry an invisible burden; their fanaticism is a reproach, not merely an eccentricity."[29] O'Connor used the grotesque in the service of "an age which doubts both fact and value, which is swept this way and that by momentary convictions.... The novels that interest the novelist are those that have not already been written. They are those that put the greatest demands on him, that require him to operate at the maximum of his intelligence and his talents...."[30]

Pointing through distortions and darkness by way of the grotesque toward the light that the dark has not overcome, Flannery O'Connor's novels and stories require not only much of their author but also the greatest intelligence of their readers. Just as there are within them various presentations of characters' or a narrator's grotesque behaviors, critics interpret O'Connor's employment of the grotesque in various ways. For example, Marshall Bruce Gentry, taking a psychological critical approach, considers O'Connor's stories as a contest between the control of authoritarian narrators and characters seeking release or salvation from grotesque authoritarianism. In this interpretation, Gentry depicts salvation as a form of psychological liberation or autonomous redemption. By contrast, Robert Brinkmeyer and Lake place more significance on

---

[28] Flannery O'Connor, "The Grotesque in Southern Fiction, *"Mystery and Manners,* 41–42.

[29] Ibid., 44.

[30] Ibid., 49–50.

O'Connor's Catholicism as they analyze the operations of the grotesque. In addition, highlighting O'Connor's reading, Lake acknowledges the influences on O'Connor of Mircea Eliade's thought on primitive religion and religious hierophanies, as well as Carl Jung's ideas, thereby richly complicating O'Connor's approach to the grotesque. Often clearing a path toward truth and salvation by a *via negativa*, O'Connor asks critics and readers alike to read situations closely, as Weil counseled, in order to discern negative from positive grotesqueries or, as O'Connor said, "distortion that destroys [from] the kind that reveals, or should reveal."[31]

Fifth, Flannery O'Connor's reliance on the grotesque arose from her adoption of the prophetic role for herself as artist. O'Connor illustrates her frequently quoted statement that "prophecy is a matter of seeing near things with their extensions of meaning and thus of seeing far things close up"[32] in her early *Wise Blood* with Enoch Emery's theft and presentation of a mummy corpse as the new jesus and with greatest mastery in "Parker's Back." In both her first novel and her final story, O'Connor depicts the modern rejection or distortions of Hebrew-Christian values close up. Then in presenting the consequent hungering search for substitute meanings to fill the void, she reaches back into the prophetic tradition of Hebrew scriptures to show readers those distant sources in twentieth-century forms. She gives Enoch, Obadiah Elihu, and Sarah Ruth biblical names, thereby linking them to a long history and large "communion of human imperfection."[33] Like the Israelites in exile succumbing to idols of Baal, Parker tries to calm his restlessness with tattoos covering his body, and finally, to win the approval of his fundamentalist wife, has the Byzantine Christ tattooed on his back. In Sarah Ruth's rejection of him when he returns with Christ on his back, Parker himself learns through suffering "that the tattoo of Jesus does more than symbolize that the Incarnation has become real for Parker, more than illustrate how Parker comes to realize that the 'stern eyes,'...are 'eyes to be obeyed.'"[34]

---

[31] O'Connor, "Novelist and Believer," *Mystery and Manners*, 162.

[32] O'Connor, "The Grotesque in Southern Fiction," *Mystery and Manners*, 44.

[33] Lake, *The Incarnational Art*, 222.

[34] Ibid., 223.

Drawing upon M. M. Bakhtin's ideas about aesthetic vision, Lake concludes that Parker becomes "a unique character in O'Connor's world."[35] He represents the aim of O'Connor's incarnational art and embodies Weil's ideas about the transforming power of creative attention, for "in aesthetic seeing you love a human being not because he is good, but, rather, a human being is good because you love him."[36]

Sixth, throughout her life as a "realist of distances," O'Connor developed and used her prophetic vision and voice ultimately as an act of love and as a means of navigating nihilism. As a prophet who perceived the whole reality as Incarnation, O'Connor took her own answerability for that vision seriously. When she sees and speaks through divine love existing at the center of the universe and manifested in the Incarnation, she addresses the vulnerability of René Descartes's contribution to epistemology by Cartesian dualisms that separated reason from faith and revelation. She understood Nietzsche's charge that the world no longer organizes toward the encompassing goal of God, and recognized the evolution of consequences from Nietzsche's pronouncement, but for O'Connor nihilism does not have the last word when mystery re-enters human experience and poses possibilities of transformation, redemption, and continuous *becoming* through the Incarnation. Nietzsche himself would not have said he was an advocate for nihilism. Rather, he explains and investigates nihilism as a consequence arising from the advent of the secular world. Differing significantly from O'Connor's understanding of nihilism, Nietzsche regarded Christianity as a form of nihilism.[37]

---

[35] Ibid.

[36] M. M. Bakhtin, *Toward a Philosophy of the Act,* ed. Michael Holquist and Vadim Liapunov, trans. Kenneth Brostrom (Austin: University of Texas Press, 1993), 62. Cited in Lake, *The Incarnational Art,* 223.

[37] For fuller, provocative discussion of Nietzsche's ideas about nihilism see Bernard Reginster, *The Affirmation of Life: Overcoming Nihilism* (Cambridge: Harvard University Press, 2009). See also Ken Gemes, "Nihilism and the Affirmation of Life: A Review and Dialogue with Bernard Reginster," *European Journal of Philosophy* 16:3 (2008), 459-466. According to Reginster, Nietzsche was centrally concerned with the possibility of cultural renewal and his claim that a cultural unity akin to that of the Greeks was needed but elusive.

INTELLECTUAL AND SPIRITUAL MENTORS: SIMONE WEIL

Although the early context of Simone Weil's intellectual life was secular and agnostic, she gave no credence to nihilism. Following her mystical experience, her search was for the truth that would enlighten her on the human condition. She felt strongly that the philosophical method, which involves precise questioning, intuitive thinking, and meditation, allowed one to discover basic principles that lead to the understanding that she sought, for she knew that the truth is one, immutable, and knowable. For her, true philosophy cannot invent anything, on the contrary, it uncovers what is already there. An entry in her *Notebooks* states that the true is the contact of the good with the intelligence. Her study of past great thinkers had the goal of discerning guideposts that indicate the path toward wisdom. In writing to her brother André, she rejected the German philosopher Nietzsche in the strongest terms.[38] Three intellectual sources that she did treasure were Plato, from ancient Greek culture; the Gospels, of the first century; and the Bhagavad Gita, a holy book of Hinduism of unclear authorship composed between 400 BCE and 200 CE. All three, she acknowledged later, focus on loving obedience to God as a way of life.

Plato. Weil searched assiduously in all her scholarly sources for enlightenment on central questions before incorporating carefully chosen fragments into her philosophical thought. Each insight into eternal truth added to her wealth of material for eventual use as analogies, allusions, and illustrations in her goal of clarifying and supporting the philosophical, and then religious, propositions she asserted. Her *Notebooks* are a mass of aphoristic notations, fragmentary entries, and intuitions. Due to his major influence on the history of Western thought, Plato's writings held Weil's attention from her earliest schooling. She studied his texts in Greek with private tutors and then continued to do so under Alain's direction. Her homage to Plato as a mystic, however, came only after her own mystical experience. She confessed to Father Perrin that after "Christ himself came down and took possession of me... I came to feel

---

[38] *Simone Weil: Oeuvres complètes*, vol. 7, no. 1, ed. Robert Chenavier, André A. Devaux, and Florence de Lussy (Paris: Gallimard, 2013), 467.

that Plato was a mystic... and my love was redoubled" (*WG* 27, 28).

To illustrate her message, Weil used key elements of Greek philosophy that centered on the need for education or apprenticeship in order to recognize the formidable stages required to arrive at knowledge of the perfect Good or God. This education would take many forms; she was steeped in the Greek idea that wisdom comes from patiently enduring suffering. Twice she cites the lines from a chorus of the *Agamemnon* of Aeschylus: "So accrues to the heart, drop by drop, during sleep, / The wage of dolorous memory: / And even, without willing it, wisdom comes. / From the gods who sit at the celestial helm, grace comes violently." She explains: "Man must learn to think of himself as a limited and dependent being, suffering alone can teach him this."[39]

Primarily, Weil esteemed Plato as a purveyor of the Greek wisdom received from the many inspired thinkers who preceded him, whose writings have not survived. Next to her comment "All human wisdom is contained in the reflections of the Greeks upon 'measure' and 'excess,'" she added, "Socrates. The tragedians."[40] She believed that contemporary society had forgotten the crucial reality of ineluctable limits inherent in the human condition and thus was perilously trying to go beyond them. In Plato, she discerned a witness to eternal truth expressed in three basic teachings: (1) God is the Good, (2) love is defined by free consent to the good, which is an absolute value, and (3) the material universe is a mediation between God and man.[41] For her, the works of Plato impart an act of love toward God, which inspires measured action based on love, eschewing excess that can destroy oneself and others.

In the following discussion, we develop four of her often-used Platonic allegories or images, which will be developed more fully in relation to O'Connor's characters and plots: the Great Beast,[42] the Cave,[43] the

---

[39] Simone Weil, *Intimations of Christianity among the Ancient Greeks*, trans. Elisabeth Chase Geissbuhler (London: Routledge and Kegan Paul, 1957), 57.

[40] Weil, *First and Last Notebooks*, 48.

[41] François Heidsieck, "Platon, maître et témoin de la connaissance surnaturelle," *Cahiers Simone Weil*, 5.4, (December 1982): 244.

[42] *Republic*, 493A–C.

[43] Ibid., 514a–520a.

Just Man,[44] and bridges—or "*metaxu*"[45]—which span the divide between the natural and the supernatural realms.

Weil's sharp criticism of the harm done by collectivities, where social pressure hinders members from acting and reacting on their own independent thinking, appears in her use of Plato's analogy of the Great Beast. The Great Beast represents oppressive public opinion, based on a tragic misconception of reality, when individuals give sway to their ego, obeying passions and appetites instead of their intelligence. The collectivity applies firm social pressure to keep dissidents from disrupting the status quo, even when it is based on injustice, due to radically corrupt social values. The difficulty of countering this wrong perspective of the world by education is illustrated in the allegory of the Cave. The uneducated populace, chained to a wall in a dark cave all their lives, prevented from turning their heads, believe the shadows of real things projected on a wall in front of them are real objects. Eventually, one prisoner is unchained and forced to go out of the cave, painfully adjusting his eyes to the sunlight that reveals the truly real objects; he is then obliged to return into the cave and force the others, against their will, up into the sun that illumines reality and the intelligence. Because too many human beings do not want to be wrested out of their comfort zone, even if they do perceive it to be founded on illusions, the person who tries to enlighten the others is often badly treated.

For this daunting task of leading others to higher knowledge, a Just Man is required; he must be determinedly obedient to his vocation, and courageous, for he will be vilified and made to suffer unjustly for his pains. He will have brought a great gift to humankind, but the passively ignorant will reject any change made to their habitual thinking, despite its being false. The ultimate Just Man is the Christ, who, at great sacrifice, has brought to the world the Good News of Salvation. His crucifixion is the model of a perfect act of obedience unto death. Now, people whose eyes are opened to the real understand that there exists something transcendental and superior to the material world, which becomes their

---

[44] Ibid., 361e.

[45] Weil preferred the Greek word "metaxu," as used by Plato to refer to intermediaries.

ultimate reality. With their new vision, they begin to recognize in the world around them a wealth of intermediaries or *metaxu* that bridge the separation between the divine and the human,[46] the infinite and finite, that is, God and man. Weil believed that earthly things are the criteria of spiritual things, that is, that earthly things, as bridges or metaxu, lead to the spiritual realm or the good and should be loved. The supernatural is known through the light it sheds on the transient sensible world. She dedicated her life to informing others of the reality of the good and to encouraging them to allow love to enlighten their intelligence.

The Gospels. Following her encounter with Christ she undertook a more thorough reading of the New Testament, finding that its wisdom held significance for understanding human beings' place in the universe. Of the Gospels, she intuitively believed that they were so beautiful that they had to be true. In her *Notebooks*, she wrote "In everything that gives the pure authentic feeling of beauty there really is the presence of God."[47] Given that the primary focus of the message that the Gospels bring is love: love of God, love of one another, and love of all creation, Weil equated love directed toward one's neighbor with justice.[48]

She saw Christ's life as the model of the perfectly Just Man and his teachings as a conception of human life that gives inspiration, insight, and knowledge of some absolute beyond the limited material world. In her thought, the wisdom of the Gospels descends directly from ancient Greek wisdom that reveals the need to seek above all else the realm and justice of our heavenly father.[49] The Gospel accounts of the Passion reveal a being, human and divine, who suffers affliction and is cast off from men and God, and who feels abandoned at his approaching death. In the

---

[46] Weil extended the meaning of Plato's *metaxu* to include all mediators.

[47] Weil, *Gravity and Grace*, 150.

[48] André Devaux, "Le Christ dans la vie et dans l'oeuvre de Simone Weil," *Cahiers Simone Weil*, 4.1 (March 1981): 7.

[49] Weil admired how "the Greeks revered the orientation toward truth, beauty, the divine, and the contemplative spirit.... In Plato and almost all the ancient Greeks, suffering is laid bare, and is seen in a being who is at once divine and human." Mary G. Dietz, *Between the Human and the Divine: The Political Thought of Simone Weil* (Totowa, New Jersey: Roman and Littlefield, 1988), 108–109.

tragedies and the *Iliad,* Greek literature also portrays the full extent of human misery in beings half human and half divine submitting to their cruel destiny.

Simone Weil writes that she intuited the truth of the Gospels by their beauty. A student in Professor Weil's first philosophy classes in Le Puy recounts discovering Weil's love of their beauty as the class read the Gospels in Greek together. After her mystical contact with Christ, all her writings become enriched with allusions to the New Testament and are indicative of the depth of her new spirituality. Her spiritual sources give her evidence that God's love is implicit throughout our material world and that even affliction bears traces of his love. Flannery O'Connor, with her own profound faith, would have recognized the multitude of biblical allusions in Weil's essays, and would have been one of the anagogical readers that O'Connor herself had so desired for her fictional creations.

Consistent with her philosophical approach to exploring a question, Simone Weil uses a profusion of citations from the Gospels to give logical proof for the truth of what she wants to convey to her readers. To support the idea that Christ truly felt separate from man and God in his agony—just as all human beings will experience such separation in turn as they enter the dark night of the soul—she cites several times the last words cried out in his agony: "My God, my God, why have you forsaken me?" (Mt 27:46; Mk 15:34).

To illustrate her belief that earthly things are the criteria of spiritual things and that God is an impersonal being, who prefers not to extend his power, Weil offers Christ's parables of the beauty of the lilies in the field and the indiscriminate distribution of the sun and the rain. The lilies do not toil or spin, but are indifferent to their future, fully accepting their destiny, just as we must accept with acquiescence and even love whatever befalls us through harsh necessity. Beauty in the world has no finality or intention; Christ directs us to see how the rain and the sunlight fall without discrimination on the just and the wicked, and he wants us to contemplate and love the beauty of all things in creation barring none.

This type of contemplation requiring patient, expectant waiting, minus any egoistic intentions, threads through Simone Weil's work: God will come to us if we wait submissively enough; we cannot even take a step toward him. We must reflect quietly on our obligations, accept the responsibility to fulfill them, eliminate any thought of our personal intentions, and pause for a deliberative moment before carrying out actions, and be without desire for personal gain. The Hindu precept of renouncing the fruits of one's actions resonated deeply with these concepts of Simone Weil. In her mind, the Bhagavad Gita and the Gospels complement each other, with the Gita expanding the notion of supernatural grace.

The Bhagavad Gita. Once in Marseille, Weil began an intense study of the Bhagavad Gita, learning Sanskrit in order to read it in the original. An important insight, gleaned from her study, dealt with the dilemma of how to sustain a desire for the "good" when one is caught in situations where elements of good and evil blatantly intermingle. This dilemma preoccupied Weil; her countrymen had to deal with oppressive Nazi invaders and to do everything necessary to drive them out. Her personal pangs of guilt still rubbed her conscience raw because she had motivated many others to maintain the active stance of integral pacifism. Hitler's invasion of Prague forced her to accept, as we noted earlier, that force must be used at crucial times to stop the expansion of evil. But how and to what extent could one deploy force to block its spread without being personally contaminated? The Greeks had shown that evil taints the handle of the sword as well as the deadly point; the Gospels echo that caveat: "They that take the sword shall perish with the sword" (Mt 26:54).

How to save the French soul while still maintaining the determination to evict the foreign intruders was Weil's obsession. The dialogue between Krishna, a god in the role of chariot driver, and Arjuna, a leader facing a moral dilemma, gave her some insights into a resolution of this conundrum. Arjuna's problem resembles that of the French caught under the boot of the Nazis: Prince Arjuna must reestablish order in his country by forcibly stopping family members who plan illegally to usurp power.

In the Bhagavad Gita, she found some resolution to the perennial problem of countering force without suffering its contamination. It is primarily in her *Notebooks* that one perceives the fruits of her contemplation of this thorny quandary. Weil harmonized Western beliefs with ideas in Hinduism as she sought glimpses of the truth pertaining to the human condition found in the lessons Krishna gives to Arjuna in this philosophical meditation. These ideas reflect elements of what she had perceived in the *Iliad* and the Gospels. All three texts contain violence, but each portrays critical moments when decisions of how to confront devastating force present themselves. In the *Iliad*, the opposing warriors fight until they and all of Troy are destroyed. As a polar opposite, Christ, in the Passion, submits his will to the Father in the midst of the evil being perpetrated on him. As a median between the other two reactions, Arjuna puts his faith in Krishna, a higher power, who tells him he must fight for justice. Krishna's dialectic with Arjuna, who doesn't want to fight his family members, valorizes the necessity to act in the world, sometimes forcefully, but only with action inspired by loving obedience to the divine and renunciation of personal gain. Krishna convinces Arjuna that he must perform his duty, or dharma,[50] as an act of submission to Krishna. To reinstall harmony and justice in his kingdom, Arjuna has to suppress his own will, be disciplined in his love for Krishna, disassociate himself from any fruits of his actions, and perform his ordained task. Even if he fights, agreeing to submit his will to that of Krishna, the self-perpetuating chaos of violence may continue, but he will not be contaminated by its inherent evil.

In her mystical philosophy, Weil stressed similar requirements for forceful action: that one reject all base actions and that one love God. The pause for reflection before confrontation corresponds to Weil's idea that a "just reading" of any peril requires quiet deliberation before taking action. To achieve a "just reading" means seeking in silence the truth of a situation, through an objective reading that comes through the supernatural. She advises that all activity have at its center some moments of stillness. Relinquishing attachment to personal advantage was a way of performing "action in inaction," which she defined in her *Notebooks* as doing only what one cannot not do. Weil intuited the vital and intimate relationship between Arjuna and Krishna as analogous to the tender love between a human soul and the divine being. Fortunately for her future readers, she persistently jotted down the inspirations she found in the

---

[50] His sacred role as protector of justice.

57

Gita throughout her later *Notebooks*; although, unhappily, death intervened before she could compose any essays on her reflections.

INTELLECTUAL AND SPIRITUAL MENTORS: FLANNERY O'CONNOR

Although her education was formally less broad and varied than Simone Weil's, Flannery O'Connor also sought insight into the truth of the human condition with her inquisitive intelligence. In his careful examination of O'Connor's library, Arthur F. Kinney surveys the works O'Connor kept in her glass-doored bookcase, wonders about books to which she refers in letters but that are not present in her collection, and concludes that from her library readers "can piece together parts of her aesthetic theory." [51] Her library included works of philosophy by Emmanuel Mounier, Etienne Gilson, Gabriel Marcel, St. Thomas Aquinas, Jacques Maritain; books by literary and political historians such as Edmund Fuller, Lord David Cecil, Alexis de Tocqueville; works by the Jewish philosopher of dialogue Martin Buber and Protestant theologian Karl Barth; the psychology of Carl Jung; Percy Lubbock's *The Craft of Fiction*; novels by Nathaniel Hawthorne and Henry James; and the scientific philosophy of paleontologist priest Teilhard de Chardin. William Lynch's *Christ and Apollo: The Dimensions of the Literary Imagination* (1960) and *The Image Industries* (1959) support O'Connor's own understanding of the relationship between theology and art and anticipate the evolution of her incarnational art.

The two thinkers to whom O'Connor refers most frequently in her essays and in her letters about her ideas on art, the artist, reality, and mystery are St. Thomas Aquinas and Jacques Maritain. In her essay on "The Nature and Aim of Fiction" in particular we find evidence of the Christian philosophy O'Connor learned from Aquinas and through Maritain's interpretation of Aquinas. She embraced Aquinas's teaching that human beings are made in the image of God through their possession of an intellectual nature. The human intelligence, the operations of the intellect, and the powers that pour forth from the soul's essence are

---

[51] Arthur F. Kinney, *Flannery O'Connor's Library: Resources of Being* (Athens: University of Georgia Press, 1985), 7.

grounded in the perfect intelligence of the Creator. Following ideas Maritain reinforced in *Art and Scholasticism*, O'Connor acknowledges Aquinas's distinctions between the intellectual virtues of the *speculative* order, the end of which is to know and to bask in knowledge, and the *practical* order in which the intellect does not rest simply in knowing but uses knowing for some work or action.[52]

O'Connor's awareness of the chasm between Aquinas's teachings and the twentieth-century world led her to write to Betty Hester on November 22, 1958, "what St. Thomas did for the new learning of the 13th century we are in bad need of someone to do for the 20th."[53] Because of the challenges against faith, the ruptures of being such as the separation of reason from imagination or the spirit from the body, and modernism's disfigurement of the intellect, which occurs when the intellect becomes "insulated from both the supernatural lights above and the irrational forces below," Maritain sought to reshape St. Thomas for the needs of his age.[54] O'Connor's view of the human situation at mid-twentieth century reflected "Maritain's insight into the spiritual situation of this century ... that no true faith could be exercised that did not reside in an intellect that was confident of its ability to know the truth. For Maritain, as for Thomas, the virtue of faith is primarily a *habitus* of the intellect."[55] *Habitus* might be considered the orientation of the practical intellect in the divine Intelligence, implying the unity of the soul imprinted with the *imago dei*.

O'Connor's interest in these ideas was essential to her art. Describing the nature of and need for this *habitus* for the artist she writes: "St. Thomas called art 'reason in making.' This is a very cold and very beautiful definition, and if it is unpopular today, this is because reason has lost ground among us. As grace and nature have been separated, so imagination and reason have separated, and this always means an end to art. The

---

[52] Jacques Maritain, *Art and Scholasticism* (New York: Charles Scribner's Sons, 1962; Notre Dame, IN: University of Notre Dame Press, 1974), 7. See particularly chapter 2, "The Speculative Order and the Practical Order."

[53] O'Connor, *The Habit of Being*, 306.

[54] Deal W. Hudson and Matthew J. Mancini, *Understanding Maritain: Philosopher and Friend* (Macon, GA: Mercer University Press, 1987), 7.

[55] Ibid., 8.

artist uses his reason to discover an answering reason in everything he sees."[56] She affirms with Aquinas that the artist working through the practical intellect "is concerned with the good of that which is made," that for a writer art means "writing something that is valuable in itself and that works in itself," and that because "the beginning of human knowledge is through the senses, ... the fiction writer begins where human perception begins."[57] For O'Connor, such passages from Aquinas and Maritain were guides and explanations for her own vocation and experience as a writer.

Paying attention to what one perceives, knows, and seeks to express was important to both Simone Weil and Flannery O'Connor, for attention aligns individual consciousness with the grace of divine intelligence and deepens human perceptions and experience of reality. For Weil attention paid to academic studies and attention in prayer "are mutually strengthening, and the joy of learning is an inchoate awakening of the human desire for God."[58] O'Connor asserts similarly that "the longer you look at one object, the more of the world you see in it; and it's well to remember that the serious fiction writer always writes about the whole world, no matter how limited his particular scene. For him, the bomb that was dropped on Hiroshima affects life on the Oconee River, and there's not anything he can do about it."[59] To offer the long, attentive look at the world or at stories requires "the kind of mind that is willing to have its sense of mystery deepened by contact with reality, and its sense of reality deepened by contact with mystery."[60] The quality of attention O'Connor advocates is essential for anagogical vision, which is the capacity to see the universe in a grain of sand and mystery in visible night stars light years away.

Flannery O'Connor's artistic interests reflect three key aims of Maritain who through his study of creativity and art wanted "to demonstrate

---

[56] Flannery O'Connor, "The Nature and Aim of Fiction," *Mystery and Manners*, 82.

[57] Ibid., 65 and 67.

[58] Hudson and Mancini, *Understanding Maritain*, 9.

[59] O'Connor, "The Nature and Aim of Fiction," 77.

[60] Ibid., 79.

the primacy of the intellect in all human action,...to reestablish the hierarchy and mystery of knowledge,...and to unify culture by referring it to God."[61] Mystical vision or wisdom for Maritain "is produced by supernatural infusion of God's grace and is consummated by the elevation of our intelligence beyond the natural limits."[62] For O'Connor, attention and awakening to mystery are necessary for anagogical vision, which enables one to see within and through surface realities a mystical interpretation of a word, a passage, a text of scripture, or an experience. How she offered her characters and readers opportunities for anagogical vision becomes the poetics of her fiction, that is, how she crafted stories aimed toward mystery and the grace of the Incarnation.

POIESIS: SIMONE WEIL

Literature that considers the mystery of the Incarnation and enlightens the intelligence in preparation for future moral choices was esteemed to a high degree by Simone Weil; she incorporated such literature into her philosophy lessons and her writings. She felt strongly that literature had a moral function in society; it needed to portray the seriousness of choices between the good and evil inherent in all decisions. Reading and thinking allow one to experience life vicariously; a reader could be exposed to the perilous consequences of bad decisions while not suffering them personally and, thus, be prepared to deal more wisely with future critical moments, when salvation is at stake. She believed that only first rate writers of genius have the aptitude for exerting a spiritual influence. Such writers prize the notion of a criterion of value, knowing that value is inseparable from human thought. In Weil's mind, the writers who compose great works have turned their whole soul toward the truth.

Serious works must be accessible to anyone who desires to understand them. Plato's writings are a vulgarization of his philosophic ideas, making them accessible to attentive readers; the same can be said for the Gospels and the Bhagavad Gita. Weil herself wrote for a common audi-

---

[61] Deal W. Hudson, "The Ecstasy Which Is Creation," Hudson and Mancini, *Understanding Maritain*, 253 and 255.

[62] Curtis L. Hancock, "Maritain on Mystical Contemplation," Hudson and Mancini, *Understanding Maritain*, 260.

ence, never for fellow intellectuals. She sought a wide audience, first from the worker class, hoping to get workers to cooperate with one another in order to enact real change in the workplace, then from the general public who needed to be concerned about the reality of God's love and its essential role in their lives. For the workers, she used a polemic style, with irony, sarcasm, and blunt unembellished challenges. When her goal evolved to drawing attention to pressing questions concerning every man's teleological purpose, she soft-pedaled her acerbic touch with a more humble and persuasive tone.

As with Plato's style, hers becomes dialectic: she doesn't offer answers, give directions, or pose questions with known answers. The readers are invited into the discussion to meditate for themselves on the mysteries of life. To transpose an eternal truth is difficult; one must be situated in the very center of that truth, seeing it with no illusions. She sought to place herself at such a point. In her art of logical dialogue, as she investigates the truth of a theory, she juxtaposes conflicting ideas to explore the validity of both sides. Framing situations in such a way makes her religious philosophy apparent. She sets guideposts that orient thinkers toward God's love and the dire importance in their accepting or rejecting it. Eternal truths need to be discovered and interpreted anew, by each generation. That being said, there is nothing relative about the truth unveiled by this necessary and continuous exploration and rediscovery.

Weil believed that the knowledge of God's providential grace existed from the beginning of time, thus age-old folklore, myths, fairy tales, legends, songs, fine literature of the ancient and recent past, plus daily experiences, her own or others', held traces of religious truths from pre-Christian times. In all her works, a reader finds allusions to a folklore that has its origins in popular culture, springing naturally from the people, and which, for the most part, has the unique character of transmitting the idea that it is not man who seeks God, but God who seeks man. Truth is to be found among the simplest of people, especially those who are in constant contact with the material world and its beauty. Even though God is absent, he has left implicit forms of his love, detectable by anyone who desires to see them, in the beauty of the cosmos.

She wants her prose to reflect the beauty of the universe, and, so, has been honing her rhetorical gifts from childhood, but she now endows

THE POETICS OF PHILOSOPHY AND FICTION

them with a spiritual purpose. Her figures of speech, such as cleverly constructed metaphors and analogies, and her interjections of Greek mythology and folklore convey a universality bathed in a Christian light. We have seen the example of Aeschylus, whose chorus sings of the painful reality of wisdom that comes through suffering by the awful grace of God and excludes no one. Prometheus, also of Greek mythology, suffers eternally for defying the gods by stealing fire and giving it to humanity, enabling development and civilization. For Weil, this Titan is an image of Christ, who brings us the Good News, but who is in turn crucified.

As with mythology, aspects of the universality of fairy tales are conveyed by a lack of any specific location and by unmerited suffering. This is the case for Cinderella, who sits in the ashes of humiliation imposed by her callous stepfamily. Nevertheless, hers is a soul supported by the natural world in the form of animals, birds, and ants who assist her in the imposed degrading tasks, as well as, the shade of her dead mother— characterized as a tree of life growing up from her grave— who provides her daughter with splendid apparel for the ball. The prince, a spirit, who searches for the owner of the lost slipper of crystal, which symbolizes purity, light, and eternity, finds Cinderella, whose suffering in her debasement draws the prince to her. Once she is found, her marriage to the prince signifies unity of soul and spirit, and the promise to enjoy immortality in paradise.[63] For Weil, suffering borne with equanimity and a persistent love of the good prepares the soul to accept supernatural grace.

Weil was sensitive to her own experiences of suffering due to an incurable sinus infection, which brought severe migraine headaches. Her personal experience had shown her that suffering can increase an individual's vulnerability to the pull of moral gravity, thus diminishing the capacity of feeling compassion for one's neighbor. She knew, nevertheless, that human emotions can be permanently transformed through new revelations. She gave the analogy of a walker's panic, when on a dark path, he sees a menacing shadow that looks like a crouching man lurking ahead. This first reaction will be completely and permanently trans-

---

[63] We are indebted to Martin Andic for his article "Fairy Tales," *Cahiers Simone Weil*, 15.1 (March 1992): 61–91.

formed once the shadow is revealed to be just a bush; re-evoking the original fear is impossible after the shadowy form has been properly identified. She sought the key to understanding this phenomenon.

Weil's skillful choice of rhetorical devices touches the sensibility of readers. Those who can read anagogically, such as Flannery O'Connor, will have a richer comprehension of her ideas. All Weil's individual works after 1938 contain traces of the whole tapestry of her religious and philosophic concepts; each piece develops one or another facet as her thought matures over the next four years. This is true even of her aphorisms, which are concise expressions of her thought as a whole. Her use of rhetorical devices makes her religious philosophy accessible and intriguing to a wide readership, as it was to Flannery O'Connor. We shall see examples of her skill in this domain throughout the following chapters.

POIESIS: FLANNERY O'CONNOR

Flannery O'Connor's interest in writing novels that have not already been written, her insistence that her works open toward mystery, and her desire for "an answering reason" in everything she sees suggest a dialogical quality in her fictional poetics, a quality expressed in the Incarnation itself as God invited an answering response from human beings to the grace of redemptive love. O'Connor's stories, which have their taproots in manners, social idioms, the language of characters and narrators, grotesqueries that carry an invisible burden, the author's devout Catholicism combined with her respect for Protestant fundamentalists, and her skills in sarcasm, satire, and irony, developed into mature fiction that educates readers in anagogical vision. By presenting divergent perspectives through the narrator and characters, among characters, and between the author and narrators, O'Connor creates a dialogue of sorts comprising contrived and distorted exchanges. As characters and readers alike encounter such exchanges and situations that are contested or distressing in the stories, both are invited to "read" (interpret) their situations differently and are pressed toward mystery, recalling Maritain's statement that "mystery exists where there is more to be known than is given to our comprehension."[64]

Because O'Connor's narrative strategies depart from traditional techniques of the modern American novel whereby "the writer construes a modern version of the self and will either show that self as beaten down to an isolated death or as fighting to be freed from constraints,"[65] readers find O'Connor stories puzzling to navigate. Who represents the authoritative perspective in O'Connor's stories? Critics such as Brinkmeyer, Gentry, Gordon, Johansen, and Lake have discussed the utility of M. M. Bakhtin's theory of language and the novel, which he calls dialogism, as a helpful approach to understanding O'Connor's poetic craft. In dialogism, the novelist does not monologically dominate the story simply in the telling. Instead, the novel "orchestrates all its themes, the totality of the world of objects and ideas depicted and expressed in it, by means of social diversity of speech types and by differing individual voices that flourish under such conditions."[66] The presentation of a multiplicity of voices in the novel—what Bakhtin calls *heteroglossia*—allows for different connections and new readings of familiar relationships and situations. In the following chapters we examine Flannery O'Connor's dialogical narrative strategies more closely to see first, how they contribute to the author's aim to embody mystery; second, how they illustrate philosophical interests akin to Simone Weil's; and third, how they educate readers in anagogical vision.

Encouraging the ability to make new readings of familiar experiences was an idea that Simone Weil believed could bring about a much-needed harmony in human interaction. In 1942, the year before her death, she completed an essay on the "Notion of Reading," which she defined as the process by which the mind makes judgments about the sense impressions received by the body. This theory stemmed from the conviction that "there was one true universal 'reading' at the heart of every situation, a 'reading' that furthered positive relationships in a just so-

---

[64] Maritain, *Art and Scholasticism*, note 4, 28.

[65] Lake, *The Incarnational Art*, 48.

[66] M. M. Bakhtin, *The Dialogic Imagination: Four Essays*, ed. Michael Holquist, trans. Caryl Emerson and Michael Holquist (Austin: University of Texas Press, 1981), 263. Cited also in Lake, *The Incarnational Art*, 48.

cial environment."[67] The ideas for this concept are found in fragmentary bits and pieces spread throughout her *Notebooks*; the finished piece allows us to appreciate her fully formed well-presented concept. Holding to the Greek idea that God needs man, she saw the true goal of mankind is to allow God, through us, to see what we see and to act through us.

What human beings see in the world around them, how they read their own and others' experiences, whether they can see through surfaces or appearances, and imagine interpretations beyond egoistic tendencies depends, Weil thought, on an implicit recognition that a hierarchy of absolute values exists in God's love outside the material world. She believed human readings could be transformed or reoriented away from fear-filled or self-aggrandizing emotions if they were aligned with the true reading intrinsic in God's love. Weil's emphasis on reading the world and the role of humans in it anticipates the importance O'Connor assigns to anagogical vision essential for seeing through illusion and distortion to the mystical and eternal presence of God. Against this backdrop of the philosopher's and the storyteller's central concerns and craft, we test how Weil's philosophy and O'Connor's fiction illumine one another as they turn their respective worlds toward God. For such a turning, attention is the bedrock.

---

[67] Simone Weil, "Essay on the Notion of Reading," trans. Rebecca Fine Rose and Timothy Tessin, *Philosophical Investigations* 13:4 (October 1990): 297-302.

Chapter 3

Attention and Apprenticeship

Simone Weil's "The Right Use of School Studies for the Love of God," "For the Love of Our Neighbor," and *Notebooks*

Flannery O'Connor's "The Artificial Nigger" and "The Displaced Person"

SIMONE WEIL

Simone Weil had a firm conviction of the importance of learning how to give complete attention to a thought, an object, a person, the cosmos, and—in her spiritual period—to God. Attention was a skill that she worked on continually, to perfect her own thought processes and actions. As we noted earlier, attention has a bodily component: a quiet pause must precede right action. She clearly valued the intellectual virtues distinguished by Aquinas of both the *speculative* order and the *practical* order, believing that authentic and pure values—truth, beauty, and goodness—in the activity of a human being can only result from giving full attention to the object. Hers was never a solely interior spirituality, but one that was always followed by a creative attention toward others. Attentive thinking, for her, is always oriented toward seeking the good; it cannot be otherwise. Attention is at the base of every one of the other concepts that we examine in the coming chapters: beauty, charity, suffering, decreation, and grace, all of which require purposeful, methodical development over time, through apprenticeship. Both attention and apprenticeship weave subtle threads throughout her writing.

Her Background

In her youth, although awkward in her physical movements, she had tried to participate in athletics and to deny herself bodily comforts, in order to prepare for any trials that might challenge her in the future. Her

1930s struggle with the workers movement, while she was teaching full time in the lycée, took enormous discipline. Although her efforts did not yield the success she desired, she never regretted the time she dedicated to convincing others to sacrifice short-term gains for the long-term benefits of having more time for reflection, along with quieter surroundings that could foster necessary habits of attention. Attention in the workplace has the obvious function of helping a worker do a good job and enjoy the satisfaction that comes with having accomplished a task well, but after her major encounter with Christ, attention took on the added dimension of nurturing a supernatural quality in prayer.

Aspects of Attention

Attention has a valuable creative element, for it can bring into existence something that was not there before: understanding, dignity, and relationships with others and with the supernatural. For Weil, the discipline of giving full attention needs a constant refining because it is difficult, requiring humility, compassion, a renunciation of self and of personal desires, and, above all, in her religious philosophy, an openness to grace. One cannot achieve the ability to give full attention without supernatural grace; the complete emptying of self with its egoistic desires goes against all that a person has embraced as self. Weil freely admits that the capacity to give full attention is so rare that it borders on being miraculous. A more detailed discussion of attention as a major aspect of Weil's religious philosophy will follow in this chapter.

Overview of the Two Essays

The comments on attention and apprenticeship that Flannery O'Connor would have found in *Waiting for God* and in the *Notebooks* illustrate the high regard Weil gave to attention and the method by which one hones one's capacity for it. These writings were composed in southern France, around the moment of her departure to accompany her aging parents from the Port of Marseille to the New York Harbor. "The Right Use of School Studies for the Love of God"[1] was written at the request of

---

[1] Simone Weil, *Waiting for God*, trans. Emma Crauford (New York:

Father Perrin, newly named director of the Dominican Convent in Montpellier, for use with his Christian Youth Group. Simone had completed "School Studies" before sailing, but had unintentionally gathered it up as she hastily packed her things to embark for Casablanca, the first stop on the two-month hazardous voyage to America over a wartime ocean. On finding the essay among all her other papers, she quickly dispatched it back to Father Perrin for his use with students.

"The Love of Our Neighbor" (*WG* 84-99), also sent to Father Perrin, is part of a longer essay entitled "Forms of the Implicit Love of God" (*WG* 83-142), made up of four shorter essays that we examine separately. She composed it during the eight months of intense activity in Marseille. Her lifelong apprenticeship in writing and thinking allowed her to be abundantly productive, as she composed, seamlessly albeit hurriedly, essays, letters, talks, and ample notations in her *Notebooks*. It is as if she had intuited that her life's journey was coming to a close. Her biographer and friend Simone Pétrement wrote, "[Simone] had acquired such mastery of her thought and her style that the words, continually beautiful and pure and with profound human resonances, flowed naturally from her pen."[2] Her friend the farmer-philosopher Gustave Thibon reflected on the last conversation he had had with her: In speaking of the Gospel, "her mouth uttered thoughts as a tree gives its fruit."[3]

In her "Forms of the Implicit Love of God," Weil makes the point that signs of God's love for his creation are embedded in the material world, and that God is secretly present in them. These supernatural guideposts are not only accessible to our love, but they also reach out to our love, if we give them our attention and allow them to function sacramentally in our lives. The three immediate conditions of our lives, in which God is implicitly present, are love of neighbor, love of the order of the world—which brings us beauty—and love of religious practices. She adds on friendship, almost as an afterthought, a relationship for which she had a special gratitude.

HarperCollins, 2000), 57-65. (Hereafter cited as *WG*.)

[2] Simone Pétrement, *Simone Weil: A life*, trans. Raymond Rosenthal (New York: Pantheon, 1977), 460.

[3] Ibid., 464.

Love for these forms of God's love can further the transformation from an implicit love of God to an explicit one. Weil believed that consent is critical to this change. At first, the response to his love can be veiled, even from one's self, until the critical moment of death when the imperative choice of whether to consent to God's love or not will be made manifest. In her religious philosophy, death is the most precious thing given to man, and it is a sacrilege to be inattentive to the importance of this final moment for others as well as for oneself. The actuality of such a consent constitutes a matter solely between God and the individual, and is not necessarily apparent to an observer.

According to Weil, in her Platonic perspective, human beings need images and symbols that create bridges between the temporal and the eternal to lead them toward the good, which is also truth. Sensitivity to the sacredness of these signs is a requisite; too many individuals see without paying sufficient attention. Since man's actual state is one of separation from God, the existence of these bridges is essential for one's spiritual progress. Weil notes in her *Notebooks*, "The world is a text containing several meanings, and we pass from one meaning to another by an effort—an effort by which the body always participates."[4]

Traces of God and his design are in the world to be discovered by us through our senses. Many things can serve as purveyors of God's grace: objects, elements of nature, people. She refers to these transcendent signs, as we noted in chapter 2, by the Greek word *metaxu*. A metaxu can lead the soul into contact with God, if faith and love are present. The efficacy of a metaxu as a spiritual bridge occurs only if there is a relation between that thing or being and a human subject. She adds: "The essence of created things is to be intermediaries. They are intermediaries leading from one to the other and there is no end to this. They are intermediaries leading to God. We have to experience them as such."[5]

---

[4] Simone Weil, *Notebooks*, vol. 1, trans. Arthur Wills (New York: G. P. Putnam's Sons, 1956), 23.

[5] Simone Weil, *Gravity and Grace*, trans. Emma Crauford and Mario von der Ruhr (New York: Routledge, 1999), 145-146. http://www.mercaba.org/SANLUIS/Filosofia/autores/Contemporánea/Weil%20%28Simone%29/Gravity%20and%20Grace.pdf?hc_location=ufi).

O'Connor's plots are rife with this type of bridge that holds the potential to lead the human toward the divine, although the potential is rarely realized. The essay on the "Love of Neighbor" with its insights into attention and apprenticeship serves as our focus in this chapter.

Development of the Concepts of Attention and Apprenticeship

Even during the time of her philosophically rationalist outlook, Simone Weil knew the importance that both attention and apprenticeship had for human behavior. In her student days with Alain, she used the very complex folktale "Six Swans" by the Brothers Grimm to explore the concept of quiet, concentrated attention focused on a pure action. The purity of the sister's attentive love in her silent efforts of sewing six shirts of the whitest and purest anemone petals to free her bewitched brothers illustrates the power of actions performed through love and given full attention, while remaining absolutely pure. Her complete dedication, despite being falsely accused and on the verge of being burned at the stake, frees the six brothers from the sorcery of the wicked stepmother, restoring their human forms held captive in the bodies of swans.

Our sixteen-year-old nascent philosopher concluded that the only real force in the world is purity; all that is pure and untainted holds a fragment of truth. She had long since perceived that folktales convey ancient wisdom known to the simplest elements in society; she later appreciated the correlation of that immemorial wisdom with the truth found in the Gospels. She came to believe that contemplation of something perfectly pure, such as the Eucharist, destroys evil in proportion to the purity of the desire.

In her lesson plans for her 1933 philosophy courses, attention holds a major place. We find the notation that all the force of the mind is in attention; it is our only force.[6] She describes a method for attention, which is essentially the same as she expresses with religious undertones in her 1942 "School Studies" essay. One must get rid of any obsession about attention, for that will not foster the necessary conditions for attention. Contrary to any compelling tendency or stress in the body, one must

---

[6] Simone Weil, *Simone Weil: Oeuvres complètes*, vol. 1, ed. André Devaux and Florence de Lussy (Paris: Gallimard, 1988), 391.

clear the mind and think of nothing, then begin afresh by giving full attention but nonactively. The importance of attention for creative thought, which Flannery O'Connor would have appreciated, is that flashes of light from pure attention are nothing other than strokes of genius.[7] She wrote in her *Notebooks*: "Extreme attention is what constitutes the creative faculty in humankind."[8]

School Studies

Her "School Studies" essay opens with this statement: "The key to a Christian conception of studies is the realization that prayer consists of attention." Her leap from a secular humanist mode to a religious philosophical attitude is reflected in the new orientation of her writing. The value of attention as a form of prayer and the need for a perpetual apprenticeship to purify its practice become a chief focus in all her writings after her encounters with Christianity. Her *Notebook* entries on attention and its requisiteness for understanding the "other," particularly in complex situations, evolve into her theory on reading (or interpreting), which we have previously introduced and on which we will elaborate further.

In her essay for the young intellectuals, she focuses on their studies as a means of apprenticeship in attention, but it is clear that her message applies to far more than just academic activities. She assures her young readers that every attempt to solve problems, despite a sense that the effort feels barren, will bear fruit elsewhere in some mysterious fashion, for the cultivation of a certain kind of attention and the acquisition of spiritual depth are internally related. She states: "Never in any case whatever is a genuine effort of attention wasted" (*WG* 58), for "every time that a human being succeeds in making an effort of attention with the sole idea of increasing his grasp of truth, he acquires a greater aptitude for grasping it, even if his effort produces no visible fruit.... If there is real desire, if the thing desired is really light, the desire for light produces it" (*WG* 59). The indispensable condition, however, Weil insists, is to have faith that attention will bring light.

---

[7] Ibid., 392.
[8] Simone Weil, *Gravity and Grace*, 117.

To illustrate her point, she alludes to an ancient Eskimo[9] folktale from Greenland that speaks of the origin of light: "In the eternal darkness, the crow, unable to find any food, longed for light, and the earth was illumined" (*WG* 59). Weil believed that any pure desire is really a desire for light.

Simone Weil, who only proposed ideas that could bear the burden of proof in human experience, had two occasions when her attention to recitation bore the fruit of spiritual joy: first while reciting George Herbert's mystical poem "Love"; second, while she was doing agricultural work in the Ardèche in southern France. In the latter situation, she had begun teaching Greek to her friend and mentor Gustave Thibon;[10] they both agreed that they would each learn by heart the Lord's Prayer in Greek. He never did, but she did, reciting it each morning with absolute concentration, starting afresh each time her mind strayed. This experience revealed to her that the quality of extreme attention is closely associated with prayer. Because of her description of the mystical light she received while practicing pure attention is worth reading in its entirety, the extensive quote is given here:

> At times the very first words tear my thoughts from my body and transport them to a place outside space where there is neither perspective nor point of view. The infinity of the ordinary expanses of perception is replaced by an infinity to the second or sometimes the third degree. At the same time, filling every part of this infinity, there is silence, a silence that is not an absence of sound but that is the object of a positive sensation, more positive than that of sound. Noises, if there are any, only reach me after crossing this silence.
>
> Sometimes, also, during this recitation or at other moments, Christ is present with me in person, but his presence is infinitely

---

[9] Weil used the general term "Eskimo," for the peoples inhabiting the regions of northern Canada and parts of Greenland and Alaska.

[10] When she left the Ardèche in southern France to go to America in 1942, she gave Gustave Thibon all her *Notebooks* up to that point in time, and said he was to do with them as he saw fit. He selected and classified certain entries, publishing the selections under the thematic title *Gravity and Grace*.

more real, more poignant, and clearer than on that first occasion when he took possession of me. (*WG* 29)

She continues to build on her prior description of a methodic apprenticeship in learning to give full attention. Attention, she explains, takes an enormous effort, perhaps requiring the greatest of all efforts; nevertheless, it is a negative effort. Neither the muscles nor the will has any place in the practice. By patient waiting and watching with attention one perfects the practice. The thoughts should be empty, not seeking anything, ready to receive in its naked truth the object that is to penetrate it. True attention given to studies, to the beauty of nature, to another in conversation, or to God in prayer involves an element of self-denial, an uncompromising intellectual honesty, and a moral requirement unconditioned by motives of self-interest. She reminds her readers that no one obtains the most precious gifts by going in search of them but rather by obediently waiting for them. The ability to give full obedient attention depends as much on grace as it does on personal effort: the reward is great. She writes in her *Notebooks*: "Each thinking creature having reached a state of perfect obedience constitutes a singular, unique, inimitable and irreplaceable mode of the presence, the knowledge and the working of God in the world."[11] The apprenticeship in attention is to prepare for the gift of grace. Every little fragment of a particular truth is a "pure image of the unique eternal and living truth, the very truth that once in a human voice declared: 'I am the truth'" (*WG* 62; Jn 14:6).

Love of Neighbor

Weil concludes her "School Studies" essay with an allusion to the legend of the Grail—that miraculous vessel that "satisfies all hunger by virtue of the consecrated Host," whose guardian is a king three-quarters paralyzed by a painful wound. The sacred Grail will belong to the first comer who commiserates with the king by asking, "What are you going through?" (*WG* 64). This legendary Grail is traditionally said to be the cup of the Last Supper and at the Crucifixion to have received blood

---

[11] Simone Weil, *Notebooks*, vol. 2, trans. Arthur Wills (New York: G. P. Putnam's Sons, 1956), 363.

flowing from Christ's side. Some historians propose that the original quest for the Holy Grail is age-old, coming from pre-Christian Celtic culture.

Weil's allusion to this legend suggests that what those who are suffering need most is fellow human beings capable of giving them attention. The fact that in this ancient legend such a sacred gift is available to the first person who offers a truly compassionate gesture to the suffering king implies that compassion, unfortunately, is only too rare. If it is Christ's commandment to love one's neighbor, to attentively look at the sufferer just as he is, and to empty one's soul of all its own contents in order to receive into itself the suffering soul in all his reality, and if this moral wisdom has existed from the beginning of man, as Weil believed, what is the underlying cause inhibiting attentive love of neighbor? Weil's response throughout her writings is: the "moral gravity" inherent in human nature.

In Weil's moral and spiritual psychology, the constant downward drag of gravity plays a key role. In the material world, gravity, the force pulling objects to earth wherever there is no counterforce, is part of the universal order she calls "Necessity"; all things are subject to this mechanism, human beings included, save for the opposing force of grace. Man's potential counterforce for good appears weak but, in reality, it is stronger. In Weil's view, human beings, as part and parcel of the universal order of the world or "Necessity," participate in the material force of gravity, physically and morally, for they are subject to an inherent moral weight that draws them persistently toward actions that favor themselves. Weil has written: "The wretchedness of our condition subjects human nature to a moral form of gravity that is constantly pulling downwards, toward evil, toward a total submission to force."[12] The sole escape is in truly desiring supernatural help; she asserts that no request for help in spiritual matters will go unsatisfied, often referring to the Gospel passage: "Which of you, if your son asks for bread, will give him a stone?" (Mt: 7:9; Lk 11:11).

Her view of this universal order comes from the Pythagorean idea of

---

[12] Simone Weil, *Oppression and Liberty*, trans. Arthur Will and John Petrie (Amherst: University of Massachusetts Press, 1973), 166–167.

mediation, a principle that unites or harmonizes contraries. There is an equilibrium in the world of flux because the continual ruptures of equilibrium compensate each other. Human beings, despite being integral participants in this system, have a limited leeway: they have freedom to accept the reality that necessity rules the universe and to love it as God's creation or to maintain an illusion that they are free to do as they please. Despite their choice, they must submit to the mechanism of necessity, under the form of illness, aging, death, natural catastrophes, and evil. If they obediently give their full attention, however, they actuate a supernatural quality that puts them beyond the limits of the mechanism that governs matter by helping them to accept such constraints as a sign of God's love for his creation. We only notice the existence of necessity when it deals us a body blow: the most challenging of times to accept it. An entry in her *Notebooks* states: "The obedience must, however, be obedience to necessity and not to force."[13]

Consequently, Weil was right to offer the phenomenon of attention as a formative notion for young people, which allows the mind to reflect with impartiality on the subject material or situation at hand, and to open itself to supernatural love, away from the pull of moral gravity. Moral gravity can allow one to reduce another to being the equivalent of a "thing" or inert matter, an act that Weil considered a sacrilege. Physical matter is at the furthest point away from transcendent love. The ultimate act in making a person a thing is by killing him.

There are many variations before such a final act of the sacrilege of making a human being into a "thing," such as social oppression, slavery, torture, mockery, and persecution. Flannery O'Connor concretizes the notion of making people into "things" in her "The Artificial Nigger" with the plaster statue of a Negro. For such sacrifices, only attention given fully and selflessly can raise a person from the depths of nonbeing. Simone Weil stresses three of the ways that moral gravity manifests itself in human actions: natural justice, as opposed to supernatural justice, degraded energies from unrealized desires, and subjective, misleading readings of others or of situations.

All three impediments overlap in their effect on human action.

---

[13] Weil, *Notebooks* 1, 150.

Egoistic interpretations or "readings" of others' actions, imposed by desire for vengeance or self-interest due to degraded energies, lead to deploying natural justice (discussed in the next section) or "that which is possible" as a criterion for action. This impulse is almost impossible to block since the soul is subject to mechanical necessity in what she calls its natural aspects. In situations where natural justice reigns, the stronger exploit the weak because they can. It doesn't occur to the victors or to the powerful that the more challenging course of treating the vulnerable as equals could be a more harmonious long-term solution for both sides. This need for immediate satisfaction applies to both individual interactions and group confrontations. As we said earlier, it is unnatural to treat someone as having equal power, when he manifestly is not equal, but such a generosity on the part of the stronger would have as a model the self-abdicating "thought" of God in creation (*kenosis*), which Weil characterizes as love.

Natural Justice

Weil illustrates natural justice with Thucydides' historic example during the Peloponnesian Wars, in which powerful Athenians confronted the hapless inhabitants of the little island of Melos. Traditionally allied with Sparta, the Melians wished to remain neutral in this bloody war, but the invaders gave them the dire alternative of cooperating or dying. The islanders refused to concede, pleading for justice and pity for their age-old city, but the haughty and murderous Athenians, with their superior strength, razed the city, killed the men, and sold the women and children as slaves. Weil focuses on the exchange between the aggressors and their potential victims in which the invading Athenians, who rejected any consideration of justice, framed the situation coldly in terms of the "possible": another term for natural or human justice. They replied to the Melian plea for honest justice with: "Let us rather deal with what is possible.... You know as well as we, the human spirit is so constituted, that what is just is examined only if there is equal necessity on both sides. But, if there is a strong and a weak, what is possible is imposed by the first and accepted by the second."

The Melians countered that the gods would be with them in battle because their cause was just, an argument that the Athenians dismissed out of hand. They disingenuously reasoned that this way of behaving was none of their making; they simply conformed to what was in their best interest:

> As touching the gods we have the belief, and as touching men the certainty, that always, by a necessity of nature, each one commands wherever he has the power. We did not establish this law, we are not the first to apply it; we found it already established, we abide by it as something likely to endure forever; and that is why we apply it. We know quite well that you also, like all the others, once you reached the same degree of power, would act in the same way. (*WG* 86)

Weil proposed that the clarity of their logic, although impressive, nevertheless created a tenebrous situation in which charity had no place. Where there is no charity there is no justice. She likened the Athenians to Romans and to all others who falsely believe in the justice of their cause simply because they are stronger. Throughout her writings, she was adamant that talk of possibility and necessity excludes the conditions for justice. The rationality of their argument lets the strong suppose they can go to the extreme limits of what seems within their reach. But in doing so, they overextend their powers and face an ultimate downfall. Such an illusion, said Weil, illustrates the mechanism of necessity or of human nature in which, when the weak pose no obstacle to the dominant, the strong inevitably exceed their limits. With no need to reconcile two wills, the weak must obey as if they were no more than inert matter and the strong stride roughshod over them.[14]

Degraded Energies

Injustice is inherent in actions that disregard limits; this indifference to immutable limitations inevitably extends to actions that automatically obey the natural order of things. Weil applies this theory to the vital energies that mobilize desire. Desire can have a higher quality or a lower

---

[14] See E. Jane Doering, *Simone Weil and the Specter of Self-Perpetuating Force* (Notre Dame, IN: University of Notre Dame Press, 2010), 186–187.

depending on its relationship to the supreme creative, self-emptying thought or divine love that is the sovereign good. In seeking to satisfy a desire, if one's possibilities of attaining it are exceeded, the energies become depleted and a void is created; the suffering that follows debases the available energies.

In her discussion of degraded energies, Weil, who sought examples for her philosophical concepts in the laws of the material universe, is applying by analogy the second law of thermodynamics to human experience, in which energies are not lost, but degraded through the process of entropy; that is, they are no longer available for useful work. Successive ruptures of equilibrium exist also in social life and in the human soul. This analogy illustrates her doctrine that human beings are subject to the same laws as the cosmos, with, of course, the supernatural exception of grace.

God created through love for love; everything that God created is good. Nevertheless, degraded energy from unassuaged desires can be the impetus toward a great deal of evil. The impulses in the soul that activate the exertion of vital energy in pursuit of some coveted object can, when they no longer serve that goal, leave a void in their wake. She believed that the soul had a terrestrial or "vegetative" part, where everything is finite, limited, subject to becoming exhausted. When a void, due to an elusive desire, is created in the soul, where once there had been energy, there are two alternatives for filling that void. On the one hand, the void could be filled through the easier path of adopting an alternative imaginary good in order to restore a spurious sense of order and balance. This choice, involving an unwillingness to accept the void, has a dangerous fallout, which she calls gravity, for "the void (non-accepted) produces hatred, harshness, bitterness, malice."[15] One mistakenly imagines that some wished-for retaliation, an evil act motivated by hatred, will restore the balance, but, instead, it perpetuates and increases the amount of evil in the world. On the other hand, one could embrace the void as part of necessity, loving it as an integral component of God's creation. This alternative choice is more difficult, though far more in keeping with the goal of a harmonious society.

---

[15] Weil, *Notebooks* 1, 139.

Only by choosing a higher goal can one advance toward truth and effect just actions. Weil explains: "The mechanism by which too difficult a situation debases is that the energy supplied by lofty sentiments is—generally—limited; if the situation requires that we should go beyond this limit, we have to have recourse to base sentiments (fear, cupidity, desire to beat the record, outward honors), richer in energy.... This limitation is the key to a good many reversals."[16] Weil discerns that even though one might start out with higher goals, in reality, base goals, such as vengeance, greed or bodily needs will often supply more consistent long-term energy than an intention grounded in justice. She observes that one makes more sacrifices to achieve an immediate satisfaction than to supply basic needs to many others far away in dire penury.

Such retrogressions led to a disdain for the afflicted rather than any generous concerns on their behalf. In Flannery O'Connor's "The Displaced Person," this condition is embodied in Mrs. McIntyre's exploitative, ungenerous reception of Mr. Guizac. Weil perceived that darker side of human nature in herself when, almost prostrate from headaches, she would want to lash out with unkind, hurtful words to diffuse her suffering to others. She understood that in moments of bitterness and disappointment, there is a tendency to want to extend evil effects beyond oneself. By harming another who is more vulnerable, we gain a sense of importance: we have filled an emptiness in ourselves by creating one in somebody else. Weil continues: "To be able to harm another with impunity—such as passing one's anger off on to a subordinate, while he is forced to keep his mouth shut—is to save oneself an expenditure of energy, which expenditure has to be met by the subordinate in question.... Energy which is economized in this fashion is immediately degraded."[17] Many examples of this phenomenon of abusive behavior by the "all-powerful" masters toward their enslaved are related in slave narratives, a literary form that is belatedly getting the attention it deserves.

"Moral degradation is a destructive, powerful thrust toward violating other beings," one scholar notes in regard to Weil's thought. "The degraded soul is driven by desires that are far from imitative of God's self-

---

[16] Ibid., 36.
[17] Ibid., 182.

emptying pure love. It is fueled by a need for affirmation."[18] Desire attains its highest quality when one desires something solely because it is good. To entertain such a desire requires attention, for when attention is manifest, gravity no longer rules human actions. Pure attention given to another, wishing only his good, is a form of reading that other person from a third view, that of God, who is pure love. When sincere attention is lacking, any interaction degrades the other.

The Notion of Reading

Weil gives several examples of a powerful group or of individuals reading their exploitative actions as right and just, for "the strong sincerely believe that their cause is more just than that of the weak." She often juxtaposes the Gospel parable of the "Good Samaritan" as a contrasting reading. The Athenians deemed that their sheer brute force justified destroying both the Melians and their ancient cherished town, so they razed it and slaughtered or enslaved the hapless victims. The vulnerable people of Melos pleaded for justice as sufficient cause for preserving their precious irreplaceable community—to no avail. A beloved home, a place where generations of people had put down their roots was destroyed, leaving bitterness and hate to fester.

A radically different reading is revealed in the creative attention given to the "anonymous flesh lying inert by the roadside." The Samaritan stops, looks, gives his attention, shares his wealth, and restores dignity to the bloodied victim of ruthless aggressors. For Weil, creative attention means giving attention to what does not exist, thus breathing life into it. She writes of

> a recognition that the sufferer exists, not only as a unit in a collection ... but as a man, exactly like us, who was one day stamped with a special mark by affliction. For this reason, it is enough, but it is indispensable, to know how to look at him in a certain way.

[18] Ann Pirruccello, "Gravity in the Thought of Simone Weil," *Philosophy and Phenomenological Research*, 57.1 (March 1997): 89. I am indebted to Professor Pirruccello for her excellent analysis of Simone Weil's concept of moral gravity.

This way of looking is first of all attentive. The soul empties itself of all its own contents in order to receive into itself the being it is looking at, just as he is, in all his truth. Only he who is capable of attention can do this. (*WG* 64–65)

Weil was intrigued with the wide variation by which people interpreted or read situations. She believed that if the mystery of reading people and situations could be understood, other mysteries in human lives would become clearer, such as how a particular criterion of values, by which people make their decisions, is adopted, and what mechanism prompts individuals to change their readings. She had contemplated the mystery of reading from her activist days until her death. Her *Notebooks* are full of reflections on the topic. It wasn't until her arrival in Marseille that she gathered her many *Notebook* reflections into her two short pieces: entitled "Essay on the Notion of Reading,"[19] and "Some Reflections on the Notion of Value."[20]

Simone Weil was deeply interested in the question of how men form the values by which they make their decisions. What criterion of values allows the group in power to consider a particular class of individuals as inferior, so they could be stripped of their dignity and possessions with impunity? Why do some individuals feel impelled to stop and help a stranger in distress and share with him all they own? She believed that her theory of reading, if truly embraced, could lead to an understanding of these mysteries and to ways of resolving potentially destructive actions. Reading a situation with a third view in mind, God's, needs a lengthy apprenticeship.

For a concrete example taken from the actual act of reading, illustrating binary effects, depending on whether there has been an apprenticeship or not, Weil cites a hypothetical situation in which an identical

---

[19] Simone Weil, "Essay on the Notion of Reading," trans. Rebecca Fine Rose and Timothy Tessin, *Philosophical Investigations* 13.4 (October 1990): 297–302.

[20] Simone Weil, "A Few Reflections on the Notion of Value," trans. Bernard E. and E. Jane Doering, *Cahiers Simone Weil*, 34.4 (December 2011): 455–486.

letter is put in the hands of two women. The letters contain the tragic announcement of the death of each woman's son. One woman reads the words, cries out, and collapses in utter despair; the other sees the letter but has no reaction. The first woman was literate; the meaning conveyed by those black marks on a paper hit her like a physical blow to the stomach, from which she will never fully recover. Every time she sees that letter, the pain will strike again. The second woman was illiterate; she only saw lines of various shapes written on paper. In sum, the black marks on the paper in themselves had no meaning, but meaning was read into them by the woman who could decipher them. Each of us reads our interpretation into events and other people's actions, which cause us physical sensations. How we read each situation depends on what we have learned from our prior experiences and to what extent we can free ourselves from our inherent egoism.

Apprenticeship in a skill can provoke positive responses. Weil often gave the illustration of an experienced boat captain navigating his boat with passengers through the midst of a terrible storm. In that hazardous situation, the chaos, extreme danger, and the desperate desire to escape were felt in the passengers' entrails; the captain, however, read the perilous storm as a formidable obstacle, but one that he could manage with his learned expertise in navigation. Whereas the same storm provoked the physical reactions of fear, helplessness, and anguish in the passengers, in the captain the storm conditions inspired courage, resoluteness, and a reassurance of his ability to carry out his responsibilities with pride.

In both situations, the material conditions exterior to the persons held no emotional content—black marks on a paper or torrential wind, rain, and high waves—but they evoked vastly different interior emotions. Weil, as a philosopher, deeply concerned about human reactions, had been indirectly exploring this phenomenon over many years. She wanted to understand the process of transforming the reactions of visceral angst into valor, a sense of adequacy, and a desire to react with all one's skill. As we saw, when a menacing shadow is discovered to be a bush, not a threatening person, the emotion of fright dissipates and is almost impossible to summon up again. She ardently believed that understanding this psychological mystery of reading could resolve many potential conflicts in their earliest stages.

She had observed how ingrained attitudes toward others could change radically in time of war or civil unrest. In peacetime, one would not think of harming, much less killing, simply at the sight of another's skin tone, facial shape, and hair color. In times of crisis, these same attributes become a cause for murder or desecration. She writes: "our entire life is cut from the same fabric, from the meanings that force themselves on us one after the other, and each of which, when it appears and enters us through the senses, reduces all ideas that might conflict with it to the status of phantoms."[21]

Weil understood that any power to change the meanings that one reads in appearances, and which impose themselves on the emotions, is "limited, indirect and exercised through work."[22] As with a workman and his tools, "every apprenticeship is learning to read in a certain way." How that experience could be honed so that the reading reflects a strong desire for truth and goodness rather than a pernicious illusion is a continuing thread in her reflections on human nature. She states: "the problem of inquiring into what criterion allows us to make a decision, and what technique enables us to pass from one reading to another ... is more concrete" than many other inquiries we could make.[23] In her thinking, the criterion of values used for judging people and events is fundamental to the notion of reading.

In her short unfinished essay on the "Notion of Value," Simone Weil explores the problem of hierarchizing the values by which one lives and makes crucial decisions. For her, this inquiry goes to the heart of philosophy, a process that uncovers the values by which one lives. Any efficacious action needs serious prior evaluation through careful reflection on the assumed criteria of values that lay behind decisions. To society's great misfortune, human beings seldom reflect on the values that orient their efforts because they implicitly believe their motives are sufficient for adopting those values. This refusal to examine one's values causes a great deal of harm to others, as we see in the microcosm of Flannery O'Connor's narratives.

---

[21] Weil, "Reading," 301.
[22] Ibid., 301.
[23] Ibid.

For Weil, individuals always direct their thoughts and actions toward some good; they cannot do otherwise, but too often the good they seek is illusory, egoistic, and destructive. This reality of the human condition demands that reflection, appropriate to the occasion, be consciously undertaken in order to discern and reorder, where appropriate, one's hierarchy of values, for determining a value and orienting oneself toward it becomes one and the same thing. Since truth is a value of thought, philosophical thinking helps individuals make decisions that move them toward truth and goodness. There is often little reflection in the characters that inhabit O'Connor's fiction; such conditions allow the careful reader to experience vicariously the evil that this negligence incurs. Simone Weil's goal in her religious and philosophical writings was to alert her readers to this real danger to their souls and to those of others.

FLANNERY O'CONNOR

Flannery O'Connor's religious convictions found in Catholic doctrine and in her sensitivity to the folk religion of her region were similar to Weil's religious ideas. Whereas Weil presented her religious philosophy in careful analysis and logical argument to awaken students, workers, and all readers to the implicit forms of God's love operating in the universe, O'Connor sharply observed the decline of reason following the Renaissance and the absence or distortions of religious values in the world. Equally intent on alerting her fictional characters and readers to this absence or to varieties of perversions, she applied her ironic gifts with prophetic audacity. Both writers drew upon the rich resources of cultural myths and legends, biblical prophets, and the Gospels to communicate their visions for humanity.

Flannery O'Connor read widely in literature, history, philosophy, and theology not to acquire intellectual mastery of those disciplines but to use them as lights by which to test her own perceptions of the darkening twentieth-century Western mind. Thus, examining Flannery O'Connor's stories through the lens of Simone Weil's works continues a practice of the fiction writer herself. The parallel readings of Weil and O'Connor offer readers a double invitation. First, they have the opportunity to notice details and actions—the sacredness of signs—in the stories to which they may not have attended in prior readings. Second, through fictional characters struggling with the impediments of moral gravity, readers may understand O'Connor's fiction more fully. In addition, the stories may mediate between readers themselves and the visible and invisible worlds they may inattentively inhabit.

All of O'Connor's stories involve the central metaphor of seeing and not seeing. Weil's writings discussed above present central aspects of attention, which require a receptive passivity of waiting and watching. Attention evokes some new insight or brings into existence something that was not present before attention was offered. When bestowed freely, pure attention bequeaths dignity to others. It provides understanding, and builds or restores human relationships. For Weil, devoted attention ultimately opens toward relationship with the supernatural. Paying attention is difficult; therefore, human beings need to be experienced in noticing and seeing beneath surfaces and beyond subjective perspectives. To enter an apprenticeship in attention requires humility, compassion, renunciation of personal desires, and an openness to the mysteries of grace.

Weil believed that human attention, directed toward God as prayer, could be developed by viewing closely an object in nature or by focusing on a geometry problem, even if a solution is not reached or a theorem understood. This insight provides wise counsel for reading "The Artificial Nigger" and "The Displaced Person." In these two well-known stories, each depicting the impediments to attention that Weil regarded as moral gravity, O'Connor offers characters and readers alike apprenticeship opportunities for developing attention. The narrative strategies that foreground the characters' attention capabilities and deficits illustrate the human need for greater experience in attention, which is essential for the love of God and the love of neighbor.

Both "The Artificial Nigger" and "The Displaced Person" draw the characters' and readers' attention with riveting visual details. In "The Artificial Nigger," Mr. Head "awakened to discover that the room was full of moonlight. He sat up and stared at the floor boards—the color of silver—and then at the ticking on his pillow, which might have been brocade, and after a second, he saw half of the moon five feet away in his shaving mirror, paused as if it were waiting for his permission to enter."[24] The narrator, attuned to cosmic signs and familiar with the idioms of southern folks, fills out the opening paragraph with numerous references to Head's seeing, gazing, and interacting with a moon personified as if contemplating itself. The reflected light of the moon hovers over Head's ruminations about the anticipated trip to the city, Nelson's waking and dressing, and their terse exchanges about the purpose of the trip at breakfast. Although the grandfather thinks his grandson would not like the city because it would be full of Negroes, "Mr. Head meant him to see everything there is to see in a city so that he would be content to stay at home for the rest of his life" (*CW* 211–212).

Visual details dominate the story as grandfather and grandson, who "looked enough alike to be brothers and brothers not too far apart in age," wait for the train to appear on tracks that "looked white and fragile" and at which "both the old man and the child stared ... as if they were awaiting an apparition" (*CW* 212, 213). Once on the train, Mr. Head pushes Nelson into a seat next to a window in which Nelson "saw a pale ghost-like face scowling at him beneath the brim of a pale-ghost hat. His grandfather, looking quickly, too, saw a different ghost, pale but grinning, under a black hat" (*CW* 214). The repeated references to an apparition and ghosts carry suggestive burdens of threat, loss, transition, and death.

Characters in "The Displaced Person" are anxiously waiting and watching, here in the presence of the peacock who had followed

> Mrs. Shortley up the road to the hill where she meant to stand.... She stood on two tremendous legs, with the grand self-confidence of a mountain, and rose, up narrowing bulges of granite, to two icy blue points of light that pierced forward, surveying everything. She ignored the white afternoon sun [suggestive of the supernatural] which was creeping behind a ragged wall of cloud as if it pretended to be an intruder and cast her gaze down the red clay road that turned off from the highway.

The peacock who lifts his glittering green-blue and gold tail to keep it

---

[24] Flannery O'Connor, *Collected Works* (New York: Library of America, 1988), 210. (Hereafter cited as *CW*.)

from dragging has his attention "fixed in the distance on something no one else could see" (*CW* 285). Acting as "the giant wife of the country-side," Mrs. Shortley gazes at Mrs. McIntyre's attire, body posture, facial disposition, and she knows that Astor and Sulk, the two Negroes, are hiding behind a mulberry tree near the toolshed to watch the entrance of the black car through the gate.

The narrator presents Father Flynn's delivery of the Guizac family of displaced persons with continuing visual detail, largely through the narrowing and widening of Mrs. Shortley's vision. Observing the welcome of Mr. Guizac, his wife, and their two children, Mrs. Shortley sees mental images of "the three bears walking single file, with wooden shoes on like Dutchmen and sailor hats and bright coats with a lot of buttons" (*CW* 286). As she watches from her vantage point, the Guizacs remind her of "a newsreel she had seen once of a small room piled high with bodies of dead naked people all in a heap, their arms and legs tangled together, a head thrust in here, a head there, a foot, a knee, a part that should have been covered up sticking out, a hand raised clutching nothing" (*CW* 287). Mrs. Shortley's intuitions and vulnerabilities—her subjective perspective—overpower the perceptions of other characters and entertain or irritate the reader through the first part of "The Displaced Person" and hover like a fearful, vindictive spirit over the entire story.

Apprenticeship Signs

Both "The Artificial Nigger" and "The Displaced Person" present elements of apprenticeship, although in more and less fruitful ways. The narrator of "The Artificial Nigger" describes the anticipated journey to the city as a trip planned by the grandfather-mentor for his apprentice grandson to help him see. The narrator compares Mr. Head to Virgil for Dante's trip to the underworld or, better still to St. Raphael, surprising associations given Head's prejudices. One of seven archangels, Raphael appears in the book of Tobit disguised as a human who travels alongside Tobiah, Tobit's son. In the apocryphal book of Enoch, Raphael (whose name means *God heals*) heals the earth after its defilement by the sins of the fallen angels.

The apprentice journey progresses in "The Artificial Nigger" through distorting subjective perspectives, overlapping circles of attention, confusing confrontations, and bravado against getting lost—all impediments to clear attention as they distract and disorient characters. Already on the train, the subjective perspectives of Mr. Head and Nelson collide when Head points out a Negro coming into the car and asks Nelson to describe what he sees. Nelson replies, "a fat man ... an old man," and Head says, "That was a nigger." And Nelson quips, "You never said they were tan. How do you expect me to know anything when you don't tell me right?" (*CW* 216). They collide again in the dining car when exerting his independence Mr. Head tries to take Nelson to the kitchen and is stopped by the authority of the Negro porter, "Passengers are NOT allowed in the kitchen." To save face, Head retorts, "And there's good reason for that," he shouts into the Negro's chest, "because the cockroaches would run the passengers out," which evokes pride in Nelson and the recognition that "he would be entirely alone in the world if he were ever lost from his grandfather" (*CW* 217–218).

The exchange between Nelson and Mr. Head suggests confusion first about what a Negro is. His grandfather did not convey accurate information about the characteristics of a Negro to which his grandson should direct his attention. The confrontation in the dining car reveals Mr. Head's inattentiveness to train dining car rules. In his disrespectful retort to the porter, Mr. Head exposes a more significant inattentiveness to or disregard for the dignity of another human being, which young Nelson interprets as pride-worthy behavior.

Once in the city, Nelson asks, "Well, how do you see all it is to see?" "You walk," replies his grandfather. As they begin, Mr. Head points out the shoe-shine stand and the weight machine, and stops to show his grandson a view of the city sewer system. Nelson is shaken, "connect[ing] the sewer passages with the entrance to hell and underst[anding] for the first time how the world was put together in its lower parts" (*CW* 220). Soon, however, Nelson observes they are walking in circles as his guide attempts to keep the dome of the station in view. To walk in circles suggests the absence of a clear direction and lack of attention for reaching that goal.

The first of Nelson's confusing confrontations occurs when he and his grandfather walk through the section of the city where "black eyes in black faces were watching them from every direction" (*CW* 221). Nelson's sight of the "large colored woman leaning in a doorway" and her ridiculing response to his question about how to get back to town consumes his visual and sensual attention as he "stood drinking in every detail of her. His eyes traveled up from her great knees to her forehead and then made a triangular path from the glistening sweat on her neck down and across her tremendous bosom and over her bare arm back to where her fingers lay hidden in her hair" (*CW* 223). As his grandfather pulls him away—"You act like you don't have any sense!"—"the sneering ghost he had seen in the train window and all the foreboding feelings he had on the way returned to him" (*CW* 223).

A second confusing confrontation for both Nelson and his grandfather springs from Mr. Head's desire to teach his tired grandson, who falls asleep leaning against a building, a lesson through trickery. Hidden around a corner out of Nelson's sight, Head startles Nelson awake with a hit on a garbage can. When Nelson jumps up, looks around, and doesn't see his grandfather, "he dashed down the street like a wild maddened pony," and knocks down an elderly woman and her groceries (*CW* 225). When Mr. Head slowly appears on the scene, Nelson grabs him around the hips to the shouted charge, "Your boy has broken my ankle." Resonant of Peter's denial of Christ, Head replies, "This is not my boy... I never seen him before" (*CW* 226). Repulsed by the denial, the gathered women drop back as Mr. Head walks away, leaving Nelson behind.

For block after block Nelson follows his mentor-turned-betrayer twenty paces behind, and Head, turning to glance at Nelson, "saw two small eyes piercing into his back like pitchfork prongs." At Head's suggestion that they get a "co'cola" somewhere, Nelson displays "a dignity he had never shown before," turning his back to his grandfather (*CW* 237). As they walk on paces apart, Mr. Head begins "to feel the depth of his denial," as his outer betrayal turns to an inward confrontation; "he could not stand to think that his sins would be visited upon Nelson and that even now, he was leading the boy to his doom" (*CW* 227). Both grandson and grandfather walk with darkening ruminations, Nelson's mind "frozen around his grandfather's treachery," and Head's face "in the waning afternoon light looking ravaged and abandoned" (*CW* 228). In relinquishing his early bravado of not being lost, Mr. Head's frantic, arm-waving exclamation to a passerby with two bulldogs, "I'm lost," with its prescient double meaning, moves grandfather and grandson to the third confrontation.

As Mr. Head recognizes that he no longer cares if he never makes the train, a figure within reach of him catches his attention: "the plaster figure of a Negro sitting bent over on a low yellow brick fence ... was about Nelson's size and he was pitched forward at an unsteady angle be-cause the putty that held him to the wall had cracked.... It was not pos-sible to tell if the artificial Negro were meant to be young or old; he looked too miserable to be either.... [Though] he was meant to look happy because his mouth was stretched up at the corners...[he had] a wild look of misery instead." Mr. Head breathes, "An artificial nigger!" When Nelson stops beside Head he repeats in Head's exact tone, "An artificial nigger!" With attentions fastened on the plaster figure, "Mr. Head looked like an ancient child and Nelson like a miniature old man." Gazing at the artificial Negro, "they both could feel it dissolving their differences like an action of mercy." Intending to say something lofty, Head instead hears himself say, "They ain't got enough real ones here. They got to have an artificial one." Quickly Nelson replies, "Let's go home before we get ourselves lost again" (*CW* 229–230).

The narrator reports that when the two step off the train as they re-turn home, the moon appears in its full splendor from behind a cloud flooding the clearing with light, turning the sage grass silver and that Mr. Head "felt the action of mercy touch him again but this time he knew that there were no words in the world that could name it. He understood that it grew out of agony.... He saw that no sin was too monstrous for him to claim as his own, and since God loved in proportion as He for-gave, he felt ready at that instant to enter Paradise" (*CW* 230–231). The third confrontation offers a severe and deeply personal mercy with pro-found social implications. Through pain and agony, grandfather-mentor has become apprenticed to fuller readings of his true situation. The mys-tery toward which O'Connor points characters and readers alike comes through Mr. Head's reluctant apprenticeship to an enlarged reality expe-rienced on his trip to the city. Mr. Head sees, as if through a glass darkly,[25] that all are lost through betrayals, both the betrayed and the betrayers; that turning others into objects, through subjective perspectives such as slavery and racism, freezes human beings into artificial figures; that the denial of Christ's image in others can be passed on to the next generation.

Obstructed Apprenticeships

In "The Displaced Person," the roles of mentor and apprentice are ambiguous from the outset, as Mr. Guizac, displaced by hatred and war, is resettled to work on Mrs. McIntyre's farm. Quickly he displays superlative mechanical skills and a disciplined work ethic put in the service of his employer-mentor, both of which threaten other hired help. In contrast to the singular apprentice journey, with physical and spiritual dimensions, taken to and from the city by Mr. Head and Nelson in "The Artificial Nigger," "The Displaced Person" presents a circle of multiple, largely nescient apprenticeships that overlap and clash. Only the Guizacs from Poland have made a physical journey for Mr. Guizac to be apprenticed as a worker on Mrs. McIntyre's farm. As a Christian and host for a family of displaced persons, Mrs. McIntyre is an apprentice of Father Flynn. Tenant farmers who work the land owned by another, Mrs. Shortley and her husband Chancey serve as tenant residents for Mrs. McIntyre, and Mrs. Shortley assumes a privileged position as self-appointed confidante to her employer. The two black workers Astor and Sulk employed by Mrs. McIntyre receive unauthorized direction from Mrs. Shortley.

All these characters are linked to one another more by accidents of geography, history, and political circumstances close to home and a world away than by choice. Their attentions are attached principally to their subjective perspectives and degraded energies through which they

---

[25] See 1 Corinthians 13:12. Flannery O'Connor frequently used windows and mirrors as mediums for seeing and through which to express her own visions. For her use of Pauline theology see Susan Edmunds, "Through a Glass Darkly: Visions of Integrated Community in Flannery O'Connor's *Wise Blood*," *Contemporary Literature*, 37.4 (Winter 1996): 559–585. See also Richard Gianonne, "Paul, Francis, and Hazel Motes," *Thought*, 59 (1984): 483–503.

navigate the tenuousness of their circumstances and their resort, in the end, to natural justice or injustice. For example, the first of Mrs. McIntyre's three husbands, the Judge, who left her the farm, rests in a fenced family graveyard in the back cornfield, and resides in Mrs. McIntyre's consciousness as she resentfully manages with help that she's seen come and go. After the arrival of the displaced person, who proves to be a knowledgeable, skillful, and conscientious worker, Mrs. McIntyre's resentment lifts as she reassesses her dependence on a chain of tenant farmers and black hirelings, concluding that "at last I'm saved! ... That man is my salvation!" (*CW* 294). She sees him not as a full person but merely as a means to satisfy her personal needs. Her discovery of Mr. Guizac's collusion to marry his Polish niece to the young Negro Sulk, however, radically reorients her subjective perspective on this object of her salvation. Now determined to dismiss Guizac she impatiently interrupts Father Flynn's recitation "when God sent his Only Begotten Son, Jesus Christ Our Lord...as a Redeemer to mankind, He...," with "Christ was just another D.P." (*CW* 320).

Throughout the first part of the story, the narrator adeptly depicts Mrs. Shortley's attention, which moves in two directions simultaneously: to that which she perceives occurring around her and to the mental images that arise internally. Her consciousness often mirrors approaching collisions or anticipates collusions. Keenly attuned to self-interest, Mrs. Shortley functions as a self-appointed liaison between Mrs. McIntyre, her husband Chancey, and Astor and Sulk, warning others and sniffing out threats to herself. In addition, however, her biblical literalism opens her to visions that suggestively link Ezekiel's vision of four wheels and his prophetic call to Babylon's history, to enslavement of Africans, to concentration camps in Europe, and to the McIntyre farm.

Anticipating her and Chancey's displacement from the farm by hordes of foreigners brought "to places that were not theirs, to cause disputes, to uproot niggers, to plant the Whore of Babylon in the midst of the righteous!" Mrs. Shortley "began to imagine a war of words, to see the Polish words and the English words coming at each other, stalking forward, not sentences, just words, gabble gabble gabble, flung out high and shrill and stalking forward and then grappling with each other." She begins to read her Bible, especially the Prophets and the Apocalypse, "with a new attention" (*CW* 300–301). Subsequently, Mrs. Shortley has her own wheels vision. "Suddenly while she watched, the sky folded back in two pieces like the curtain to a stage and a gigantic figure stood facing her. It was the color of the sun in the early afternoon, white-gold. It was of no definite shape but there were fiery wheels with fierce dark eyes in them, spinning rapidly all around it….She shut her eyes in order to look at it and it turned blood-red and the wheels turned white. A voice, very resonant, said the one word, 'Prophesy!'" (*CW* 301).

When Mrs. Shortley overhears Mrs. McIntyre tell the priest that she intends to give Mr. Shortley his month's notice, she sets her face, which "was an almost volcanic red," to frenzied preparations for departure. Loaded and crammed into the car, Mrs. Shortley's stroke precipitates her final vision: "Fierce heat seemed to be swelling slowly and fully into her face….There was a peculiar lack of light in her icy blue eyes. All the vision in them might have been turned around, looking inside her." After she thrashes around, grabbing everything she can get hold of, "Mr. Shortley's head, Sarah Mae's leg, the cat, a wad of white bedding, her own moon-like knee…then all at once her fierce expression faded into a look of astonishment and her grip on what she had loosened." The narrator's description of Mrs. Shortley's eyes in death, that they "seemed to contemplate for the first time the tremendous frontiers of her true country" (*CW* 304–305), recalls Weil's conclusion that death is the most precious thing given to human beings; therefore, it is a sacrilege to be inattentive to the final moment of choice, both for oneself and for others, to consent to God's love.

Largely frozen into objects by others' perceptions and actions, Chancey, Astor, and Sulk exhibit little agency throughout the story. Anxious about her own position, Mrs. Shortley prophesies to Astor and Sulk that "all you colored people better look out. You know how much you can get for a mule…. Before it was a tractor, it could be a mule. And before it was a Displaced Person, it could be a nigger. The time is going to come when it won't be no more occasion to speak of a nigger" (CW 297). Twice in the story Chancey refers to himself as a dead man, first when Mrs. Shortley warns him as he lies in bed pretending to be a corpse that Guizac prowls and probably knows about his still. Chancey responds, "Don't worry me now. I'm a dead man" (CW 297). Second, after

94

Mrs. Shortley's stroke the two girls ask "'Where we goin, Ma? Where we goin?' They thought she was playing a joke and that their father, staring straight ahead at her, was imitating a dead man" (*CW* 305). The energies of human beings treated as objects become deflated, void-like, and vulnerable to turning diabolical.

Before her departure and death, Mrs. Shortley prophesies an inevitable outcome of natural justice, that is, the final collusion in death on the farm. Responding to Mrs. McIntyre's euphoria about the speed with which Mr. Guizac, using the tractor, the cutter, and the wagon, will be able to cut the whole bottom cane in two days, Mrs. Shortley mutters, "Maybe if don't no terrible accident occur" (*CW* 296). When Mr. Shortley returns in part 3 to Mrs. McIntyre's procrastination in letting Mr. Guizac go, "he didn't know how long he could put up with her shilly-shallying" (*CW* 319). In the absence of Mrs. Shortley, Mr. Shortley begins to talk more, practices on himself, and "finds that he had a gift for it....He began to complain and to state his side of the case to every person he saw, black or white." To Mrs. McIntyre he says, "All men was created free and equal, and I risked my life and limb to prove it. Gone over there and fought and bled and died and come back on over here and find out who's got my job—just exactly who I been fighting" (*CW* 323).

Mrs. McIntyre's inaction combined with Mr. Shortley's degraded energies that he has turned into active gossip about her business convinces her of "a moral obligation to fire the Pole and that she was shirking it because she found it hard to do. She could not stand the increasing guilt any longer and on a Saturday morning she started off after breakfast to fire him" (*CW* 324). On the frosty ground she passively witnesses a collusion of the subjective perspectives—misreadings of others and one's situation by the desire for vengeance in the service of self-interest—of Mr. Shortley, Sulk, and herself as the tractor wheels roll over Mr. Guizac, breaking his backbone.

The departure of all Mrs. McIntyre's hired help, the auction of her cows below market price, her nervous affliction that confines her to bed, and her declining eyesight depict the consequences of natural justice where the strong exploit the weak. Only the priest makes visits once a week with a bag of bread crumbs to feed the peacock and explain the doctrines of the church, ineffectual for inspiring consent to the love of God. This fictional set of failed apprenticeships in attention that render love of neighbor on the McIntyre farm impossible depicts in microcosm the perennial imitations of human egocentrism, rebellion, and force from the biblical history of Babylon to the twentieth-century conflagrations and devastation of the Second World War.

O'CONNOR'S *AS IF* AND WEIL'S *METAXU*

One of Flannery O'Connor's consistent fictional devices is her reliance on *as if* constructions to bring to consciousness something that is not readily apparent to a character or to suggest relationships between aspects of reality, between the real and the imagined, between manners and mystery or for converting utilitarian language into a means of revelation. To the extent that this construction may loosen attachments to a person's exclusively subjective perspectives or suggest revitalization of degraded energies or the transfiguration of injustice into supernatural justice, it is necessary to pay attention and to learn to read others and situations as accurately and fully as possible. Johansen has described these *as if* constructions collectively as a territory, even a liminal space, that bridges between one perception and another or, more likely, between something perceived or experienced and something intuited or only vaguely perceived.[26] Edward Kessler interprets the *as if* as an intermundium, a "bridge between the real and the imagined, but it is a bridge that cannot carry her [O'Connor as poet-storyteller] or us to the other side."[27] As Kessler explains, the interaction between the "*as* of direct analogy with the indefinite, conditional *if* ... denies the merger of the dual entities that constitute metaphor."[28] O'Connor assiduously avoided collapsing the two sides of a metaphor, for both were necessary for expressing the ineffable. "The complex meanings evoked by O'Connor's *as if* center on power," Kessler notes, "an inexplicable energy acting on the mind and on or

---

[26] Ruthann Knechel Johansen, *The Narrative Secret of Flannery O'Connor: The Trickster as Interpreter* (Tuscaloosa: University of Alabama Press, 1994).

[27] Edward Kessler, *Flannery O'Connor and the Language of Apocalypse* (Princeton, NJ: Princeton University Press, 1986), 55.

[28] Ibid., 57.

through external nature. This power cannot be named; language can only render its effects."[29]

Simone Weil's concept of *metaxu*, which translates as "intermediary," may provide a fruitful interpretation of the ways in which O'Connor employed the *as if.* Throughout her *Notebooks* Weil uses the term *metaxu* to signify those things that serve as bridges between the human spirit and God. According to Eric O. Springsted and Diogenes Allen,[30] Weil's theory arises from her sacramental view of the world in which all manner of things encountered in it may purvey God's grace or convey an inexplicable power beyond immediate human understanding. For O'Connor who also expressed a sacramental vision of the world often beyond the perception of her characters, the *as if* provided the sign through which she could convey a relationship between the human and the divine, the natural and the supernatural.

The *as if* constructions in "The Artificial Nigger" mediate linkages between creation and the supernatural with examples such as the moon pausing *as if* waiting permission to enter, or the miraculous moonlight that casts a composure of ancient wisdom on Mr. Head's eyes *as if* they belonged to the great guides of men. The references to an apparition or to reflections in the windows that looked *as if* they were ghosts imply spiritual connections beyond the physical forms of both grandfather and grandson. The weight of moral gravity can also be mediated through the *as if* as happens when the black waiter brushes Head and Nelson aside *as if* they were flies, or when Nelson, staring fixedly at the black woman, feels *as if* he were reeling down through a pitch black tunnel, a psychic underworld. The *as if* poignantly mediates acts of betrayal and resentment with spiritual possibilities when Nelson's mind freezes around his grandfather's treachery *as if* he were trying to preserve it for the final judgment, or when Mr. Head stares *as if* he were returning from the dead. O'Connor's *as if* constructions, or her version of metaxu, carry her stories forward on two levels simultaneously: the temporal, natural level

---

[29] Ibid., 62.

[30] Eric O. Springsted and Diogenes Allen, *Spirit, Nature, and Community: Issues in the Thought of Simone Weil* (New York: State University of New York Press, 1994).

with intersecting dimensions of the mysterious and the ineffable, or the inexplicable, presented through the *as if*.

The *as if* constructions in "The Displaced Person," although still suggesting bridges between the natural and the supernatural, pull inexorably toward disquiet and death. From the beginning, nature appears in the form of the white afternoon sun creeping behind a ragged wall of cloud *as if* it pretended to be an intruder. This pretended intrusion of the sun suggests Weil's idea that God watches through nature but never intrudes on it or humanity. The peacock's appearances, with its long blue reed-like neck drawn back *as if* its attention were fixed in the distance on something no one else could see or *as if* it had just come from some sun-drenched height to be a vision for them all, link the physical farm with the supernatural. The bird's beauty and the exquisite "eyes" of its tail, which produces new feathers annually, combined with the information of the legend that its flesh does not decay, sustain the peacock's association with immortality and with Christ. Mrs. Shortley's anxieties about her own displacement next to a family displaced by war and the bones of death are mediated by visions reminiscent of Ezekiel's fiery wheels with fierce dark eyes in them and of the sky full of white fish, another symbol associated with Christ, but these are carried lazily on their sides by some invisible current and pieces of the sun, submerged some distance beyond them, *as if* they were being washed in the opposite direction. The allusions to Ezekiel's prophecy to the valley of dry bones[31] bind the supernatural strength of God's spirit to the enduring history of human sins and violation and to the temporal McIntyre farm as the story rolls slowly toward its final violence. The *as if*s in O'Connor's fiction mediate not only between nature and the supernatural; they bridge the real and imagined, even the distorted imagined as when, after discovering Guizac's

---

[31] In Ezekiel 37, the prophet is led into the valley of dry bones where the Lord directs him to prophesy to the bones saying that the Lord will cause breath to enter them, and they will live. In Ezekiel 38, the prophet is again directed to prophesy against Gog and to warn the people that on the day when Gog comes against Israel, there shall be a great shaking in the land of Israel; "the fish of the sea, and the birds of the air, and the animals of the field, and all creeping things that creep on the ground, and all human beings that are on the face of the earth, shall quake at my presence…" (Ez 38:20).

plan to marry his niece to Sulk, Mrs. McIntyre begins to peer at him *as if* she were seeing him for the first time; his whole face looks *as if* it might have been patched together out of several others. And the *as if* prefigures the story conclusion when Mrs. McIntyre's narrowing gaze closes entirely around his diminishing figure on the tractor *as if* she were watching him through a gunsight. Confirming that the farm is her place and immediately preceding the Saturday morning death of Mr. Guizac, Mrs. McIntyre folds her arms *as if* some interior violence has already been done to her, and she looks *as if* something were wearing her down from the inside.

Two figures, one in each of these two stories, may function as metaxu, potential bridges between human beings and the supernatural. In "The Artificial Nigger" the plaster imitation of a small black figure set with putty on a fence bridges the breach between grandfather and grandson caused by Mr. Head's denial of Nelson. As they both stand gazing at the artificial Negro they feel *as if* they are faced with a great mystery and an act of mercy. Here paradoxically a plaster imitation of a race of people turned into objects becomes a bridge for reconciliation and clearer vision.

In "The Displaced Person" Mr. Guizac comes as a man from another country, one who offers efficient service to Mrs. McIntyre and her farm, and for a brief period of time she describes him as her "salvation." When his aspiration for his niece runs counter to racial prohibitions, Mrs. McIntyre links Guizac directly to Christ as she angrily informs Father Flynn she wants to be rid of him with "Christ was just another D.P." In death, Guizac is turned into an object, a thing, through limited subjective perspectives and the diabolical actions emanating from a void within Mrs. McIntyre and the thwarted desires of the farmhands, which silently collude in death.

CONCLUSION

Flannery O'Connor's "The Artificial Nigger" and "The Displaced Person" illustrate the power of moral gravity to inhibit the development and exercise of pure attention essential for reading the world, people, and all situations accurately. According to Weil, attention purely offered that is free of egocentric interests opens one to God and to the supernatural.

The impediments of subjective perspectives, degraded energies, and commitment to natural rather than supernatural justice inevitably produce debased readings of others and the world. Inadequate readings can become institutionalized in all varieties of damaging social, cultural, religious, or political systems of oppression such as slavery, anti-Semitism, racism, and Islamophobia. In contrast to Weil's social actions, what O'Connor did not express in social-political activism against the injustices of racism or the devastations of war, she addressed poetically through fiction animated with and shaped by her knowledge of biblical, prophetic, scriptural heritage and her Catholic sacramental view of creation.

Chapter 4

Beauty and Charity

Simone Weil's "Letter to a Priest" and "Love of the Order of the World"
Flannery O'Connor's "Good Country People," "The Lame Shall Enter
  First," and "Revelation"

SIMONE WEIL

Apologia for Loving the Beauty of the World.

Simone Weil's sacramental vision focused on the sacredness of every person, which is best protected in a just society with all members attentive to their mutual obligations. A just society fosters conditions in the material world that help individuals orient their actions toward the teleological purpose of life and diminishes those hindrances that, on the contrary, create obstacles on the path toward salvation. In the essay "Forms of the Implicit Love of God," her main dialectical assertion is that God has planted the seeds of a virtual love in each soul, allowing the individual, when he encounters implicit signs of God's love, to recognize what is already known. When no interior or exterior barriers impede the vision, each person can discern divine love in the incarnated traces embedded in the material world and in the relationships between human beings.

We have already seen that compassionately sharing a morsel of bread with another in affliction can be a spiritual exchange, a form of communion, for both benefactor and receiver. Weil expands this idea in "Love of the Order of the World" by stating that "there is no contradiction between love of the beauty of the world and compassion."[1] When we turn our face toward matter with loving consent, we love the order of the world or the beauty of the world, which is the same thing (*WG* 100). In this chapter, we look at the bases of Weil's assertion that beauty is an

---

[1] Simone Weil, *Waiting for God*, trans. Emma Craufurd (New York: HarperCollins, 2001), 116. (Hereafter cited as *WG*.)

implicit form of God's love, as well as her comments on the impediments that prevent one from loving the beauty of the world. Contemplating beauty in silence has the virtue of deepening the quality of our attention turned toward God and toward our fellow man, as well as enlarging the possibilities of overcoming hurdles blocking the path.

In "Love of the Order of the World"—the second section of "Forms of the Implicit Love of God"—Simone Weil sheds light on actions that imitate God's divine act of withdrawing so that the rest of the cosmos might exist. She writes: "By loving our neighbor we imitate the divine love that created us and all our fellowmen. By loving the order of the world, we imitate the divine love that created this universe of which we are a part" (*WG* 99). God loves his entire creation; the secondary or lesser loves in the material world must be loved in the context of a greater love of the cosmos. These inferior loves serve as ladders or metaxu, opening onto supernatural love, but they also can detract by creating false gods or idols. Each moment of reverence, however modest, that we devote to beauty should be considered in the larger context that embraces God's love for the universe, its beauty, and its obedience to harsh necessity. Too often, human beings ignore or squander priceless occasions for giving sacramental attention to the beauty of the universe.

Weil's letter to Father Couturier delineates the many ways that the Christian faith has, in her opinion, neglected or dismissed the beauty and truth in pre-Christian faiths. In ancient times, they who lived closer to nature saw spiritual significance in the stone or wood that they fashioned, in the animals they sacrificed for food, in the vegetation symbolizing divinities, in the relationship between the sun, the moon, and light as an oracular vision of the Trinity. Plato, in *Timaeus*, enigmatically describes the astronomical constitution of the universe "as a sort of crucifixion of the Soul of the World...."[2] For Weil, these ancient religions intuited "the mystery of the beautiful in nature and in the arts (of the very first order) as a sensible reflection of the mystery of faith."[3] She comments in her *Notebook*: "I believe that the mysteries of the Catholic reli-

---

[2] Simone Weil, *Letter to a Priest*, trans. A. F. Wills (London: Routledge & Kegan Paul, 1953), 23.

[3] Ibid., 60.

gion are an inexhaustible source of truths concerning the human condition (… and an object of love). Only nothing prevents me from believing the same thing with regard to other mysteries, or from believing that some of these truths have been directly revealed elsewhere."[4]

She maintains that not only has the Christian Church, in its teachings, disregarded the sacramental gift of beauty that reflects God's love, but its missionaries crassly trampled on the beauty in other peoples' traditional means of paying homage to God's creation. Such was the "[d]estruction of America through massacre, of Africa through slavery, the massacres in Southern France, etc."[5] This desecration disdains the reality that, while the Christian religion explicitly asserts certain truths, which other religions honor implicitly, conversely, other religions explicitly acknowledge truths that are only implicit in Christianity.[6] Since Weil conceives beauty as an integral truth in God's creation, a means of honoring other religions would be by recognizing beauty everywhere as a metaxu.

The Rationale

In her essay on the love of the order of the world, Weil argues for the essential role beauty plays for engendering virtue, justice, love of God and of our neighbor. Beauty is unique, for the universe "has in it no finality beyond universal beauty itself" (*WG* 112). Just as with the heartwarming effects of a smile from a friend, an end in itself that inspires one to strive for Good, "The beauty of the world is Christ's tender smile for us coming through matter. He is really present in universal beauty. This love of beauty proceeds from God dwelling in our souls and goes out to God present in the universe. It is like a sacrament" (*WG* 104). Beauty is its own good, yet it mirrors our desire for good. Being an end in itself, beauty cannot be used as a means, but it can infuse an inexhaustible supernatural energy for serving others and inspire a yearning for immortali-

---

[4] Simone Weil, *The Notebooks of Simone Weil*, vol. 1, trans. Arthur Wills (New York: G. P. Putnam's Sons, 1956), 190.

[5] Simone Weil, *The Notebooks of Simone Weil*, vol. 2, trans. Arthur Wills (New York: G. P. Putnam's Sons, 1956), 345.

[6] Weil, *Letter to a Priest*, 33.

ty.

She evokes St. Francis as an example of a person whose pure delight in the beauty of creation made him revel in his poverty, his life as a vagabond, and his very nakedness, "in order to have immediate contact with the beauty of the world." She elevates his life and poetry to the level of sacramental perfection. "When joy is a total and pure adherence of the soul to the beauty of the world, it is a sacrament (the sacrament of St. Francis)."[7]

Weil speculates that a total incarnation of the faith would be possible if a sense of beauty were made true and pure. Such a reverence for beauty would sweep all secular life in a body to the feet of God. Beauty entices the beholder to love God, by returning his love through developing a deeper spirituality practiced in silence and attention to the needs of our neighbors in affliction. For beauty to serve its purpose, however, one must have faith that God is behind creation, that creation is an act of incarnation: the original enduring Incarnation. She believed that this incarnation was perfected by "the creation of beauty; God created the universe, and his son, our firstborn brother, created the beauty of it for us" (*WG* 104).

The prior section on love of our neighbor and the following section on love of religious practices frame and support the essential importance of love of order of the world. While the first two loves are rarer, the beauty of the world is more accessible. Beauty is present in all the preoccupations of secular life. Beauty is almost the only way by which we can allow God to penetrate us. A "sense of beauty, although mutilated, distorted, and soiled, remains rooted in the heart of man" (*WG* 102). Weil reminds her readers often that a human being is made of carnal matter, and beauty is the means by which the good seduces the flesh in order to penetrate directly to the soul. But counterfeit beauty can also seduce the soul with treacherous effects.

Even with all its risks, having the soul love beauty is God's trap. In his pursuit of humankind, God sets beauty as beguiling bait. For Weil, God hastens into every soul that opens to him, so that he can love and

---

[7] Simone Weil, *First and Last Notebooks*, trans. Richard Rees (New York: Oxford University Press, 1970), 83.

admire the tangible beauty of his own creation. To illustrate this concept, Weil used the ancient myth of "The Hymn to Demeter" as an analogy. For her, "the foundation of mythology is that the universe is a metaphor of the divine truths."[8] "The Hymn to Demeter" recounts that when the heavens were smiling, as was the entire earth and all the swelling ocean, a, young maiden, Kore,[9] reaches out to pick a beautiful fragrant narcissus.[10] Instantly caught, she is dragged under water to another world, and made to eat a pomegranate seed, which keeps her permanently trapped between the two worlds; writhe as she might, she cannot get free.

Weil explains that the girl is the soul; the scent of the narcissus is the sentiment of beauty that makes the whole world smile. The desire to seize beauty is a trap; God uses seduction and violence to capture the soul as soon as it reaches out to beauty. It can no longer escape. Having tasted an instant of divine joy, the soul is bound forever. Weil concludes: "The action on the part of God and the passivity on the part of the soul in the process of salvation — there lies the great lesson to be drawn from this myth, a lesson which can only be revealed."[11]

To approach the beauty of the world, the soul must be set in the direction of love, loving necessity, despite its coldness and separation from the good. When God created the world by withdrawing, he left two other forces to rule in his place, as previously mentioned: "the blind Necessity attaching to matter, including psychic matter of the soul and the autonomy essential to thinking persons" (*WG* 99). The more we choose to embrace necessity by loving it, the closer we come to the beauty of the world. Contemplation of the contradiction of loving both necessity, despite the suffering it can bring, and of loving the world's beauty can lead us to a higher truth: to the Good—to God. Weil uses Job as an example. Because Job steadfastly maintained in his anguish the truth of the human condition, God, in his wisdom, showed Job a divine revelation. Weil claims: "The beauty of the world is the cooperation of divine wisdom in

[8] Ibid., 191.
[9] Weil uses Kore, Cora, and the virgin daughter interchangeably.
[10] This is a version of the Homeric hymn of Demeter, Persephone, and Hades.
[11] Weil, *Notebooks* 2, 382.

creation" (*WG* 104).

Thus, beauty is a means not an end; she writes:

> A beautiful thing involves no good, except itself, in its totality, as it appears to us. We are drawn toward it without knowing what to ask of it. It offers us its own existence. We do not desire anything else, we possess it, and yet we still desire something. We do not in the least know what it is. We want to get behind beauty, but it is only a surface. It is like a mirror that sends us back our own desire for goodness. It is a sphinx, an enigma, a mystery that is painfully irritating. We should like to feed upon it, but it is merely something to look at, it appears only from a certain distance. (*WG* 105)

She exhorts us to "love the country of here below. It is real; it offers resistance to love. It is this country that God has given us to love. He has willed that it should be difficult yet possible to love it" (*WG* 114). By contrast, our heavenly country is a challenge to love because we do not know it, although by imagining it as we please, it becomes too easy to love, but then we risk loving a fiction. The book of Job offers us a vital lesson if we wish also to receive the gift of having the full beauty of the world revealed to us.

FLANNERY O'CONNOR

Flannery O'Connor's sacramental view of life and art makes it easy for one to imagine the resonance O'Connor found with Simone Weil's ideas about the beauty and the order of the world derived from a divine source. In her essay "Novelist and Believer," O'Connor cites St. Augustine, who "wrote that the things of the world pour forth from God in a double way: intellectually into the minds of the angels and physically into the world of things," as support for her own conviction. For O'Connor, "the artist penetrates the concrete world in order to find at its depths the image of its source, the image of ultimate reality,"[12] what Weil considered the Real. Images, metaphors, and analogies of the earth's forms and activities

---

[12] Flannery O'Connor, "Novelist and Believer," *Mystery and Manners*, ed. Sally and Robert Fitzgerald (New York: Farrar, Straus & Giroux, 1957, 1979), 157.

drift over many of O'Connor's stories, tying the narration of human actions to a cosmic order: the moon gazing across a room in "The Artificial Nigger"; the huge red sun like an elevated Host drenched in blood at the end of "A Temple of the Holy Ghost"; a white-gold sun in a sky folded back preparing for Mrs. Shortley's vision in "The Displaced Person"; a river that makes a child count in "The River"; woods in which unimaginable murders occur or are consumed in fire that appear in "A Good Man Is Hard to Find," "A Circle in the Fire," or "A View of the Woods"; a telescope pointed through an attic window toward the stars in search of a dead mother in "The Lame Shall Enter First"; a swinging bridge extending upward from the earth through a field of living fire found in "Revelation"; a burial in the earth and echoes of bread distributed on a hillside in *The Violent Bear It Away* with echoes from the Gospel of Matthew.

Flannery O'Connor weighed Weil's ideas seriously, including the questions such as those Weil raised in her "Letter to a Priest" and letters to Father Perrin about the Christian disregard for pre-Christian beliefs or the neglect of pagan influences on Christian faith. In a letter to Betty Hester on September 30, 1955, O'Connor specifically refers to Weil's letters to Father Perrin on her hesitations about joining the social structure of the church. O'Connor reports that in reading Etienne Gilson's *History of Christian Philosophy in the Middle Ages*, she discovered "various answers to Simone Weil's questions to Father Perrin and Father Couturier. St. Justin Martyr anticipated her in the 2nd century on the question of the Logos enlightening every man who comes into the world. This is really one of her central questions and St. Justin answered it in what I am sure would have been her own way."[13] Justin concluded that the seeds of Christianity or the Logos, which existed in the Hebrew understanding of the Word, predated Christ's incarnation. His *Apologies* and his *Dialogue with Trypho* permitted him to include Greek philosophers such as Socrates and Plato as unknowing Christians.[14]

---

[13] Flannery O'Connor, Letter to "A," September 30, 1955, *The Habit of Being: Letters of Flannery O'Connor*, ed. Sally Fitzgerald (New York: Vintage Books, 1979), 107.

[14] M. J. Edwards, "Justin's Logos and the Word of God," *Journal of Early*

O'Connor would have agreed with Weil that beauty exacts looking and silent contemplation, central to her ideas about attention. Embracing Romano Guardini's view that "the roots of the eye are in the heart," O'Connor asserted that "for the writer of fiction, everything has its testing point in the eye, an organ which eventually involves the whole personality and as much of the world as can be got into it."[15] O'Connor's gift for seeing made it possible for her to survey clearly the state of beauty and order in her twentieth-century section of the world. Of her capacity to see, Marion Montgomery observes,

> This Georgia poet has an eye for detail, out of which she builds metaphor that is as close to earth as Saint Teresa in the kitchen or as an illiterate Georgia country boy on any dirt road from Crawford to Plains. And she recognizes in her gift of seeing an engagement with the earth as crucial to her existence as to her art, a recognition which sets her quite apart from the poet as detached observer.... Her fiction is held close to the earth by seemingly ugly, but familiar local details. We discover that her birds are fiercely petty, like the shrike, or scavengers, like the buzzard. She keeps us close to the grass and to that flesh which is grass, as Isaiah cries to us. Even the lovely peacock, for all his beauty, can scramble awkwardly only a few feet above the earth, being loveliest when both feet are in the dirt, so that he may spread his tail and condense the universe for the poet's eye.[16]

For Weil and O'Connor, human values ideally arise from the love of beauty and love of the order imprinted in the world. Natural disasters or human actions out of harmony with the beauty and the order of the world that produce destructive outcomes, Weil calls harsh necessity, as

---

Christian Studies, 3 (January 1995): 261–280. Edwards argues that Justin's *Apologies* "cannot be elucidated from the pagan schools alone, and that the womb of his Logos-doctrine was the *Dialogue*, where the term is used to confer on Christ the powers that were already attributed in Jewish literature to the spoken and written utterance of God," 262.

[15] Flannery O'Connor, "The Church and the Fiction Writer," *Mystery and Manners*, 144.

[16] Marion Montgomery, *Why Flannery O'Connor Stayed Home* (La Salle, Ill: Sherwood Sugden, 1981), 12–13.

we have seen, also a part of the order of the world to be accepted and loved by human beings. With her keen eye for seeing beneath surfaces and behind pretense or disordered behaviors, O'Connor employs irony and satire to depict situations of harsh necessity caused by human beings' ignorance of or indifference to beauty and the world's divine order. Reading the fiction beside Weil's philosophical and theocentric ideas grounds the stories in the sacramental order respected by Weil and O'Connor but perverted by O'Connor's characters, overlooked by casual readers, and lost to societies entangled in normalized systemic injustices such as poverty or racism and the arrogance of individual and collective thirst for power.

In contrast to Weil's philosophical, elegantly reasoned descriptions of beauty and order, O'Connor signals order indirectly through metaphors and analogies drawn from the backwoods pastures of the earth. Mixed with these earthy details, she anthropomorphizes cosmic elements such as the moon, the sun, the river, a museum mummy called Jesus, which preside over the struggles of human beings to know their place in a two-dimensional reality, one human and temporal, the other divine and eternal. The readers' conclusions about the outcomes of these varied struggles in each story—whether or not they unveil a transcendent beauty and order of the world—depend on answers to at least two questions that we will test with "Good Country People," "The Lame Shall Enter First," and "Revelation": Are O'Connor's characters changed, and if so, how? Can we interpret O'Connor's view of the world from the outcomes experienced by her characters?

According to Weil, beauty is the principal way human beings allow God to penetrate them; therefore, beauty is present in all the aspects of secular life. Indeed, God pursues humankind by using beauty as a trap because, however distorted, a sense of beauty remains in the human heart. In "Good Country People," Hulga rejects the beauty of her first name Joy and the love Mrs. Hopewell, albeit imperfectly, wishes to give her; instead, she claims to believe in Nothing and is vulnerable to the Bible-selling con artist fascinated with the curiosity, if not the beauty, of her artificial leg. "The Lame Shall Enter First" offers several examples of beauty traps that are ignored or misperceived. The young Norton, a vulnerable offspring of beauty, exhibits physical and emotional hungers unacknowledged by his father. Rufus simultaneously enjoys the beauty of cunning required in a life of crime while eschewing the beauty of Sheppard's warped charity. In "Revelation," Ruby Turpin is an outspoken advocate for the beauty of the world as she creates it in her own image and revels gratefully in her good disposition, her cottage, and her fields.

Caught in these beauty traps, are these characters changed either by externally directed encounters or by internal shifts in consciousness? Hulga's external encounter simply leaves her without a leg to stand on. Norton's grief and loneliness have been channeled to death through his unwary trust in an unreliable teacher. Sheppard's ingratiating charity toward Rufus is overpowered by an awakened love for the beauty of his son moments before he discovers his little body hanging from the attic rafters. Ruby's external encounter with Mary Grace's book stimulates self-examination, which leads to a vague appreciation of some secret life exhibited by her pigs and an altered vision of the classes of humanity.

In a critical attempt to understand the nature and consequences of the portentous, often violent, acts of grace visited on O'Connor's characters, Frederick Asals examines the sources and results of such acts. Do the experiences of assault or shock arise from some inner longing of the character, or are they purely externally directed—perhaps, in Weil's terms—as pursuit of them through the trap of beauty? He argues for external direction, because O'Connor projected her own prophetic consciousness "onto her characters, causing them to be relentlessly pursued by God, while they remain in rebellion or revolt."[17] Because of O'Connor's prophetic proclivities, Asals characterizes her stories as anthropotropic, coming from *tropos,* the Greek root for turning, and *anthro* for man, which means the turning of the divine toward human beings. According to Asals, in O'Connor's stories God pursues human beings, stripping them of their worldly virtues yet separated from the transcend-

---

[17] Frederick Asals, *Flannery O'Connor: The Imagination of Extremity,* (Athens: University of Georgia Press, 1982). Susan Srigley, *Flannery O'Connor's Sacramental Art* (Notre Dame, IN: University of Notre Dame Press, 2004), 144. See also See also Abraham Heschel, *The Prophets* (New York: Harper and Row, 1962), particularly the chapter titled "Event and Experience," in which the terms *anthropotropic* and *theopotropic* are used.

ent. If there is a transformation of a character's inner vision from the confrontation, it occurs simply as a shift in consciousness, implying a psychological more than a spiritual change. Asals's conclusion that the characters usually remain rebellious after their encounters seems to foreclose the possibility that the stories could be theopotropic, that is, a turning toward or longing of human beings for God or engagement in a reciprocal pursuit of relationship with the transcendent.

While Weil believed that God pursues human beings and not the other way around, humans are to be receptive and responsive to divine initiative. Susan Srigley argues with Asals's contention that O'Connor's fiction is entirely anthropotropic, leaving characters in rebellion against God's pursuit: "What occurs in such an interpretation is an effective narrowing of the meaning of the experienced vision itself; it has no other purpose than to inform Ruby [for example] that 'the first shall be last and the last shall be first.' The purpose of the vision is thus reduced to a radical separation between the human and the divine." Following Asals's interpretation, Ruby's experience "constitutes a removal of the worldly order of virtues...rather than a transformation of Ruby's *worldly* understanding of the measure of her virtue."[18] For O'Connor and Weil who regarded the world as a key medium through which the divine communicates beauty and order, the capacity for human response to the divine initiative, as in transformed vision of and orientation toward that order, must remain possible.

The discussion of the anthropotropic or theopotropic orientation of O'Connor's stories is important for interpreting O'Connor's notions of the world's beauty and order. Although she never claimed a personal mystical experience such as Weil's, O'Connor was greatly influenced by the mystical tradition, which shaped her own sacramental vision. The writings of the Desert Fathers, Teresa of Avila, the Catherines of Genoa and Siena, John of the Cross, Baron von Hugel, and Evelyn Underhill were influential. If in her stories refusal of transformation seems to have the final word in a character, as it does in Mrs. McIntyre, Hulga, or Manley Pointer, the beauty and order of the world shine through the rebellion, which exposes impartial or imperfect vision—or what might be

---

[18] Srigley, *Flannery O'Connor's Sacramental Art*, 144–145.

called harsh necessity—not a "world" separated from the transcendent order. Indeed, rebellion or revolt contains meaning in reference to the order rejected. In Weil's ideas about the beauty and order of the world, and O'Connor's fictional embodiment of similar perceptions, the internal and the external are not separate. The anthropotropic invites theopotropic awareness. God's search for humans and humans' longing for— even apparent rejection of—God are intertwined. Love of the supernatural—the beauty and order of the world—evolve through the dust of the physical world, material objects, the loved beauty of persons, and the cosmos, any of which can turn into obstacles.

SIMONE WEIL

Obstacles to Loving the Beauty of the World

Weil's religious philosophy weighs carefully all the obstacles that hinder humankind from being beguiled by the beauty of the world as seen in harmonious relationships between individuals and groups. She had confronted a good many of those challenging aspects of human nature during her experience with the workers' movement. That involvement was in a context of secular humanism, which held that any problem rationally considered ought to be resolvable. She found, however, that, given the moral gravity inherent in human nature, rational arguments alone were insufficient to achieve congruous collaboration in a social group. The conflicting tensions were too formidable and egoistic. Social pressure among and against the workers was relentless; the factory owners wanted more profits, the union leaders wanted more power, and the workers desperately needed decent living conditions. No one was willing to give credence to the others' points of view. The members of each group considered only their own needs. These seemingly intractable parameters of human behavior have universal application.

Forceful social coercion seeking conformity rears its ugly head against any attempt to alter the status quo, especially when the change sought involves innovative sharing of society's goods. Means, such as money, power, prestige, meant to be useful for obtaining a goal, become ends in themselves. The "social" becomes imbued with an aura of idolatry, requiring unquestioning loyalty to a leader, a church, a social class, an ideology, a nation. Too many individuals, seeing themselves as the center of their own universe, refuse to acknowledge that others have valid perspectives on the world. Implicit threats hover over anyone who dares to think independently, so that those who speak up for truth quickly face a hostile backlash. Consequently, what might be a situation of harmony and beauty becomes controlling, ugly, and threatening, quashing any incipient attempt to consider a situation objectively, with detachment and a charitable attitude toward the other.

Weil experienced the phenomenon of ostracization herself from her comrades on several occasions when she openly refuted the widely accepted propaganda that Stalinist Russia was a true workers' state; that the German Communist workers, though seemingly strong and stalwart, could buck the coalition of National Socialists and the rich German bourgeoisie; or that Marx was more important than the truth. In 1934, Weil moved on from the workers' movement to do further experimental study on the causes of collective tyranny, producing a long essay: "Reflections Concerning the Causes of Liberty and Social Oppression" that she called her "Testament." Alain named it a "work of the very first magnitude."[19] Her observations about the tenuous relationship between the individual and the collectivity remain valid today. In retrospect, she never regretted the efforts spent on the political and social scene, during which she observed objectively many of the less commendable realities of human nature. Two *Notebook* entries read: "To contemplate the social is as good a way of detachment as to retire from the world. That is why I have not been wrong to rub shoulders with politics for so long," adding that "meditation on the social mechanism is in this respect a purification of the first importance."[20]

Plato's Great Beast and Idolatry

After her conversion from placing full confidence in rationality to

---

[19] Simone Pétrement, *Simone Weil: A Life*, trans. Raymond Rosenthal (New York: Pantheon Books, 1976), 231.

[20] Simone Weil, *Gravity and Grace*, trans. Emma Crauford and Mario von der Ruhr (New York: Routledge, 1999), 166.

believing in the individual's need for grace, Weil's writings all have a salvific preoccupation. To illustrate the dangers that encroach on the aspiration for Good from social constraint, idolatry, egotism, and fear of alienation from a group, she alludes to Plato's image of the Great Beast (*Republic,* book 6). She writes: "The Great Beast. It is a real animal. It is susceptible to force and crushes weakness. It does not look upon humility as a virtue."[21]

In this analogy, Plato compares society to a mob-like beast, whose humors and desires must be indulged to keep it under control. The animal tamers learn ways to make the savage bear or lion gentler and to interpret its sounds, which they praise as words of "wisdom." They take no interest, however, in the vital task of distinguishing worthy ideas from base prejudices, or the good from the evil, or the just from the unjust. One can infer from Socrates' comments a parallel between that type of manipulative handler and self-serving politicians who, in order to stay in power, learn the moods and pleasures of the motley multitude in the assemblage. Simone Weil agreed with the main point in the analogy: that the unfettered Beast, in the long run, controls the individuals not the other way around—to no one's lasting advantage.

For Weil, this similarity between a great beast and a mob represents the treacherous dominion of the social element, which can force conformity to group biases, whether they be good or evil. Such constraint is perilous, for it can encourage all forms of idolatry, but mainly the idolatry of allowing the collectivity to serve as a false god, giving its members cover for evil acts without demanding accountability. She states: "The service of the false God (of the Social Beast in whatever form it may be) purifies evil by eliminating the horror of it. Nothing seems ... evil to him who serves the false God, except lapses in the performance of his service. The service of the true God allows the horror of evil to subsist, and even renders it more intense. Whilst one has a horror of this evil, at the same time one loves it as emanating from the will of God."[22]

She believed that the collectivity is the object of all idolatry that chains us to the earth, for it compels individual members to submit to the

---

[21] Weil, *Notebooks* 2, 370.
[22] Ibid., 504–505.

general will rather than use their intellect. Lacking the fortitude to oppose the throng, they soon find themselves accomplices in evil. In Weil's judgment, the Catholic Church by its use of *anathema sit* has been a totalitarian great beast dedicated to entrenching and expanding its own existence. She explains: "The authority of the Church has a rightful claim to attention only. For each truth in particular, adherence should proceed by an interior illumination of intelligence and love."[23] Although she primarily aimed her barbs at the Catholic Church, her criticisms apply to all churches that favor indoctrination or the social aspect over the essential goal of spreading the message of the Gospels. It is thus that religion becomes piously disguised idolatry. "A society with divine pretensions, like the Church, is perhaps still more dangerous on account of the ersatz form of good it contains than on account of the evil that sullies it."[24] She contends that "the majority of the pious are idolaters"[25] who adhere to a false or illusory idea of God. Though she esteemed the values of a city where a people can feel rooted in a culture, a language, their own history, she warned against the superficial social feeling that can deceptively manufacture an imitation of faith, which to her mind is very dangerous. Weil's originality has been to take the basically religious notion of idolatry and to extend it to the collective or the "social," while still keeping its religious nature.[26]

Attachment/Detachment

Although a person is naturally led by the beautiful, detachment and silence are necessary correlatives to distinguish the true good from the ersatz good. These attributes are rarely found within a vociferous crowd, in which the mob culture predominates and the individuals are attached to a multitude of self-serving interests. In her mind, attachment can manufacture illusions, so whoever truly wants to be in touch with reality ought to be detached. Detachment, albeit vital for seeing the beauty of

---

[23] Weil, *First and Last Notebooks*, 133.

[24] Weil, *Notebooks* 1, 296.

[25] Weil, *First and Last Notebooks*, 308.

[26] See Patricia J. Little, "Le refus de l'idolâtrie dans l'oeuvre de Simone Weil," *Cahiers Simone Weil* 2.4 (December 1979): 212.

the world and for recognizing the other as a full person, is counter to our nature. It requires renunciation, waiting, and patience. Weil notes in her *Notebook*: "To detach our desire from all good things and to wait. Experience proves that this waiting is satisfied. It is then [that] we touch the absolute good."[27] Thus, to have access to the beauty of the world one must not want to harvest or gather the goods of this world, but rather desire to cultivate a detachment analogous to that of St. Francis.[28] Harvesting is consuming or eating, but the beauty of the world requires just looking. In human life, looking and eating are two different operations.

Weil suggests that maybe "vice, depravity, and crime are nearly always or even perhaps always, in their essence, attempts to eat beauty, to eat what we should only look at" (*WG* 105). Vice, depravity, and crime leave poverty and ugliness in their wake, giving rise to self-loathing within the victim and aversion rather than compassion within the observers. This chain of events leaves the sufferer bereft even of the ability to use the freely accessible beauty as a means to lift his spirits. "The soul that is prevented by circumstances from feeling anything of the beauty of the world, even confusedly, even through what is false, is invaded to its very center by a kind of horror" (*WG* 106). For Weil, this is a travesty of the worst kind. She found validation for separating looking from eating in age-old wisdom from the Upanishad: "Two winged companions, two birds are on the branch of a tree. One eats the fruit, the other looks at it" (*WG* 105). She asserts that these two birds are the two parts of our soul.

Self-Centeredness

A noisy agglomeration of individuals has little space or time for quiet contemplation of the beautiful; this lack of stillness allows an indifference toward beauty to develop, leaving a void vulnerable to being filled by an individual's sense of his or her own importance. Weil alerts her readers to this major obstacle of self-centeredness that keeps humankind from seeing the true light and hearing the true voice. When individuals see themselves each as the center of the world—the main focal point in

---

[27] Weil, *Gravity and Grace*, 13.

[28] See Alain Birou, "Le Beau, 'Présence réelle de Dieu dans la Matière,'" *Cahiers Simone Weil*, 17.1 (March–June 1994): 45.

space, time, and values, a sort of imagined divinity here on earth—they are living an illusion, one that is hard to abandon. Using God's renunciation of power in creating the universe can be a model for man to renounce his imaginary likeness to God and to power. She writes: "To empty ourselves of our false divinity, to deny ourselves, to give up being the center of the world in imagination, to discern that all points in the world are equally centers and that the true center is outside the world, this is to consent to both mechanical necessity in matter and free choice at the center of each soul. Such consent is love" (*WG* 100).

FLANNERY O'CONNOR

The prospect of self-emptying and consenting to love that is not manipulated staggers the human imagination. O'Connor's "Good County People," "The Lame Shall Enter First," and "Revelation" offer concrete fictional illustrations of the obstacles that make a consent to love difficult. Weil questioned all obstacles that inhibit the ability to recognize the presence of beauty and the supernatural in the temporal, physical world. All three stories depict characters given opportunities to experience gratitude or to express charity. These qualities nurture love of neighbor, which, Weil asserts, imitates the divine love that created the universe. She warns, however, that love of one's neighbor or love of religious practices is harder than loving the beauty and order of the world because beauty is more accessible and easier to love. "Good Country People," "The Lame Shall Enter First," and "Revelation" depict impediments to gratitude and caritas for one's neighbor, and require the reader to assess how well or poorly the narratives disclose the supernatural through the beauty of the world, even when it is ignored or denied.

Secular Humanism

Both Weil and O'Connor considered secular humanism not merely a distraction but a fundamental disorientation from divinely infused reality. Echoes of secular orientation are particularly audible in the clichéd conversations that Mrs. Hopewell and Mrs. Freeman exchange in the kitchen or in the garden in "Good Country People." Finding it difficult to settle her mind on any point, Mrs. Freeman reverts to "well, I wouldn't of said it was and I wouldn't of said it wasn't." Several of Mrs. Hopewell's favorite sayings are "nothing is perfect ... that is life! .... [W]ell, other people have their opinions too."[29] Despite Mrs. Hopewell's displeasure that her daughter Joy Hulga refuses to believe in anything, she and Mrs. Freeman continue to chatter: "'Everybody is different,' Mrs. Hopewell said. 'Yes, most people is,' Mrs. Freeman said. 'It takes all kinds to make the world.' 'I always said it did myself'" (*CW* 265). Hulga, who has a PhD in philosophy, believes in Nothing, has no patience for her mother's desire to make her daughter at least more socially, if not genuinely, appreciative, and as a secularist, seems intent on dispelling the religious illusions of others.

In "The Lame Shall Enter First," Sheppard is the city recreational director who works on Saturdays at the town reformatory. Bearing the markings of a sociologist, Sheppard turns his secular sensitivity to "helping boys no one else cared about," paradoxically demonstrating love of neighbor while ignoring the grief of his own son (*CW* 597). Of his role as a counselor at the reformatory Sheppard thinks his closet-sized office might be a little like a confessional, though he had never been in one and "his credentials were less dubious than a priest's; he had been trained for what he was doing" (*CW* 599). When Rufus refutes Sheppard's suggestion that someday Rufus may go to the moon with "I ain't going to the moon and get there alive, and when I die I'm going to hell," Sheppard replies, "We can see it. We know it's there. Nobody has given any reliable evidence there's a hell" (*CW* 613).

Through the clientele seated together in the doctor's waiting room in "Revelation," O'Connor captures a secular humanist atmosphere lacking in natural beauty. Amidst the plastic fern in a gold pot, a table cluttered with heavily fingered magazines, a green glass ashtray overfull with cigarette butts and blood-spotted cotton wads, patients display their prejudices, seek recognition from others, and laugh heartily at Claud's racist joke. Mrs. Turpin's gesture toward congeniality and beauty by commenting on the lovely wall clock with a brass sunburst face is met by the announcement that if Mrs. Turpin wanted one like it she could get it

---

[29] Flannery O'Connor, *Collected Works* (New York: Library of America, 1988), 264. (Hereafter cited as *CW*.)

with green stamps. Mary Grace's apparent ability to infer Mrs. Turpin's vanity, her great impatience with the object of her inference, and the general lack of progress of the human race on display in the waiting room ironically mirror the secular title of the book she is reading, *Human Development*.

The Great Beast

For Weil, all forms of social oppression, one of which she describes with the analogy of the Great Beast, present nearly impenetrable obstacles to recognizing and affirming a supernatural order in the world. The Great Beast exerts social pressure that prevents individuals from thinking independently or departing from collective opinions. O'Connor implies the ways academic disciplines may encourage conformist thought in "Good Country People," "The Lame Shall Enter First," and "Revelation." Disciplines such as philosophy (Hulga), sociology (Sheppard), psychology and human development (Mary Grace), the Bible and religion (Rufus and Manley Pointer) provide systems and methodologies for thinking, conforming, and interpreting others' behaviors and the world.

Although O'Connor never wrote directly about the Great Beast of the U.S. history of slavery or the long arc of that legacy that abides in much of her fiction, the narrator's depiction of the waiting room in "Revelation" exposes the Great Beast of economic and social class distinctions among landowners, tenant farmers, and Negroes through clothing, speech patterns, expressed and unvoiced prejudices, through disparities in education, through Ruby Turpin's image of the heap of human beings arranged by race and class, and in condescending gaze and silence. Following Mary Grace's assault on Mrs. Turpin, the flattery Ruby's black workers give her when they see the dark lump on her forehead gives audible evidence of language habits based on power positions. This familiarly irritating exchange with her workers precedes Ruby's continuing fixation: how could she be a warthog from hell and herself, too? As she bends over the pen to watch the pigs "appear to pant with a secret life," her Job-like question roared over the pen, "Who do you think you are?" returns to her as an echo from beyond the wood (*CW* 653). Reminiscent also of Jacob's dream of a ladder between earth and heaven as he wrestled with his own thirst for power and deceitfulness, Ruby's earlier vision of the heaps of humanity turns into "a vast swinging bridge extending upward from the earth through a field of living fire" (*CW* 654). At the head of the line are "whole companies of white-trash, clean for the first time in their lives, and bands of black niggers in white robes, and battalions of freaks and lunatics shouting and clapping and leaping like frogs" (*CW* 654). Ruby Turpin's proud appraisal of her status in the world has been altered by the blow to her head. For the first time she uneasily confronts the reality that divine justice does not depend on rank or clean hog parlors, and it burns through self-righteous merit. Those she has regarded as lowly may indeed be first, and she and Claud may be coming on behind "with a tribe of people whom she recognized at once as those who, like herself and Claud, had always had a little of everything and the God-given wit to use it right" (*CW* 654).

False Piety

Flannery O'Connor was less a philosophical idealist than Simone Weil, who believed that human beings should strive for perfection as a goal. Despite her sacramental view of the world, O'Connor believed that human beings could not perfect themselves. In a May 4, 1963, letter to Sister Mariella Gable, she confessed, "Ideal Christianity doesn't exist, because anything the human being touches, even Christian truth, he deforms slightly in his own image."[30] Placing oneself at the center of the universe and false piety are closely linked means by which human beings deform the beauty and order of the world and pervert offerings of gratitude and charity. In the three stories discussed here, several characters—Hulga, Manley Pointer, Sheppard, and Ruby Turpin—regard themselves and their interests as the center of the world. Hulga stomps into a room when she arises to announce her importance; she sneers at the escapades of Glynese and Carramae, Mrs. Freeman's daughters. She scoffs at her mother's tepid, mock interest in religion yet obsequiousness toward the Bible salesman. She persists in her atheistic belief in Nothing as she asks her mother, "Woman! do you ever look inside? Do you ever look inside

---

[30] O'Connor, "Letter to Sister Mariella Gable," *The Habit of Being*, 516.

and see what you are *not*?" (*CW* 268). Hulga further reveals her self-righteous personal regard when she decides to disabuse Manley Pointer of his piety. But performing as the center of his universe of deception and trickery, Pointer has other ideas. Feigning to be "real simple, ... just a country boy," he convinces Mrs. Hopewell that he is "salt of the earth," before subsequently seducing Hulga with his false piety and absconding with her artificial leg.

Sheppard's desire to mentor the juvenile Rufus held for petty crimes in the reformatory and simultaneously teach his ten-year-old son gratitude thinly veils Sheppard's view of himself as the center of his own universe measured by altruistic behavior. Sheppard's intention to turn Rufus from a small-minded life of crime to one of abundant, family inclusion depends on sustaining Sheppard's illusions about Rufus's behavior and activities, on offering Norton as an innocent for Rufus to mentor, and on repeated clashes with the police in defense of Rufus. Ultimately it leads to the death of his grieving son. Sheppard's irreligious piety is exposed sharply by Rufus's defiant resistance to social improvement strategies and his religious declarations: to Norton he says, "God, kid, how do you stand it? He thinks he's Jesus Christ." To Sheppard's statement that he is going to save Rufus, Rufus hisses, "Save yourself. Nobody can save me but Jesus" (*CW* 609, 624).

When Ruby Turpin and husband Claud enter the waiting room, a gathering place for the infirm and afflicted, she fills the space not only with her size but also with her self-righteous piety through which she dominates her universe. From her moment of entry, Ruby surveys the waiting occupants; notes that there is only one chair available; pushes Claud, who has an ulcer on his leg, into it; silently judges the five- or six-year-old child who was not told to move over or give up his seat for her; and selects a fashionable woman, whose social standing she interprets to be equal to her own, with whom to converse. In the microcosm of the waiting room, the narrator masterfully captures attitudes of the social situation in the 1950s and '60s South through the verbal exchanges of patients whose social positions Mrs. Turpin assesses by their shoes, clothes, speech habits, and behaviors.

The narrator intersperses Ruby's pious private reflections on her good disposition with an imagined conversation with Jesus about who she might have been if she hadn't been created as herself—"'All right, make me a nigger then—but that don't mean a trashy one.' And he would have made her a neat clean Negro woman, herself but black" (*CW* 636). The story characterizes a slight range of attitudes toward race from Mrs. Turpin's weariness from "buttering up niggers" who "don't want to pick cotton any more" (*CW* 639, 638) to the white-trash woman's view that "they ought to send all them niggers back to Africa. That's wher they come from in the first place," and the pleasant lady's response that she "couldn't do without [her] good colored friends" (*CW* 640).

Although Mrs. Turpin's expressed and nonverbal judgments expose her false piety and her distorted order of the world, the presence of Wellesley student Mary Grace in the waiting room adds another view of the world.[31] Displaying ugly, silent displeasure toward Ruby Turpin's self-righteous social and moral underdevelopment, Mary Grace hurls the book titled *Human Development* at Ruby, assaulting her self-image and preparing her for a glimpse of beauty and a revised order of the world.

---

[31] Jean Cash, *Flannery O'Connor: A Life* (Knoxville: University of Tennessee Press, 2002). See particularly Cash's discussion of Flannery O'Connor's friendship with Maryat Lee, a Wellesley College graduate, artist, and political activist for civil rights. Cash writes, "Though [Lee] majored in Bible history at Wellesley, studied theology with Paul Tillich at the Union Theological Seminary, and took a master's degree in religious drama from Columbia, her chief interests were secular rather than spiritual" (228). Upon reading "Revelation," Maryat Lee wrote in her journal, "...[it] has knocked me over. Wellesley girl in doctor's office throwing a book at a typical O'Connor chatty lady smug & fat—telling her to go back to hell that she was a wart hog—& then interesting the girls mad eyes drive the woman into a vision of her & her kind being *last* in line to the Kingdom. Just sent wire. 'Flannery I'm floored with Revelation Love Raygrace.' Shortly thereafter O'Connor gave Lee half interest in Mary Grace, the "Wellesley girl." [Raygrace is Lee's pseudonym drawn from Rayber and Mary Grace.] 236.

Idolatry

If people who live in figurative caves or grow up in ugliness resulting from their own choices or the actions of others are unable to see the beauty and order of the world, they substitute idols for love of neighbor or love of beauty and order. Manley Pointer takes Hulga, who according to her mother chooses ugliness, to the remote cave-like hayloft at the edge of the farm where no one can or will be seen clearly. There he seeks to capture her soul by stealing her artificial leg, necessary to her for both mobility and identity.

Manley and Hulga are linked in their perverse intentions to exploit what each sees as the vulnerability of the other: Hulga seeks to disabuse Manley Pointer of his pseudo religious piety as he performs limb rape of a philosopher who espouses no religious faith and whose soul stands on an artificial leg of Nothingness. Confirming the illusions of residents who inhabit the Hopewell farm, including ignorance of what has just transpired in the hayloft, the narrator reports Mrs. Hopewell's observation as she sees Manley Pointer cross the meadow to the highway, "Why, that looks like that nice dull young man that tried to sell me a Bible yesterday ... He must have been selling them to the Negroes back in there. He was so simple, ... but I guess the world would be better off if we were all that simple" (*CW* 283).

Trapped in poverty and his psychic cave of crime and circuitous flights from police, Rufus uses his elevated shoe as a mark of self-respect and identity. The old shoe serves him as an idol of his cunning, self-reliance, and location in the prevailing social system. Sheppard's offer of a new shoe symbolizes transformed life that Sheppard seeks to offer through compassion, generosity, and sociological charity. Rufus remains hostage in his cave of rebellion and defiance; for Sheppard the idolatry of altruism obstructs both a genuine love of neighbor, including for his son, and a clear view of reality that is the beauty and order of the world.

The cave metaphor is most explicit in "Revelation" where patients wait together as if in a purgatorial space, displaying their fears, prejudices, and idolatries, and anticipating medical treatment inadequate for the distresses exhibited. The narrator refers to shadows cast from outside through the curtains onto the wall of the waiting room, first as the medical messenger on a bicycle arrives and second as the ambulance passes the window to pick up Mary Grace after her violent outburst. Ruby Turpin idolizes her good disposition, which obstructs both her love of neighbor and her recognition of beauty and order beyond her own manipulation.

There is another important, though critically overlooked, reference in the story to interpreting dimly detectable figures or deciphering writing on a wall. Srigley links Ruby's looking at the ceiling of her bedroom as she lies in bed— "she was looking straight up as if there were unintelligible handwriting on the ceiling" (*CW* 648)—to the story of Belshaz'zar in the book of Daniel. "Belshaz'zar insists on using the purloined temple vessels for his own purposes, praising the gods of 'silver and gold, of bronze, iron, wood and stone' to the exclusion of the 'God in whose hand is [his] breath.'"[32] Like Belshaz'zar, Ruby Turpin honors her status and possessions, and lying in bed tries to decipher the meaning of the attack. Only after her injury does her sight clear as she

> gazed, as if through the very heart of mystery, down into the pig parlor at the hogs.... A red glow suffused them. They appeared to pant with a secret life. Until the sun slipped finally behind the tree line, Mrs. Turpin remained there with her gaze bent to them as if she were absorbing some abysmal life-giving knowledge.... A visionary light settled in her eyes. She saw the [purple streak in the sky] as a vast swinging bridge extending upward from the earth through a field of living fire. (*CW* 654)

The bridge carried people, in reverse order of her previous imaginings, with Claud and her, whose "virtues were being burned away," in the rear (*CW* 654). Leaving her perch on the edge of the pigpen, the locus of her vision that leads her through physical animal life to mystery and beauty, Ruby's view of her place in the order of the world is being transformed.

---

[32] Srigley, *Flannery O'Connor's Sacramental Art*, 153. Srigley interprets the Daniel passage: According to the story, when writing appears on the wall of the king's palace and none of the king's servants can interpret it, the queen asks the king to consult Daniel. Daniel reports (5:25) that the message inscribed is *Mene, Mene, Tekel, Parsin* and that Belshaz'zar's kingdom has been found wanting because of its "impiety and excessive pride" (153).

SIMONE WEIL

Caritas and Contemplation of Beauty

Weil was very attentive to the mystery of beauty in visions, in actions, in the universe, and in works of fine art: music, literature, painting. The mysterious unity between beauty and the good in such contemplation had always engrossed her due to its transformative power, within oneself and in relationships with others, particularly the marginalized. Her interest deepened, once she accepted that the good is God, and she saw the good bathed in a spiritual light. Contemplation of beauty reflected in relationships between human beings, a form of caritas,[33] helps form habits of attention, with the necessary detachment and inner silence. This entails looking not eating and having compassion for the suffering of others. She believed that the contemplation of beauty leads a person to obedience to the Good.

We have already commented on her sensitivity to the radiance of the Gospels and the recitation of the "Our Father" in Greek. When she was in the Rhone Valley, she would often be found in deep contemplation of a beautiful natural landscape, and her attentive recitation of George Herbert's poem "Love" became a form of prayer. Thus, she wanted to share with others the vital message that attentiveness to beauty, which reflects the whole of creation operating through the indifferent laws of necessity, gives a privileged access to God and his love. She believed that the soul oriented toward love becomes closer to the beauty of the world by contemplating and loving necessity (*WG* 114).

Beauty and the Good

In one of her early philosophy topoi written for Alain, "Le beau et le bien," Weil elaborated on the inseparable relationship between beauty and good.[34] Any object, creation, or act that is beautiful has as its source

---

[33] In Christian theology, caritas is the highest form of love; applied to Weil's concepts, it is selfless "love," as of God for man and man for God; it is human compassion for one's neighbor, the equivalent of Greek *agapē*.

[34] Simone Weil, *Simone Weil: Oeuvres complètes*, vol. 1, ed. André Devaux and Florence de Lussy (Paris: Gallimard, 1988), 60–73.

the eternal, something that is and cannot be otherwise. She speaks of a temple beautifully made of stone, a piece of music whose beauty would be altered with a change of a note, and a dance, in which all the movements or parts harmoniously fit together. It is in contemplating these artful creations that one perceives an element of eternity, of goodness, even in their fragility. A part of any of these beautiful creations evokes the goal of the whole: "A fragment of the temple is still beautiful because we see in it the symbol of the entire temple, thus all in the universe is beautiful because it symbolizes the entire universe."[35] This criterion of beauty reflecting the good can apply to acts whose source is caritas, which stem from compassion and love of the world as it exists, accepting necessity in all its brutal effects. "Thus, the beautiful, in an act, as in a work of art, has only itself as a finality."[36]

Alexander the Great

Weil gives as an example an incident that occurred during the trek of Alexander, king of Macedonia, over the desert, at the head of his severely dehydrated troops.[37] At a critical point, a soldier brings a helmet containing the last drops of water to Alexander, who was also parched to the extreme. The great military leader takes the offering, remains motionless for a moment; "the troops and their commander look fixedly at each other, the universe is filled with silence and the expectant waiting of all the men." Suddenly, Alexander looks at his bone-dry troops, then at the water, and pours the water into the sand; "their anticipation is fulfilled."

For Weil, the significance of this event exemplifies the spiritual importance of a freely chosen sacrifice, which merits contemplation: Alexander was attentive to the direness of the situation. He had detached himself from his own desire, preferring to look rather than drink; by choosing suffering with his men, he obeyed a higher law. Weil concludes that while it is not exceptional to be thirsty, it is of great importance to refuse to satisfy one's thirst at the expense of separating oneself from oth-

---

[35] Ibid., 63.
[36] Ibid., 68.
[37] Ibid., 405n3. This anecdote comes from Plutarch's *Lives*.

ers. If any aspect of Alexander's sacrifice were altered, it would not be as beautiful or as deserving of contemplation.

She opens her essay on the beautiful and the good with "man lives in three ways: thinking, contemplating, and acting," summing up here the essential criteria for morality in human behavior. Thinking always has truth as its ultimate purpose; contemplation of the order of the world constitutes a contact with the beauty of the world; both must be followed by action. A critical element in the narration of Alexander's "refusal to obey the animal" in himself is the moment of silence: the moment for contemplation, the space for Alexander to read the value of a shared humanity with his thirsty men. His actions reveal that he did not consider himself, despite the vast difference in rank, as the unique center of the universe; he understood that each of his troops also had his own personal perspective on the world. The beauty and justice of his action arise from the impersonal aspect of a gesture that serves no purpose but to "redeem suffering men through voluntary suffering": an imitation of the Passion. It was not one specific man making a gesture, but it was a willing human submission to necessity.

Eighteen years later, an entry in her *Notebooks* refers to Alexander and the helmet filled with water. "Faith, justice; [t]hese come from a sense of right inner disposition and a sense of reading. It is the inner disposition that produces the correct reading, and there is no other criterion. Certain acts proceed from us when we are in such and such a state, without any particular intention motivating us while we are carrying them out. Such is the case with ... Alexander and the helmet filled with water."[38] Alexander's inner disposition was to not separate himself from his men, either through privilege or in suffering, so, he did not attend to his own needs while his men went without water. For Weil, his deliberate action was beautiful because it was good; Weil considered this type of voluntary suffering as bordering on saintliness.

Charity and Gratitude

The teaching in the Alexander allusion parallels the lesson in the

---

[38] Weil, *Notebooks* 1, 298.

parable of the Good Samaritan, in which faith and a sense of justice produce, once again, a correct reading. The Samaritan's reading of a deeply unjust situation leads him to treat as an equal a being who was exposed to others' disdain. Once again, the stronger makes the weaker a gift of the quality of being human, of which fate had deprived him. In this way, the stronger imitates the original generosity of the creator, for whom creation is not an act of self-expansion but of restraint and renunciation.

For Weil, charity and gratitude are inseparable; when both have their model in God's act of creation and in his Passion, the result is beautiful and merits contemplation. When the stronger is truly generous, the gratefulness of the weaker becomes supernatural because of the participation in supernatural compassion, leaving the self-respect of the weaker absolutely intact. This kind of charity or caritas requires a detachment from one's own desires. If the thought that it is better not to command when one has the power to do so fills the whole soul and controls the imagination, it constitutes true justice and faith. The charity of the giver, as well as the gratitude of the receiver, when they are pure, obtain a sacramental beauty, and provide nourishment for the contemplative part of the soul.

Detachment: Part 2

Of the various qualities that can be inculcated when contemplation of beauty becomes an ingrained habit—attention, looking without eating, compassion—perhaps the most challenging are those of detachment and of obedience. To become truly detached from all that we consider ourselves and our possessions is to emulate Christ, but it can be painful. "He emptied himself of his divinity. We should empty ourselves of the false divinity with which we were born.... An imaginary divinity has been bestowed upon man in order that he should strip himself of it, as Christ did of his real divinity."[39] For Weil, that is the way to bear witness to the truth, to recognize that one is made of human material, that one has no inherent rights.

For Weil, detachment is necessary to truly love God with a love that

---

[39] Weil, *Notebooks* 1, 217, 229.

is pure and free from all desire, other than an aspiration toward the absolute good. Here, we continue our prior description of detachment, focusing on the contemplation of beauty. For beauty asks only to be looked at, so the desire that it awakens can lead us beyond the visible to the supernatural. The beauty of the visible world can become a metaxu if cherished as an opening to a higher good. And going beyond material goods to the supreme good means a total suppression of our egoistical desires, and of what we consider the essence of our being. Detachment causes pain because we have become attached to the carnal pleasures in life, and we think that we have a right to continue enjoying them, so we mitigate that pain by indulging in hatred and lies. This pain, activated by our doing without our illusory pleasures, detracts from our willingness to conform our entire being to divine will.

In true contradictory form, detachment means giving up the desire even for that which is good; in effect, it is "to renounce everything that is not grace; and not to desire grace."[40] The goal is to create a void into which grace can enter. The void is the nothingness that preceded creation. For Weil, an act of decreation allows a return, at least virtually, into the uncreated state. Before the creation of our physical selves, we had no desires or illusions; if we can come close to emulating that condition as physical beings, we are in a state of readiness to accept grace. Desires and illusions block the possible entry of grace into the soul, so we must be detached from any fruits of our action, and act for the action not the fruits. Alexander illustrated this sort of inaction in action (*agir nonagir*) when he poured the water into the sand. He acted, but sought no benefit from his action. Intangible results of his gesture were realized, not because his purpose was to that end, but because he accepted necessity and was obedient to it.

Obedience and Obligation

Obedience to necessity or the laws of the universe, which we must accept as our destiny, accompanies detachment. We must allow our free will to be guided by grace, so that we can direct our attention to the ab-

---

[40] Ibid., 130.

solute good, rather than the relative goods, such as carnal loves. Perfect obedience is the *summum bonum* for Weil; obedience is the power of renouncing our own personality, for it is in this way that we are made in the very image of God. For us, the fullness of being is in obediently following the divine model of God's renunciation; such renunciation is the creative and ruling principle of the universe.

Weil gives us a road map for knowing the will of God, along with the encouraging idea that such knowledge is accessible to all who seek it with the sincerity of their whole being. Many aspects of a person's psyche may, nevertheless, hinder the accurate interpretation of God's will. Given that God created the world and withdrew, leaving it to operate under the laws of necessity, according to Weil's philosophy, both the good and the bad are the result of the way God created the world.

> The will of God. How to know it? If we produce a stillness in ourselves, if we silence all desires and opinions and if with love, without formulating any words, we bind our whole soul to think 'Thy will be done', the thing which after that we feel convinced we should do (even though in certain respects we may be mistaken) is the will of God. For if we ask him for bread he will not give us a stone.[41]

There is, in addition, the obligation to help others know the truth concerning the beauty accessible to all and to help them take the sometimes arduous and dolorous path toward God. Weil uses the analogy of the mouth of a labyrinth for the beauty of the world. The unwary individual who enters must find his way in the dark, alone, away from all that is familiar, uncertain of the right direction, fearful of danger ahead. He must go on, for then, at the center of the labyrinth, "God is waiting to eat him." After being eaten and digested by God he will be transformed and must exit the labyrinth, with the obligation to stay near the mouth and gently push in all those who come near to the opening.

This metaphor, which closely resembles Plato's analogy of the Cave, aptly describes Weil's own experience of being taken by Christ (*WG* 27) and her dedication to the task of compelling the rest of humanity gently

---

[41] Ibid., 233.

into the maze toward salvation. Her vocation to carry the message to others has the intent that they too will take a turn at the mouth of the labyrinth, persuading more individuals to enter.

FLANNERY O'CONNOR

Purgatorial Space and the Mouth of the Labyrinth

As Flannery O'Connor read Weil in the summer and fall of 1955, she may have intuited that Weil herself had experienced the labyrinth of which she writes. In an October 30, 1955, letter to Betty Hester, O'Connor noted the remarkable distance Weil had come in her thinking, apparently from her secular philosophy to her religious philosophy following her mystical experience. Traversing that arduous intellectual, psychological, and spiritual path required significant courage.

In the same letter, O'Connor reported that she had also been reading St. Catherine of Genoa's treatise on purgatory, in which O'Connor acknowledged she herself was a strong believer.[42] St. Catherine's acceptance of divine beauty at the heart of life and her commitment to acts of charity echo Weil's ideas about the unity of beauty and the good. Catherine's beliefs about purgatory enlarge our understanding of O'Connor's fiction in relation to Weil's idea about the walk to the center of the labyrinth.

St. Catherine's conception of purgatory appears similar to Weil's convictions about detachment, obedience, and obligation, all of which contribute to the soul's awakening to the beauty and order of the world and to love and charity expressed toward the neighbor. According to St. Catherine, purgatory is not merely a cleansing place between death and entry into paradise. The entire Christian life is one of purgation, for Catherine believed that the only true progress in earthly life is the development of the human soul. A human being's recognition of separation from God yields great pain, so purgatory provides the opportunity to be cleansed of all hindrances to participate in God. Indeed, souls in purga-

---

[42] O'Connor to "A," October 30, 1955, *The Habit of Being*, 113. See also subsequent letters mentioning St. Catherine of Genoa, 118, 121, and a March 16, 1960, letter to Dr. T. R. Spivey, 382.

tory become exempt from self-love because they are being cleansed of pride and cannot turn their thoughts back to themselves. Through the experience of purgation, the soul becomes more and more like God and recognizes, as St. Catherine claimed, that "God is my best self."[43] To this claim O'Connor wrote that St. Catherine "realized probably what Jung means [about the Self] but a great deal more." O'Connor concluded "that the kind of 'belief' Jung offers the modern, sick, unbelieving world is simply belief in the psychic realities that are good for it. This is good medicine and a step in the right direction but it is not religion."[44] One is truly oneself only in God, in detachment from the illusions of egoism and in obedience to God and the obligations of love.

St. Catherine's belief that the Christian life invites and requires purgation offers further entry into the mystery of Flannery O'Connor's fiction. In a long letter to Hester, O'Connor reflects on the role of purgation in her fiction and in her own life, first experienced as she struggled with the creation of Hazel Motes and then in depicting Mrs. McIntyre's condition, at the end of "The Displaced Person," which is a beginning of suffering. Mrs. McIntyre's helplessness to herself is "very like that of the souls in Purgatory."[45] Through Mrs. McIntyre, O'Connor "show[s] a present agony of spirit when one refuses the necessity of the right action of the will toward a recovery of being. To such an agonized [woman as Mrs. McIntyre], the world is a sort of hell ... and perhaps in some degree a purgatory."[46] Srigley's perceptively illustrated analysis of purgatorial vision in "Revelation" encourages readers to consider that all of O'Connor's fiction provides purgatorial space for characters and readers alike to accept or refuse the cleansing from pride and self-deceit. Her allusions to biblical figures such as Jacob, Job, Daniel, and other prophets who encountered and warned about separation from God and disobedience, along with her depiction of devastating historical events spawned by the lures of pride and lust for power, reveal the perennial challenges to

[43] Catherine of Genoa, *Purgation and Purgatory, the Spiritual Dialogue*, trans Serge Hughes (Mahwah, NJ: Paulist Press, 1979).

[44] O'Connor, Letter to Spivey, March 16, 1960, 382.

[45] O'Connor, Letter to "A," November 25, 1955, *The Habit of Being*, 118.

[46] Montgomery, *Why Flannery O'Connor Stayed Home*, 155.

the human soul.

In contrast to Simone Weil, who explains philosophical paths leading to the supernatural realities, Flannery O'Connor principally narrates the conditions that prevent the soul from participating in the beauty of the supernatural order. The kind of vision O'Connor desired for her readers, that is, anagogical vision that can see different levels of reality in an image or situation, also influences the ways her characters do or do not respond to their purgatorial experiences. They must be willing to have their "sense of mystery deepened by contact with reality, and [their] sense of reality deepened by contact with mystery."[47] O'Connor implies that to experience mystery one must be both a realist and a poet: "poetry is always dependent on realism, that you have to be a realist or you can't be a poet … [and] where the poet and the realist are truly combined you have St. Catherine of Genoa maybe."[48]

The three stories considered in this chapter give three responses to the experience of purgation. If characters must be both a realist and a poet to see different levels of reality in their situations, or to detect beauty and the mystery of the supernatural, neither Mrs. Hopewell nor Hulga exhibits those capacities. In fact, O'Connor explained that "Mrs. Hopewell is a realist but not a poet, whereas Hulga has tried to be a poet without being a realist."[49] At the end of the story Hulga is stranded in the hayloft with only one leg, while Mrs. Hopewell and Mrs. Freeman dig up onion shoots from the ground.

In "The Lame Shall Enter First," death itself provokes the purgatorial space that Sheppard and Norton enter. Sheppard responds by heightening acts of charity motivated as much by self-interest and instruction for Norton as by genuine compassion either for his son or Rufus. The child Norton is vulnerable to confusing manipulation by his father and Rufus. Sheppard fails repeated opportunities to see Rufus's hoodwinking actions realistically. Only when it is too late does he experience "his image of himself shrivelled until everything was black before

---

[47] Flannery O'Connor, "The Nature and Aim of Fiction," *Mystery and Manners*, 79.

[48] O'Connor, Letter to "A," December 8, 1955, *The Habit of Being*, 121.

[49] Ibid.

him ... and a rush of agonizing love for the child rushed over him like a transfusion of life" (*CW* 632) right before he finds his dead son.

The character most responsive to her experience of purgation is Ruby Turpin. This prideful racist and classist woman reveals the struggle involved in stripping away prejudices as she confesses to her black workers what Mary Grace called her, joining them for a brief moment in shared suffering. Although she quickly reclaims a position of superiority, calling them idiots under her breath for their excessive solicitousness toward her, the attack and her confession to her workers prepare her for the vision over the pigpen and of the swinging bridge of souls in altered order. Mrs. Turpin possesses the capacity to "read" her situation anagogically. Her self-appraisal has been shattered sufficiently so that she can see through, however ambivalently, to the mysterious possibility of a reordered reality.

Weil's metaphor of the labyrinth and O'Connor's purgatorial spaces may serve similar purposes. Both make possible the evolution of the soul toward its true identity, which is participation in God. Set in the often unacknowledged beauty and order of the world, O'Connor's stories invite characters and readers to enter purgatorial spaces, or the mouth of the labyrinth, to be cleansed of illusion and to walk toward the center to be consumed by God.

Chapter 5

Suffering and Affliction

Simone Weil's "The Love of God and Affliction"
Flannery O'Connor's "The Enduring Chill" and *The Violent Bear It Away*

SIMONE WEIL

In chapter 4, we examined how the beauty of the order of the world is an end in itself; its radiance is freely offered for mankind's contemplation and love, with no finality beyond its existence. Beauty, as a product of the order of the world, brings joy and incites individuals to reach out to touch its loveliness. Weil notes in her *Notebooks*: "Beauty is the harmony of chance and the good."[1] In his pursuit of humankind, God deploys the appeal of beauty in his desire that his gift of supernatural love be accepted. If joy alone enticed human beings to love God, life would be easy, perhaps too easy, allowing individuals to think they were cocreators equal to God and in control of their own existence. Such is not the case, however, for there is a pendant to joy, which is suffering.

Suffering, as well as joy, can also bring individuals into perfect contact with God's love: the primary goal of human existence. Simone Weil tells us in "The Love of God and Affliction" that "joy and suffering are two equally precious gifts both of which must be savored to the full, each one in its purity, without trying to mix them. Through joy, the beauty of the world penetrates our soul; through suffering, it penetrates our body."[2] In her discussion on beauty, Weil refers to its source as the order of the world; the term she favors for the suffering that comes from the workings of the world is "necessity."

Suffering comes in varying degrees, all of which are "ways we can

---

[1] Simone Weil, *The Notebooks of Simone Weil*, vol. 1, trans. Arthur Wills (New York: G. P. Putnam's Sons, 1956), 266.

[2] Simone Weil, *Waiting for God*, trans. Emma Craufurd (New York: HarperCollins, 2001), 78-79. (Hereafter cited as *WG.*)

participate in Christ's affliction and thereby love God with as near a perfect love as human beings in this life are capable of."[3] Other causes of suffering, beyond necessity, are evil acts perpetrated by others, producing great pain, or by ourselves, resulting in acute remorse. Plus, there is anguish that results from very bad choices. Transcending the suffering from the above causes, which can be heartrending, but not necessarily degrading, there is an extreme suffering: affliction[4] that can crush the very soul of the sufferer. Weil herself had great difficulty reconciling the coexistence of God's love and the reality of misery imposed by chance on innocent victims. As a philosopher of deep Christian feelings, yet steeped in Greek Stoicism, she believed "that the virtue of the Stoics and that of the Christians are one and the same virtue," for the "true Stoical virtue is love" (*WG* 49). In consequence, she sought to find some use for suffering since it exists, noting in her *Notebooks*: "The tremendous greatness of Christianity comes from the fact that it does not seek a supernatural remedy against suffering, but a supernatural use of suffering."[5]

Our discussion of Weil's concept of suffering, up to this point, has stressed that by means of suffering, which strips individuals of their sense of self-importance, one gains the potential for sharing in the suffering of Christ. She cites St. Thomas: "Not to seek not to suffer, or to suffer less (in affliction), but to seek not to be affected by suffering."[6] Such a desire can only be fulfilled with the gift of grace, for which the sufferer needs to empty himself of a false sense of divinity and of any illusions of personal merit. God shared his divinity with us in order that we might have something of value to give back. Weil uses the image of a parent who gives his child funds, so that the child can buy a present for the parent. The self we enjoy benefits from being destroyed voluntarily by love from within, for when the destruction is imposed from without, the suffering becomes

---

[3] Diogenes Allen, "Natural Evil and the Love of God," *Religious Studies*, 16.4 (1980): 455.

[4] "Affliction" is the translation for the French word *malheur*, which has no real equivalent in English. It includes the concept of misfortune falling by chance on someone.

[5] Simone Weil, *The Notebooks of Simone Weil*, vol. 2, trans. Arthur Wills (New York: G. P. Putnam's Sons, 1956), 386–387.

[6] Weil, *Notebooks* 1, 106.

extreme and too often degrading.

The reality is that at the onslaught of pain, the sufferer is forced to endure it to the very end, at which point, the realization of a person's full dependency on something higher makes itself manifest. Suffering reduces the will to nothing, so that in time the victim might stretch out his arms, stop, look up, and wait patiently for the divine gift of love. This experience embodies Aeschylus's theme of wisdom that comes drop by drop through suffering, which threads its way throughout her *Notebooks*. She repeats her concept, crucial to her philosophy, that human beings need to see themselves as integral parts of the entire cosmos, suggesting that through suffering the sufferer's body becomes one with the universe.

In "The Love of God and Affliction," Weil pursues humankind's relationship to the supernatural in the most extreme case of suffering: affliction. She writes: "So long as the play of circumstance around us leaves our being almost intact, or only half impaired, we more or less believe that the world is created and controlled by ourselves. It is affliction that reveals, suddenly to our very great surprise, that we are totally mistaken."[7] Thus, she introduces the conundrum of affliction and its vital function.

In her essay, Weil explores the possibility of a closer contact with God due to intense suffering, but she also indicates the great risk to a person's relationship with the supernatural if that person were to deny the inexorable laws of necessity that caused the pain, and thereby reject God's creation. The dangers of such an outcome caused her great anguish. She wrote to her friend Maurice Schumann: "I feel an ever-increasing sense of devastation, both in my intellect and in the center of my heart, at my inability to think with truth at the same time about the affliction of men, the perfection of God, and the link between the two."[8]

The Existence of Affliction

Since the entire gamut of suffering exists, and Weil knows that God is good and can only create that which is good, she seeks to discern some

---

[7] Simone Weil, *Simone Weil: Selected Writings*, ed. Eric O. Springsted (New York: Orbis Books, 1998), 65–66.

[8] Simone Weil, *Seventy Letters*, trans. Richard Rhees (London: Oxford University Press, 1965), 178.

purpose for it within the realm of his goodness. She considers suffering, in its various degrees, and particularly affliction, a call to participate in the Cross of Christ, as the very heart of Christianity, for the "Trinity and the Cross are the two poles of Christianity, the two essential truths: the first, perfect joy; the second, perfect affliction."[9] Affliction impels us to accept our suffering lovingly as part of the world God created. Such an embrace of misfortune requires compassion, consent, renunciation of illusions, obedience, and recognition of impassive necessity and callous evil as the sources of suffering.

To endure the harsh aspects of the human condition and to sustain others in their suffering, she calls, in her last letter to Father Perrin, for a new type of saintliness, one that would include all the qualities just listed above. She wrote: "Today it is not nearly enough merely to be a saint, but we must have the saintliness demanded by the present moment, a ... sanctity...almost equivalent to a new revelation of the universe and of human destiny. It is the exposure of a large portion of truth and beauty hitherto concealed under a thick layer of dust." She continues on with a comparison saying that the world needs saints of genius, just as a plague-stricken town needs doctors (*WG* 51).

This call for a new and original kind of sanctity is typical of her dialectic style, with no definite conclusion, but an indication of a way to proceed. One must reflect on the present, see what is needed, then obediently take the necessary actions. An appropriate analogy might be the person who has been wrenched from his chains in the cave, forced to move up into the light, where he receives God's grace to recognize the pure good. This transformed person, however, must now return into the cave (or the world as it is) and inform others of the truth, which will enable them to see their familiar surroundings in a new reflection of supernatural light.[10]

The task is acutely challenging—even more so under the duress of pain—driving the sufferer desperately to seek and share the knowledge of

---

[9] Weil, *Selected Writings*, 59.

[10] Emmanuel Gabellieri, *Être et don: Simone Weil et la philosophie* (Louvain: Éditions Peeters, 2003), 311–312.

the truth of the human condition. The eternal quandary of why deep suffering exists in a world created by God's love motivates the desire to understand and to comply, if possible. Cataclysmic effects from the laws of the cosmos indiscriminately devastate human lives. Evil actions engender an indomitable desire in the sufferer to spread the pain to others, inciting an endless cycle of maleficent acts. No one is exempt from the misery due to either cause. Basic to Weil's dialectic on the knotty problem of affliction and the evil that generates it is her profound conviction, which she repeats in many variations, that God created through love and for love. He did not create anything except love itself, and the means to love, having created love in all its forms.

Background

This 1942 essay was written during a period of frenetic writing in the midst of preparations to leave Marseille for the United States. Weil, deeply distressed at the menace of affliction hovering over the entire French population cruelly dominated by Nazi occupiers, was still subject to mind-numbing headaches, and to the debilitating psychological "mark of a slave" received during her work in the factories (*WG* 25). While collaborating with Father Perrin on a study concerning the love of God, she slipped the first half of this essay to him without a word, at one of their last encounters. Perrin describes her silent offering to him "as if it were a precious gift offered to a friend, without wishing to trouble him."[11] Father Perrin eventually published the initial part in the first printing of *Attente de Dieu*.[12] The second part, which she sent back to Marseille from her layover in Casablanca, was joined to the first and the essay was published in its entirety in a separate collection.[13] Although she wrote it in two separate sittings, the combined parts read smoothly with no break, forming a seamless and well-crafted whole.

As usual, she is speaking from experiential knowledge. In one of her

---

[11] Joseph-Marie Perrin, *Mon dialogue avec Simone Weil* (Paris: Nouvelle Cité, 1984), 128.

[12] First published in Paris by La Colombe in 1950.

[13] Simone Weil, "Amour de Dieu et le Malheur," in *Pensés sans ordre concernant l'amour de Dieu*, coll. "Espoir" (Paris: Éditions Gallimard, 1962).

letters to Father Perrin, Simone confesses to him that an infinitely tender love has given her the "gift of affliction," and that in gratitude she is asking him, her friend and mentor, to help share with a wider public her reflections on the painful dilemma of suffering, with its potential glorious reward (*WG* 52).

In one of the last letters to him describing her unworthiness to suffer affliction, she hastens to assure him that she is not unaware nor ungrateful for God's mercy, but on the contrary, she knows its richness "with the certainty of experience" (*WG* 43), and wants others to know of it too. Once again, she spoke from personal observation:

> God's mercy is manifest in affliction as in joy…. But it is not the outward results of affliction that bear witness to divine mercy. The outward results of true affliction are nearly always bad…. It is in affliction itself that the splendor of God's mercy shines, from the very depths, in the heart of its inconsolable bitterness. If still persevering in our love, … we end by touching something that is not affliction, not joy, something that is the central essence, necessary and pure, something not of the senses, common to joy and sorrow: the very love of God. (*WG* 43–44)

Father Perrin, struck by the beauty of the text and the humility of the author, writes, "'The Love of God and Affliction' corresponds to what is deepest and most profound in her [and] also the most difficult and most exceptional."[14]

Although Flannery O'Connor would have read only the first half of the essay in *Waiting for God*, the ideas expressed in the second part elaborate on those in the first, particularly with an increased stress on Christ's Cross as redemptive suffering and on the gift of our sharing in Christ's agony.[15] In her *Notebooks*, Weil notes the subtle differences between redemptive and expiatory suffering; both, however, fall on the victim by blind fate. The former is visited on a pure being, whose compassion tears at his own flesh; the physical pain is experienced as God's mercy spreading throughout the world. The latter is the shock of anguish in return for the evil, of which one has been the agent.

---

[14] Perrin, *Mon dialogue*, 128.
[15] The full essay in translation is in Weil, *Selected Writings*, 41–71.

All these thoughts, originally jotted down in staccato form in her *Notebook* entries, relate to the ideas used in "The Love of God and Affliction." They reflect the mystery of the contradiction between God's love that is real and affliction that is also only too real.

Definition of Affliction

For Weil, "Human misery is not created by the extreme affliction that falls upon some human beings, it is only revealed by it."[16] Affliction is a "pulverization of the soul by the mechanical brutality of circumstances,...which imposes itself upon a man quite against his will."[17] Unmasking humankind's dependence on God under all circumstances, even the most crushing, is her goal. To endure harsh suffering that attacks a person physically, mentally, and socially requires the utmost effort both to maintain an unwavering consent and to continue in a loving orientation toward God. This perseverance is extremely difficult, for affliction can destroy the integrity of a person's sense of self. "Affliction is anonymous before all things; it deprives its victims of their personality and makes them into things" (*WG* 73). Just as observers can look on an afflicted person with the shock of horror and turn away, a self-loathing on the part of the afflicted turns the revulsion inward, leaving him emotionally incapable of seeking solace. Even the mental torment caused by the loss of someone dear can cause physical pain. Corporal torment is integral to affliction because, as Weil believes, our body participates in any real learning, and pain guarantees that affliction has not been forged by imagination. "Affliction contains the truth of our situation,"[18] and it can be a bridge to the supernatural, although apprenticeship is needed to appreciate its challenging reality.

Compassion for the Afflicted

Social degradation leaves one humiliated and alienated from others' compassion, and suffering leaves one mute with shock, unable to express

---

[16] Weil, *Notebooks* 1, 262.

[17] Simone Weil, *Simone Weil: Selected Writings,* ed. Eric O. Springsted (New York: Orbis Books, 1998), 65.

[18] Ibid., 66.

even the feeling of debasement. Those who have never suffered affliction have no idea of how harrowing it is, and those who have been mutilated by affliction are in no state to help others; they are perhaps not even capable of wanting to do so. Thus, compassion for the afflicted is a more astounding miracle than walking on water, healing the sick, or even raising the dead, according to Weil. To understand the afflicted, one must have knowledge of affliction, for those who have not seen the face of affliction or are not prepared to, can only approach the afflicted behind a veil of illusion or falsehood. They run away if the look of affliction is revealed by chance on the face of the afflicted.

For Weil, affliction is impersonal, it falls on an individual by chance and is inequitable, although the anguish, beyond simple suffering, is specific and irreducible. Taking possession of the soul, affliction stamps it with the mark of slavery. One can recover from a temporary distress, such as a toothache, however painful at the time, by picking up the threads of one's prior life, but with affliction, one never fully recovers. Weil reminds us that the glorified body of Christ retained the stigmata. Christ's life and crucifixion demonstrate the epitome of affliction. The element of chance transmits the reality that every human being is vulnerable to being struck down to the level of a "half-crushed worm" from one instant to the next. Weil writes: "Extreme affliction, which means physical pain, distress of soul, and social degradation, all at the same time, is a nail whose point is applied at the very center of the soul, whose head is all necessity spreading throughout space and time" (*WG* 81). It is an immensity of force, blind, brutal, and cold, which transfixes the center of a soul.

A person in affliction quivers like a butterfly pinned alive to a tray, but he must continue to want to love. The book of Job, which Weil considered "a pure marvel of truth and authenticity from beginning to end" (*WG* 70), recounts the tale of a soul transfixed. Job, the incarnation of a just and innocent man, suffered the most profound affliction, yet, because his soul remained ever turned toward the truth of God, he was rewarded by seeing the full glory of God. Wanting to love is the essential element.

Suffering in its extreme form can fall on believers and nonbelievers indiscriminately. Weil is convinced, however, that once the potential for love germinates, God pursues relentlessly, coming at his own time, yet everyone has the power to consent to receive him or to refuse. If one obdurately continues to refuse, he stops coming. "If we consent, God puts a little seed in us and he goes away again. From that moment, God has no more to do; neither have we, except to wait. We only have not to regret the consent we gave him…. On the whole, however, the seed grows of itself. A day comes when the soul belongs to God, when it not only consents to love but when truly and effectively it loves" (*WG* 79–80). By contrast, a sorrow that is not centered on an irreducible core of such a nature is mere romanticism or literature.

Consent

Weil speaks of this seed in her correspondence with the poet Joë Bousquet, whose physical and mental agony caused him to be very ambivalent about God's love. His denial was worrisome to her. She first met him around the time she was composing "The Love of God and Affliction," and her ensuing correspondence with him resonates with the ideas in her essay. In Joë, she had an attentive reader whose life was at a tipping point, and, in her opinion, his thinking deeply on the full meaning of his more than two decades of pain could bring him immense spiritual benefit. Bousquet's lower body had become paralyzed after a bullet had fractured his spine during World War I, leaving him bedridden and in constant searing pain over the previous twenty-four years. In spite of an aura of spirituality enveloping him, his refusal to regard questions of good or evil, which on the imperative level she considered necessary for the well-being of his soul, distressed her. She wanted him to be fully cognizant of the importance of consenting to the good of creation, despite his terrible torment, for the alternative would be to default into evil.[19]

The critical moment of choosing between good and evil—consenting to God's love or repulsing it—must not be squandered. She knew the seriousness of the Gospel message: "Whoever believes in the Son has eternal life, but whoever rejects the Son will not see life, for

---

[19] Simone Pétrement, *Simone Weil: A Life*, trans. Raymond Rosenthal (New York: Pantheon Books, 1976), 465.

God's wrath remains on them" (Jn 3:3). She alerts Bousquet that when his decisive moment for consent occurs, he will be able to forgive that bullet that entered his body and "all the universe that directed it."[20] She writes in this essay, "Each time that we have some pain to go through, we can say to ourselves quite truly that it is the universe, the order and beauty of the world, and the obedience of creation to God that are entering our body" (*WG* 78).

The Duke O' Norroway

In one of her last letters to Bousquet, she illuminates God's implacable desire for him by recounting a Norwegian folktale, "Three Nights," which vividly illustrates God's pursuit of man by both torment and beauty, as well as the real possibility of God terminating the quest after a firm rejection of his offer of love. In her *Notebooks*, Weil alludes many times to the fragment of age-old wisdom contained in the folktale that is also called the "Bull of Norroway." Although the details vary in her many allusions, the lesson she infers from the myth remains constant. This is the version of "Three Nights" that she recounts to Joë Bousquet.

A young woman has married a prince who during the day has the form of an animal. One night the young bride destroys the animal skin, which causes her husband to disappear. As she searches for him, barefoot, clothes in tatters, exhausted, an old woman on the wayside gives her three magic hazelnuts. At long last, the grieving spouse finds the prince's palace, but he is on the verge of marrying again, having forgotten the past. The wife, entering the household as a kitchen maid, opens the first hazelnut, which reveals a splendid gown that she uses to tempt the ersatz fiancée to give her one night in the prince's chamber. The intended accepts but gives the prince a heavy narcotic, and, despite the spouse's heartbreaking song, "Far have I sought ye, near am I brought to ye, Dear Duke O' Norroway, will you turn and speak to me?" the prince does not wake up. The second night, the scene is repeated. On the third and last night—for the young wife has only three magic hazelnuts, thus, only

[20] Simone Weil and Joë Bousquet, *Correspondance* (Lausanne: Éditions L'Age d'Homme, 1982), 42.

three sumptuous garments for bribes—the prince awakens just before daybreak, as the opiate is wearing off. As soon as he recognizes his true love, he chases off the other woman.

In Weil's interpretation of the tale, the spouse is Christ, who, indefatigably, stalks the wayward soul, in this case the prince. The unscrupulous fiancée is the siren appeal of the flesh that distracts the fickle soul from its true destination with illusions of pleasure. There are "two unions of the married pair, the first one at night, and the second one openly, obtained by ruse and the arts of seduction, but in the last resort with consent."[21] Eventually God enthralls the soul, using beauty and suffering. The intention is to signal that God marshals all the devices at his command, even violence, as we saw in the fate of the young maiden, Kore, and the narcissus, to strip away the veil of distracting illusions and sensual pleasure, enabling the soul not only to perceive the real but to consent and to embrace it. Weil often uses the metaphor of force or violence to show God's firm intent to capture the soul.

Her comment on the Hymn to Demeter is: "Tearing a girl away from her mother's side, against her will—the greatest and most painful form of violence that it is possible for men to commit—is what serves us as an image of grace."[22] She compares this to Plato's analogy of the cave: "The captive in the Cave who is violently compelled to turn round and walk towards the opening, and who tries to rush back to his wall, and is again dragged forward by force—that is Kore in the Hymn to Demeter.[23] Her illustration of the point of the nail applied to the center of the soul or the man quivering like a butterfly pinned alive to a tray shows "affliction as a marvel of divine technique" (*WG* 81). These examples reveal in stark images the difficulty in getting individuals to redirect their sights toward the love of God and away from love of self, with all its comfortable illusions. Weil's metaphors "illustrate that we are at best receivers, not controllers, of transformative grace, and that grace changes us forever."[24]

---

[21] Weil, *Notebooks* 2, 382.

[22] Ibid., 401.

[23] Ibid., 384.

[24] Ann Pirruccello, "Simone Weil's Violent Grace," *Cahiers Simone Weil*, 19.4 (December 1996): 402. See Professor Pirruccello's article for an excellent

Human will is weak, and many distractions can lure a soul away from dealing directly with the real, such as desire for power, money, fame, and luxuries; affliction itself could be a serious deterrent, for despair can ensue. By remembering that love is a direction, not a state of the soul (*WG* 81), keeping this thought firmly in mind throughout the ordeal, and devoting all energies toward remaining obedient to necessity, one can arrive at the real or the truth. She writes: "Each thinking creature having reached a state of perfect obedience constitutes a singular, unique, inimitable and irreplaceable mode of the presence, the knowledge and the working of God in the world."[25]

Obedience

This attitude of acquiescence and submission appears to be an about-face from the earlier feisty revolutionary Simone in the atmosphere of secular humanism, when she organized worker revolts, participated in protest marches, wrote scathing polemics. The transition from self-reliance to deference stems from the shattered sense of dignity and self-respect that occurred during the oppressive experience in the metallurgy factories, under the daily crushing constraint of speed and output. In this situation, to her astonishment, instead of feeling hot-blooded revolt rising within her, she had succumbed to the docility of a beast of burden marked by the red-hot iron that branded the most-despised Roman slaves.

Her second contact with Christianity in a small Portuguese village gave the concept of slavery a spiritual underpinning. After hearing ancient canticles sung with heartrending sadness by wives of fishermen on the festival of their patron saint as they processed around the boats about to transport their loved ones on dangerous fishing expeditions, she wrote: "There the conviction was suddenly borne in upon me that Christianity is pre-eminently the religion of slaves, that slaves cannot help belonging to it, and I among others" (*WG* 26). This moment crystalized for her the essentiality of Christ's obedience on the Cross and the need to emulate his submission; nevertheless, she remains fiercely adamant that oppres-

---

overview of the issue of grace and violence.

[25] Weil, *Notebooks* 2, 363.

sive external force must be resisted at every turn.

Delineating the two conflicting objects of obedience, self-centered illusions or truth, she notes:

> We can obey the force of gravity or we can obey the relationship of things. In the first case, we do what we are urged to by the imagination which fills up voids. We can affix thereto, and often with a show of truth, a variety of labels to it, including righteousness and God. If we suspend the filling up activity of the imagination and fix our attention on the relationship between things, a necessity becomes apparent which we cannot help obeying. Until then we have not the notion of necessity, nor have we the sense of obedience.[26]

Suffering must be loved as part of the network of relationships that make up the order of the world. Christ's total obedience in his filial relationship with the Father, even to submitting to crucifixion, reveals the way to God, despite his absence. Christ's lament, "My God, My God, why have you abandoned me?" received no answer. The isolated afflicted soul that persists in the love of the silent God rejoins Christ on the Cross, and comes into the presence of God. "The just man loves.... He who is capable not only of listening but also of loving hears this silence as the word of God.... Necessity is the vibration of God's silence."[27]

Weil's insights in "The Love of God and Affliction" sum up her spiritual path, during which she sought to interiorize a harmony with the beauty of the world, all in single-minded obedience to a supernatural love of God. She knew that passing through the trials of suffering and affliction, one must remain faithful to the desire to see the face of God, not only in the beauty of the sky but also in the servitude created by necessity. Only affliction and beauty are piercing enough to penetrate our souls. The goal is to read matter's pure obedience expressed in the movements of the cosmos, accepting necessity's indifference to good and evil. If seen in that light, matter becomes beautiful as it perfectly obeys God, as do the lilies in the field and the constantly forming folds of the ocean waves.

In her *Notebooks*, one finds: "Obedience is the only pure motive, the

---

[26] Weil, *Notebooks* 1, 155.
[27] Weil, *Selected Writings*, 70.

only one which does not in the slightest degree seek a reward for the action, but leaves all care of reward to the Father who is in secret, and who sees in secret.... The obedience must, however, be obedience to necessity and not to force."[28] Obedience to God leads to a unity of necessity and freedom.[29] In truth, she reminds us that "the only choice given to men, as intelligent and free creatures, is to desire obedience or not to desire it" (*WG* 76), for "as soon as we feel this obedience with our whole being, we see God" (*WG* 77). Since obedience to the cosmos, however, is never obedience to human oppression and constraint, she wants the word "necessity" to take the place of the word "constraint."

Learning to read the obedience of the universe to God in all things is like mastering a trade, requiring time and effort (*WG* 78). Whether we accept or refuse the apprenticeship, we still remain subject to necessity, but by accepting, we obey a new set of laws: the laws governing supernatural things. Weil concedes that God has created a world that is difficult for human beings to understand, for it contains the whole range of good and evil and holds the full spectrum of joy and affliction. Such a world enjoins the imperative obligation for compassion to alleviate avoidable suffering from sinister acts.

Moral Gravity

Within the compass of evil, Weil suggests three types: physical and cosmic events, faults and sins of human beings, and suffering and affliction. Having touched on the first and third, we will look more closely at the category that deals with human sins and faults, which result directly from inherent moral gravity on the part of human beings. Since her religious philosophy is founded on the existence of an absolute good that resides outside our material world, all aspects of life on earth contain an necessary mixture of good and evil, as do human beings. This pull downward toward adverse behavior, she refers to as moral gravity. Humankind's goal, just as hers was, must focus on efforts, in every possible form, to diminish the evil that harms human souls, despite the reality

---

[28] Weil, *Notebooks* 1, 150.
[29] Simone Weil, *First and Last Notebooks* (New York: Oxford University Press, 1970), 90.

that its eradication can never fully occur.

Sin, in Weil's spiritual economy, is that which directly affects one's personal relationship with God; as for evil acts, she prefers the words "crime" or "fault." Although God bears no responsibility for sins or crimes since man shares in the composite of good and evil, the supernatural is omnipresent in human life to make grace available to counter any separation of humankind from God. Sin engages acts that break the ties between God and his creatures; faults and crimes disintegrate relationships between people. The tendency toward ego-satisfying behavior, weighed down by the inexorable force of moral gravity, inclines individuals toward imagining pretexts that fabricate affirmative reasons for legitimizing questionable behaviors, bathing them in a salutary light. "In the same way as pretexts are necessary for unjust wars, a promise of some false good is necessary for sin, because we cannot endure the thought that we are going in the direction of evil."[30] Since humankind inherently prefers the good, any light shown on the motivation makes the veil of illusions more fragile, for evil is blind and flees the light.

Weil was obsessed, as we have seen, with the social origins of suffering, both malignant and redemptive. By the two analogies already presented—Plato's image of the Great Beast and Thucydides's narration of the Melians' decimation by the Athenians—she alerted her readers to the negative consequences of actions stemming from injustice and violence—in psychological and physical forms. In the former case, often a stainless victim will absorb, by his own redemptive suffering, the violence emanating from a quarrelsome crowd encouraging intemperate actions. In the latter case, an act of pure malicious evil, the whole population of Melos, down to the smallest child, were innocent victims forced to bear the impact of Athenian brute force. Where there is an expansion of malice, Weil notes, depravity multiplies in perpetrator and victim alike; however, redemptive suffering can often be the catalyst to limit a spread of evil. Seeking underlying principles useful for understanding how evil can be contained, Weil explored the example of Antigone's redemptive suffering in Sophocles' tragedy of the same name.

---

[30] Simone Weil, *Gravity and Grace*, trans. Emma Crauford and Mario von der Ruhr (New York: Routledge, 1999), 58.

Sophocles's Antigone

This Greek tragedy illustrates for Weil the potential of individuals' willingness to offer up their lives rather than submit to transgressions that perpetuate evil. She saw in Antigone the same extreme and absurd love that led Christ to the Cross. Although the narrative of Antigone has multiple perspectives, our interest here is the integration that we discern between the text and Weil's theology.[31]

Antigone, with compassion for her brother Polyneices's soul, despite his seditious attack against Thebes, feels the sacred obligation to cover his body with soil to protect it from shameful desecration by birds of prey and wild animals. Her rebellious act, punishable by death, defies the king's dogmatic decree that the body of a declared traitor in civil uprisings must be left unburied. Antigone is afraid and does not want to die, but is committed to the "unwritten and inscrutable laws of God."[32] Creon, her uncle and future father-in-law, defends his exercise of arbitrary power with the rational argument: "An enemy, even when he is dead does not become a friend."[33] Antigone's response, based on the folly of love, is simply: "I was born not to share in hate, but only in love."[34] She then offers her own body up to his unjust punishment, saying, "It is for having done what is right that so much wrong is done to me."[35]

Creon, who has co-joined the idea of order in the city to his own personal dignity, is caught between love for his son and concern for his own prestige. He, nevertheless, coldheartedly has Antigone immured alive and left to die of isolation and starvation, as an affirmation that his decrees, right or wrong, must be obeyed. Eventually forced to confront with horror the appalling consequences of his hardheaded decision, he rushes to set her free, but he is too late, she has already assumed her own destiny. Creon, with all his self-righteous pronouncements, watches as

[31] Simone Weil made her own translations from Greek into French, which were then translated into English.
[32] Simone Weil, *Intimations of Christianity among the Ancient Greeks*, trans. Elisabeth Chase Geissbuhler (New York: Routledge, 1998), 21.
[33] Ibid.
[34] Ibid.
[35] Ibid., 23.

his grief-stricken son commits suicide before his eyes, and then discovers that his wife too has ended her life on hearing of their beloved son's death. The spectators are led to imagine Creon's state of grievous affliction endured in expiation for his hubristic defiance of limits.

For Weil, Sophocles is the Greek poet "whose quality of inspiration is the most visibly Christian."[36] She sees in the tragedy of Antigone a manifestation of the saying: "We ought to obey God rather than men."[37] Her self-sacrifice is a witness to a timeless truth. Under Creon's authoritarian rule, Antigone's willingness to suffer and die for her belief in a common humanity under God reveals the futility of Creon's willful violation of sacrosanct boundaries. Weil considers Antigone as "a perfectly pure being, perfectly innocent, ... who voluntarily gives herself up to death to preserve a guilty brother from an unhappy fate in the other world...." She "loved beyond reason," and suffers from the "curse born of a sin transmitted from generation to generation until it strikes a perfectly guiltless person who suffers all the bitterness of it. Then the curse is ended."[38] Antigone's affliction, likened to Christ's, was redemptive suffering. From early on, Weil's driving intuition was that virtue consists in keeping within oneself the evil that one suffers, not entertaining a false sense of freedom by extending it to others through delusionary tactics.

Weil notes: "*At a given moment* one is not free to do anything whatever. And one must accept this internal necessity; accept what one is, at a given moment, as a fact, even one's shame."[39] She treasured contradictions for the learning opportunities they offered; she believed that the contemplation of equally valid opposing ideas is a means to arrive at a timeless truth.

Antigone exemplifies the new and admirable type of sanctity, of which Weil spoke in a letter to Father Perrin: she accepted the affliction imposed on her and absorbed the evil into herself, dying in the process. This saintliness, a fruit of humility, accords a major place to compassion,

---

[36] Ibid., 8.

[37] Ibid., 9.

[38] Ibid., 10. (See Sophocles's tragedy *Oedipus Rex* for an explanation of the curse.)

[39] Weil, *Notebooks* 1, 56. Weil's italics.

where the viable person identifies with the less viable to the point of losing his own life for the other. Its source is in pure attention to others, in an open acceptance of God's love, and in reflective thinking that seeks the light of truth in a situation.

Weil tells us that compassion, beauty, joy, and affliction are integral to the Christian faith, which "comes to flower and fruit at every time and every place where there are men who do not hate the light."[40] These ideals attracted both Simone Weil and Flannery O'Connor, who dedicated their lives and artistic talents to enlightening their readers on the importance of living life in accordance with eternal values.

FLANNERY O'CONNOR

Simone Weil's statement that both joy and suffering are "equally precious gifts...which must be savored to the full, each one in its purity" would have appealed to Flannery O'Connor who, by personal necessity and temperament, gave unusual attention to the conditions of bodily and spiritual suffering. Her empathy for Mary Ann, the young patient at Our Lady of Perpetual Help Free Cancer Home, and her desire to protect Mary Ann's suffering from objectification have previously been noted. As a child herself, O'Connor visited suffering children at St. Mary's Home, founded in 1873 by the Sisters of Mercy to care for homeless girls after the Civil War. She described the effects of such visits in a letter to Betty Hester in October 1957, during the time she was working on her second novel and writing "The Enduring Chill."

> When I was a child [St. Mary's] was a creaking house on a dreary street and I was occasionally taken there to visit the Sisters or some orphan distant-cousins; also probably as a salutary lesson. "See what you have to be thankful for. Suppose you were, etc."—a lesson my imagination played on exhaustively. I don't suppose that orphanage was so bad, there was doubtless plenty of love there but it was official, and you wouldn't have got yours from your own God-given source. Anyway to me it was the ultimate horror.... From time to time, they were allowed to spend the day with me— miserable occasions for me, as they were not other children, they

---

[40] Weil, *Selected Writings*, 68.

were Orphans. I don't know if they enjoyed coming or not; probably not.... Anyway I have been at least an Imaginary Orphan and that was probably my first view of hell. Children know by instinct that hell is an absence of love, and they can pick out theirs without missing.[41]

That O'Connor's imagination played exhaustively on orphans and homelessness is apparent in many of her stories that depict characters lost, wandering, or yearning for places to be at home. In his essay on *The Violent Bear It Away*, Gary M. Ciuba suggests that "the solitude to which O'Connor gravitated by illness, vocation, temperament, and spirituality made her live out on a daily basis the strangeness and separation that she detected in the children at St. Mary's." Similarly to Weil, who found that suffering could bring one into contact with God's love, O'Connor recognized in the St. Mary's children and from her own experiences of loss and diminishment that our deprivations can be blessings, which made it possible for her to "adopt orphanhood as a sign of the ongoing loss out of which she created her fiction."[42] Her interest in artistic depictions and investigation of suffering and affliction is evident in her parallel work on her second novel, for which she had signed a contract with Harcourt, Brace in 1955, and "The Enduring Chill." These two works interpret in fiction experiences of suffering and affliction that Weil explored philosophically.

After working on *The Violent Bear It Away* for more than a year, in November 1957 Flannery O'Connor set the novel aside to begin writing "The Enduring Chill." O'Connor's correspondence reveals her ambivalence about the story, vacillating between appreciation and dislike as she worked, tore it up, began again, and revised extensively. After selling the story to *Harper's Bazaar* in 1958, she continued to revise even in the gal-

---

[41] Flannery O'Connor, Letter to "A," October 5, 1957, *The Habit of Being: Letters of Flannery O'Connor*, ed. Sally Fitzgerald (New York: Farrar, Straus & Giroux, 1979), 244. Also cited by Jean Cash, *Flannery O'Connor: A Life* (Knoxville: University of Tennessee Press, 2002), 4, and by Brad Gooch, *Flannery: A Life of Flannery O'Connor* (New York: Little, Brown, 2009), 27.

[42] Gary M. Ciuba, "Not His Son," *Dark Faith: New Essays on Flannery O'Connor's The Violent Bear It Away*, ed. Susan Srigley (Notre Dame, IN: University of Notre Dame Press, 2008), 59.

ley stage, and after its publication in January 1960, still was not fully satisfied with the ending. The profound contrasts between Asbury's real and illusory suffering and Tarwater's tormented flight from his vocation embody in fiction the differences between suffering and affliction that Weil explicated in "The Love of God and Affliction," and suggest O'Connor's personal struggle with her vocation as prophet and artist.

Art and Death in Life

"The Enduring Chill" presents a quixotic dance around life and death, which Asbury Fox considers "was coming to him legitimately, as a justification, as a gift from life."[43] The aspiring artist Asbury living in New York as he tries to write a play on the Negro, with whom he has little concrete experience, returns ill to Timberboro, convinced that he is dying. The narrator reflects Asbury's physical exhaustion upon his arrival in the "chill gray sky and a startling white-gold sun" and his psychological attitude toward home in his observation of "the single block of one-story brick and wooden shacks" which he imagines transformed "into mounting turrets of some exotic temple for a god he didn't know" (*CW* 547). From the outset the narrator mirrors his physical malady and consequent irritation at having to come home to die in familial, medical, religious, and racial conflicts, all of which make visible the illusions to which Asbury himself seems blind.

Wracked by physical sickness and frustrated by his unrealized dream of becoming a sophisticated New York artist, Asbury reveals impatience and disrespect in response to Mrs. Fox's comments about the temperature or observations about how the town has changed as they drive from the train station to their home. He considers his father, who had died twenty years earlier, "one of the courthouse gang, a rural worthy with a dirty finger in every pie" (*CW*, 554). In New York he had written his mother a letter, which filled two notebooks, to disclose all the things she had done wrong but were hidden by her self-satisfaction. Hostility prevails between Asbury and his sister, whom he snidely calls a sleeping dog

---

[43] Flannery O'Connor, *Collected Works* (New York: Library of America, 1988), 560. (Hereafter cited as *CW*.)

as she rests in the backseat of the car. And Mary George concludes that his illness is psychosomatic; "Asbury can't write so he gets sick. He's going to be an invalid instead of an artist" (*CW*, 563). In addition to coming home for his grand exit from life, Asbury makes clear his egoistic superiority.

Illusory Suffering

When Asbury's mother suggests with concerned practicality that he see their local physician, he expresses similar condescension for Dr. Block, whom the narrator describes in Asbury's mind as "the enemy of death" because he was taking blood samples and "wouldn't prescribe until he knew what was wrong...." (*CW* 562). The narrator further discloses Asbury's psychological arrogance by presenting him as a seeker with limited religious or spiritual depth of inquiry. While attending a lecture on Buddhism in New York, prior to returning home, he fastens his attention on a priest whom he asks for his opinion of his friend Goetz's remark that "salvation is the destruction of a simple prejudice, and no one is saved." To this the priest replies, "there is a real probability of the New Man, assisted, of course, by the Third Person of the Trinity" (*CW* 550), which listening Buddhists intensely reject. And then the priest hands Asbury his card: Ignatius Vogle, S.J. Once at home, his mother suggests that she invite the retired Methodist minister Dr. Bush to speak with him in his suffering, which Asbury rejects, and demands she locate a priest, preferably a Jesuit because they are intellectually "foolproof" in their ability "to discuss something besides the weather" (*CW* 561).

Father Finn, who interestingly announces himself from "Purrgatory," confronts and exposes Asbury's egoistic commitments to intellectual abstractions about art, religion, theology, the Holy Ghost, the New Man, and Death itself. In humorous bypassing exchange, the priest and Asbury discuss topics such as James Joyce, whom the priest does not know; the myth of the dying god; who God is; the reality of the Holy Ghost; Asbury's announcement that he is dying; and Fr. Finn's conclusion that "The Holy Ghost will not come until you see yourself as you are—a lazy ignorant conceited youth!" (*CW* 566–567). Through the association of Fr. Finn with purgatory, the narrator signals that the exchange between

Asbury and Fr. Finn will fulfill two traditional purposes of purgatory: to expose the sins of Asbury and to relieve or cleanse him of his attachments to those sins. In their conversation, Asbury persists in his commitment to intellectual abstractions. Finally, in exasperation, Fr. Finn calls Asbury lazy and ignorant, disclosing the necessary truth of Asbury's condition before the appearance of the Holy Ghost.

In the midst of such contemptuous dismissals of family, doctors, and clergy—"this [entire] collapsing country junction"—Asbury wants "some last significant culminating experience that he must make for himself before he died—make for himself out of his own intelligence" (*CW* 568). His imagination lands on the memory of what he considers communion—shocking for its superficiality—that he had when smoking with the Negroes—"when the difference between black and white is absorbed into nothing" (*CW* 558). Despite their refusal to drink the unpasteurized milk with him, he now asks to say good-bye to them. Their deferential assertions of how well Asbury looks throughout their visit and prediction that "you'll be up and around in a few days" (*CW* 570) anticipates the diagnosis from Dr. Block that Asbury has contracted undulant fever from unpasteurized milk, consumed in defiance of the rules of the farm.

The Implacable Holy Ghost

In "The Enduring Chill," Flannery O'Connor illustrates suffering produced by one's own actions. Relying on his own intellect and commitment to ideas about Art, Religion, the New Man, and Death, Asbury has already dismissed any supernatural use for his suffering; it is the last thing he would have considered. Suffering does not strip him of self-importance which, according to Weil, offers the potential for the descent of grace, but instead clings to his illusions. Careful readers will note, as does the critic Kessler, the diminished presence of the *as if* construction in this story, which limits the play of mystery through metaphor and freezes Asbury in his story. However, following the disclosure of the real source of his suffering, "a blinding red-gold sun moved serenely from under a purple cloud. Below it the treeline was black against the crimson sky. It formed a brittle wall, standing *as if* it were the frail defense he had set up in his mind to protect him from what was coming" (*CW* 572, emphasis added).

Although the visual of the sun moving from under a purple cloud may be unnoticed by Asbury, O'Connor's regular use of colors assists both attentive characters within a story and readers to read situations anagogically. In this case, the gold for regal, the purple representing suffering, and the red associated with blood would not be missed as symbols used in Christian liturgical worship. For a would-be artist ignorant of his own ignorance but only now, at the end of the story, stripped of his brittle defense and his will reduced to nothing, the Holy Ghost descends as a fierce icicle-like water stain. Described by Jesus as an Advocate in John 14, the Holy Spirit mediates between God and human beings, restoring relationship between the supernatural and the natural.

That Flannery O'Connor interrupted her work on *The Violent Bear It Away* to write "The Enduring Chill" and wrestled with it for eight years is significant for our reflections on suffering and affliction. In noting that Asbury failed his god Art, Kessler suggests that O'Connor may have failed art, too, by directly naming the Holy Ghost. She "has overpowered fictional illusion, exposing the 'meaning' that O'Connor in her other stories manages to keep hidden behind metaphor."[44] As an artist and a devout believer, O'Connor struggled with the specter of human suffering and affliction brought about by one's own poor choices or illusions or by the evil actions of others. According to Kessler's criticism, her presentation of Asbury's self-inflicted suffering and his true condition appears to be more didactic than guided by metaphors opening to mystery. On the contrary, we think by being explicit about the Holy Ghost, she also insinuates God's relentless pursuit of human beings even through their frigid denials and release to frozen humility.

The Violent Bear It Away

In all her fiction Flannery O'Connor explores what it means for human beings to bear the image and likeness of God. Weil also wrestled with that question as she attempted to reconcile the problem of human suffering—whether caused by the sins of a person's own choices or by

[44] Edward Kessler, *Flannery O'Connor and the Language of Apocalypse* (Princeton, N. J.: Princeton University Press, 1986), 131.

evil acts perpetrated against a person—with an all-loving God. After her trip to Lourdes in the spring of 1958, O'Connor returned home and made progress on her second novel, which she had laid aside while writing "The Enduring Chill." As with "The Enduring Chill," her correspondence reveals ambivalence about the demands the second novel made on her as she considered human nature. Writing a week apart to two different correspondents she quips first that "from here on out my novel will have to be forced by will. There is not pleasure left in it for me." Five days later she reports that "the little vacation from the Opus Nauseous [*The Violent Bear It Away*] seems to have done me some creative good anyway as I am at it with something like vigor, or anyway, have been for the last two days or so."[45] "The Enduring Chill" and *The Violent Bear It Away* make palpable the gradations of suffering and its extreme of affliction experienced and explored by the author and readers alike.

Simone Weil describes affliction as a crushing of the soul that destroys a person's sense of self, takes possession of the soul, stamping it with "the mark of slavery." Social degradation produces humiliation that impedes others' compassion, and self-loathing turns revulsion inward. As discussed earlier in the description of these two authors' contexts, both Weil and Flannery O'Connor identified examples of affliction in their societies, and experienced it themselves.

Weil saw the social degradation produced by totalitarianism spreading across Europe and the crushing boot of Nazism in France afflicting the French people. O'Connor contends with the personal and cultural affliction that has tenacious roots in the slave history of the United States, two world wars, and the challenges of existentialism expressed by Camus and Sartre in their own grappling with suffering.[46] Interpreting O'Connor's depiction of the influence of nihilism in the twentieth century, Richard Gianonne persuasively argues that Hazel Motes, the Misfit, and Tarwater are "all ardent, even principled, exponents of nihilism. If pure or single-minded of heart, they are not clean of hands. They are killers. Strikingly, they are also seekers," and as such "they draw God's

---

[45] O'Connor, Letter to "A," May 17, 1958, and Letter to Cecil Dawkins, May 22, 1958, *The Habit of Being*, 282 and 284.

[46] Richard Gianonne, "Dark Night, Dark Faith," Srigley, *Dark Faith*, 9.

compassion."[47] Although the outcome for the Misfit after his confessed confusion about Jesus to the Grandmother before he shoots her is unclear, Hazel blinds himself and turns to Jesus, and Tarwater embraces his prophetic vocation. Following the theological openness of St. Thomas, O'Connor had considerable sympathy for unbelievers who also seek the truth. Weil had similar respect for unbelievers, writing, "Of two men who have no experience of God, he who denies him is perhaps nearer to him than the other. The false God who is like the true one in everything, except that we cannot touch him, prevents us from ever coming to the true one. We have to believe in a God who is like the true God in everything, except that he does not exist, since we have not reached the point where God exists."[48] O'Connor's capacity to see herself in the other—the orphaned or unbelievers—permitted her to regard unbelief or denial as one way to God and perhaps a veil over belief.

Seeds in the Blood

In *The Violent Bear It Away*, Flannery O'Connor presents the complicated family history of affliction through the patriarch-prophet of old Mason Tarwater who, though he dies in the first chapter of the novel, continues to contend with his nephew George Rayber for the soul of Mason's great-nephew Francis Tarwater.[49] Several essays in Srigley's collection *Dark Faith* freshly examine the complexities of this family line— the meaning of kinship, lost childhood, absent or neglectful parenting, abandonment, exploitation—headed in the novel by Mason, who called himself to be a prophet. He embellishes his personal story with biblical narratives of Adam, Abel, Enoch, Noah, Abraham, Moses and the bush that flamed for him, Jezebel, Job, Jesus, the Resurrection, Judgment Day, and, seeking to pass the mantle of prophecy to young Francis Tarwater, he compares himself and his great-nephew to Elijah and Elisha. The biblical stories that chronicle experiences of homelessness, exile, abandonment, and betrayal, O'Connor suggests, have placed seeds of human history in the Tarwater family.

---

[47] Ibid., 11.

[48] Weil, *Gravity and Grace*, 115.

[49] For excellent essays on *The Violent Bear It Away*, see Srigley, *Dark Faith*.

The seeds of George Rayber's affliction were deposited in his blood during the first seven years of his life when he lived with his neglectful insurance man father and Mason's sister whom Mason considered a drunken whore. Rayber's early life was a confusing time of neglect, abandonment, and resentment, reminding O'Connor's readers of Harry Ashfield in "The River." When his uncle Mason rescues Rayber to live with him, "he did not yet understand the full meaning of his home life, [though] he is an intelligent, sensitive child who clearly felt the neglect and indifference of his parents [which] left an indelible mark on his personality."[50] Rayber responds positively to the caring attention of Mason and accepts his baptism and instruction about Jesus and his own place in the redemptive scheme of life. However, John Desmond points out, this new knowledge fills him with internal conflict about which "father"—his birth father, his adoptive father, or the Lord Jesus—to honor in his heart, "propel[ing] him into a state of moral and psychological confusion"[51] that will follow him into adulthood and solidify his estrangement from himself and others. Rayber's confusion is heightened when his biological father comes to Powderhead to take him home. Even though he doesn't adopt the neglectful habits of his birth family, he returns to Powderhead at age fourteen to renounce Mason, his adoptive father, who evoked in him feelings of love about which he is ambivalent and ashamed.

In a September 13, 1959 letter, O'Connor tells John Hawkes that old Mason and Rayber provide the governing tension of *The Violent Bear It Away*. Even after Mason's death, they contend for the pulverized soul of young Tarwater. The seeds of Francis Tarwater's affliction have been passed from one generation to the next. Young Tarwater proudly claims he was born in a wreck to a mother who lived only long enough following the car crash to give birth to Tarwater. Upon hearing about the wreck, his father shot himself, effectively orphaning the baby. As brother of the baby's dead mother, Rayber initially assumes informal, bloodline custody of Tarwater, which old Mason contests because of his resentment against Rayber's turning Mason into an object of his scientific re-

---

[50] John Desmond, "The Lost Life of George Rayber," Srigley, *Dark Faith*, 37.

[51] Ibid., 38.

search while Mason was once visiting him. Mason kidnaps Tarwater to save him from the godless influences of secularism and instead to provide him with a larger, religious family history. The challenges facing young Tarwater repeat in the present what has occurred across generations: "Resolving the identity crisis as the child of such ambiguous fathers is … complicated for Tarwater [as it was for Rayber]. The youth defines himself through and against his birth parents as well as two quasi-adoptive parents—one, a member of the living dead; the other, a dead old man who lives in memory—before discovering the possibility of a more ancient lineage."[52] Following his great-uncle's death, Tarwater faces two commandments given him by Mason to fulfill. First, he is to bury Mason properly, and second, if Mason himself has not baptized Rayber's young son Bishop prior to his death, Tarwater is to perform that sacred rite. These orders launch Tarwater toward the city where Rayber and Bishop live, and hound him until the end of the novel.

Contending for the Afflicted Soul

Despite his self-protective resistance against Rayber's intentions to rehabilitate him, young Tarwater's sojourn in the city increases his suffering. In her essay on "The Love of God and Affliction," as we noted, Weil acknowledges that suffering in its extreme form can befall believers and nonbelievers alike and that suffering offers the potential for love to germinate from the suffering. This is the seed that Weil referred to when one consents to affliction. Whether the seeds of affliction Flannery O'Connor fictionally drops in the blood of the Tarwater family are simultaneously seeds that offer the potential for love and evoke consent from the afflicted that Weil considers desirable depend on the responses the three generations of Tarwater men give to their experiences of affliction.

Believing himself to belong to the ancient lines of biblical prophets, many of whom suffered hostility and rejection, Old Mason interprets the world as a sorely afflicted place to which, following a long line of biblical mentors and fundamental religious convictions, he calls himself to prophesy about the ways of God. Kidnapping his great-nephew to give

---

[52] Ciuba, "Not His Son, *Dark Faith*, 64.

him freedom from Rayber's social-scientific experimentations, Mason instructs young Tarwater that Jesus is the bread of life and that "as soon as he [Mason] died, he would hasten to the banks of the Lake of Galilee to eat the loaves and fishes that the Lord had multiplied" (*CW* 342). Young Tarwater is secretly afraid that Mason's "madness, this hunger, ... might be passed down, might be hidden in the blood and might strike some day in him, and then he would be torn by hunger like the old man, the bottom split out of his stomach so that nothing would heal or fill it but the bread of life" (*CW* 343).

Immediately following Mason's death, Tarwater exhibits responses to the seeds of affliction in his blood that cage him between Mason's prophetic imprints on Tarwater's consciousness and Rayber's attempt to mold Tarwater into a more rational and enlightened human being. Although young Tarwater shares Mason's commitment to freedom, he does not understand that Mason's freedom is rooted in submission to the Lord as he interprets him. In contrast, Tarwater wishes to be autonomous through his own acts of will that avoid limits and obligations, such as fulfilling burial and baptismal prescriptions. As he contemplates moving the fence that Mason had set in the middle of the corn patch, and asserts that there is nothing to hinder him from anything except the Lord—"and He ain't said anything. He ain't even noticed me"— Tarwater begins to feel that with the stranger's voice speaking to him "he was only just now meeting himself, as if as long as his uncle had lived, he had been deprived of his own acquaintance" (*CW* 344, 352).

Rayber responds to his affliction by violently rejecting everything that Mason taught him and stands for, which divides him against himself. To defend against emotion and his own suffering, he becomes a rationalist dedicated to quantitative data gathering and sociological analysis. When Tarwater flees Powderhead for the city, he discovers Rayber's house full of books and papers, not food or moonshine, which were abundant in Mason's house. Rayber is a utilitarian, dependent on a mechanical hearing aid, and confused by his own emotions. He regards his mentally handicapped son Bishop, who evokes hated love in him, as a problem. When Tarwater arrives, Rayber sees Tarwater not as a flesh-and-blood person but only as someone he can shape in his ideal image.

Into the contention between Tarwater's and Rayber's responses of willfulness and rationality to their affliction, O'Connor places two figures of children who present a third invitation, the way of love.[53] In the middle of the novel, both Rayber and Tarwater listen to the physically crippled and psychologically exploited twelve-year-old child preacher Lucette Carmody deliver the message of John's Gospel, "Jesus is the Word of God and Jesus is love. The Word of God is love and do you know what love is, you people? ..." (*CW* 412). Even though speaking abstractly of love, Lucette's preaching frightens and infuriates Rayber, as he turns off his hearing aid and moves away from the window where he is watching and listening. Tarwater, on the other hand, becomes silent and recognizes in his body a hunger for bread.

As part of Tarwater's family education, Mason tells Tarwater in the first chapter that Rayber's one child has been preserved from being corrupted by his parents by being dim-witted. Bishop confounds the emotions of both his father and Tarwater who resist his dependence and cognitive limitations, even as they are drawn to him. Although Bishop embodies delight, wide-eyed and open-mouthed wonder, sensitivity to music, water, dance, touch, and nature, neither Rayber nor Tarwater expresses compassion toward him, and both are embarrassed by his sensual openness. Weil frequently reminds us that the material world is our bridge to the supernatural world, to which our senses give us access. "Whereas his father and cousin resist opening themselves to the world for fear of feeling obligated to it or feeling love for it, Bishop puts up no such resistance. He instinctively understands himself to be vitally connected to the world and to other people."[54] Scott Huelin's essay invokes Weil: "Bishop's wondering gaze and receptive mouth might remind us of what Simone Weil has called creative attention, the ability to see things not only as they are but as they might be: this, Weil argues, is the beating heart of neighbor."[55]

---

[53] Scott Huelin, *The Violent Bear It Away* as Case Studies in Theological Ethics," Srigley, *Dark Faith*, 118–135. Huelin helpfully associates the affliction responses of Rayber, Tarwater, and Bishop with three positions of theological ethics in the Western tradition: reason, will, and love.

[54] Ibid., 126.

[55] Ibid., 127.

With Bishop's baptism as the focal point of conversation at the Cherokee Lodge prior to Tarwater's and Bishop's baptismal-drowning boat ride, the tension of Rayber's and Tarwater's responses to affliction peak. Rayber puts two solutions to Tarwater: First, since baptism is simply an empty act of spilling a little water and a few words, Rayber gives Tarwater permission to perform it with a glass of water. Second, the way of being born again the natural way is through your own efforts and intelligence. Suggesting that his emotional compulsion toward Bishop (to drown him) is more complicated than Tarwater's, Rayber says they must fight the compulsion in the same way. Tarwater replies, "It ain't the same. I can pull it up by the roots, once and for all. I can do something. I ain't like you. All you can do is think what you would have done if you had done it. Not me. I can do it. I can act" (*CW* 451). Only a short time later, as Rayber rests in the lodge and Tarwater and Bishop ride in the boat, Rayber hears the bellow of Bishop and knows that Tarwater has acted. What Rayber could not do because he considered it a meaningless act and because of his own mistrust of his emotions, Tarwater has done. And the conflicted love for his son against which Rayber guarded himself leaves him in this moment empty and emotionless. "[Rayber] stood waiting for the raging pain, the intolerable hurt that was his due, to begin, so that he could ignore it, but he continued to feel nothing. He stood lightheaded at the window and it was not until he realized there would be no pain that he collapsed" (*CW* 456).

Transfiguring Affliction

Intensifying his personal affliction with the baptismal-murder of Bishop, Tarwater heads away from Cherokee Lodge and the city toward Powderhead with trousers still wet with lake water. Fleeing the influence of his great-uncle's directives compounded by confusion and guilt over having baptized and drowned Bishop, Tarwater is picked up by a driver of an auto-transit truck. He rides in the truck as forbear reluctant prophet Jonah did in the belly of a whale fleeing his call to prophesy to the people of Nineveh. On his tortured return to Powderhead—"and to know the place for the first time"[56]—Tarwater confronts in himself the original act of violence: "to separate oneself from others through an illusion of and desire for autonomy or independence,"[57] that is, to resist submission to God's completing work in oneself.

In the truck Tarwater mixes nonsensical comments to the driver about baptism and drowning, relives memories from the past, expresses hunger but refuses food, hears voices which O'Connor considers wrestling with the devil, and finally encounters the stranger in the man wearing lavender who obliterates his senses with powerful liquor and rapes him. His violation, a metaphor for the world's rape, Kessler argues, moves Tarwater from the foot of the Cross—the greatest possible distance from divine Presence—to be nailed to it, as it were. When he wakens, he sets fire to the place where he was violated, and when the voice whispers one last time "Go down and take it....It's ours. We've won it" (*CW* 475), he "shuddered convulsively ... tore off another pine bough," and set it afire to watch the grinning presence of his adversary be consumed in flames (*CW* 475). The violence inflicted upon Tarwater that strips him naked comes not from God but precedes consent to his afflictions and grace to obey his vocation. As we have seen previously, O'Connor frequently depicts in her stories and novels unexpected, often shocking, acts of violence that precipitate profound reversals of perception or direction. These she considered preparation for the intrusions of grace necessary for the recalcitrant, unseeing, and hard of hearing.

With O'Connor's own poetic prose, the final chapter of *The Violent Bear It Away* reverberates with seeds of poetry opening to transfigured vision. The narrator's description of Tarwater's homecoming reveals Powderhead to be familist but vastly changed for him. He returns as if to see the place for the first time and as part of a mystical community.

As he looked, his hunger constricted him anew. It appeared to be

---

[56] T. S. Eliot, "Little Gidding," *Four Quartets* (New York: Harcourt Brace Jovanovich, 1943, 1971), 59.

[57] Huelin, "Only Love Overcomes Violence," 128. See also Susan Srigley, *Flannery O'Connor's Sacramental Art* (Notre Dame, IN: University of Notre Dame Press, 2004), 91–95.

> outside him,
> surrounding him. He sensed a strangeness about the place
> as if there might already be an occupant....
> A deep quiet pervaded everything....
>
> He became conscious of the very breath he drew.
> Even the air seemed to belong to another. (*CW* 476)

After he sees the grave marked with a rough cross in which Buford has faithfully buried Mason, Tarwater looks at the field Buford has just crossed.

> It seemed no longer empty but peopled with a multitude.
> Everywhere, he saw dim figures seated on the slope and
> as he gazed he saw that from a single basket the throng was being
>   fed....
> His hunger was so great that he could have eaten all the loaves
>   and fishes
> after they were multiplied....
>
> He felt his hunger no longer as a pain but as a tide.
> He felt it rising in himself through time and darkness,
> rising through centuries,
> and he knew that it rose in a line of men whose lives were chosen
>   to sustain it,
> who would wander in the world,
> strangers from that violent country where the silence is never bro-
>   ken
> except to shout the truth....
>
> He threw himself to the ground
> and with his face against the dirt grave, he heard the command,
> GO WARN THE CHILDREN OF GOD OF THE TERRIBLE
>   SPEED OF MERCY.
> The words were as silent as seeds
> opening one at a time in his blood,
> binding him to an ancient lineage, an extended human community. (*CW*
>   477–478)

As Weil has reminded us and O'Connor embodies narratively through Tarwater, "God's mercy is manifest in affliction as in joy....The outward results of true affliction are nearly always bad...It is in affliction itself that the splendor of God's mercy shines, from the very depths, in the heart of its inconsolable bitterness. If still persevering in our love,... without ceasing to love, we end by touching something that is not affliction, not joy, something that is the central essence, necessary and pure, something not of the senses, common to joy and sorrow: the very love of God" (*WG* 43-44).

Chapter 6

Grace and Decreation

"Forms of the Implicit Love of God" and the *Notebooks*
"A Good Man Is Hard to Find" and "A View of the Woods"

SIMONE WEIL

Simone Weil experienced something akin to the love of God in her friendship with Father Joseph-Marie Perrin. Weil and Perrin had only known each other eleven months before the long-awaited passage came through for Simone and her parents to leave the port of Marseille and embark on a hazardous three-month voyage across the Atlantic to the United States. A mutual friend, Hélène Honnorat, a fervent Catholic, had introduced Simone into some Catholic circles in Marseille after Simone had told her, "I am as close to Catholicism as it is possible to be without however being Catholic."[1] Hélène later recommended that she meet Father Perrin, who might direct her to some agricultural employment in the region, which she ardently desired. Despite their vast differences, theirs was a meeting that seemed fated to occur; it is hard to imagine how two souls could have benefitted more from their mutual dedication to an absolute love of the truth. Father Perrin was just four years Simone's senior, yet his letters, as their friendship flourished, all have the tender, loving, and accepting address, "Mon cher enfant." No one was more understanding of her intense desire to love God in the most total, obedient, and unconditional way. She confided to him that she could not think of him without thinking of God.[2]

Hélène, four years younger, was a professor in a lycée for girls in Marseille, and had been in the Lycée Duruy while Simone was studying with Professor Le Senne. Hélène, anxious to serve Simone's desire to

---

[1] Simone Pétrement, *Simone Weil: A Life*, trans. Raymond Rosenthal (New York: Pantheon Books, 1976), 394.

[2] Joseph-Marie Perrin, *Mon dialogue avec Simone Weil* (Paris: Nouvelle Cité, 1984), 12.

know Catholicism as well as possible, introduced her to various members of the clergy. Although each identified unorthodox elements in Simone's ideas and detected a certain skepticism about the church's authoritarian dictates, they all noted admirable traits of authenticity, nobility, rectitude, and poverty of spirit. After a few discussions with them, however, Simone confided to Hélène, "As our conversations proceeded, I saw myself getting further and further away from baptism."[3] Given these interactions between a more traditional clergy and a probing young intellectual, one can better understand Flannery O'Connor's referring to Weil with the rhetorical question we noted earlier: "What is more comic and terrible than an angular intellectual proud woman approaching God inch by inch with ground teeth?"[4] Nevertheless, at the same time, as Simone was tacitly maintaining her independence vis-à-vis the church, she was composing a prodigious number of profoundly spiritual essays, among them, the pieces that compose *Waiting for God*.

This collection of writings with deep spiritual content reveals an urgency to share her "deposit of pure gold,"[5] given the approaching departure amidst the dangers of wartime. On the brink of leaving, she had let drop the remark to Hélène that the ocean might make a splendid baptismal font. In this sixth and final essay on Weil's spiritual insights into our human condition, we explore two more of her fundamental concepts: a fairly traditional view of grace, but dependent on an innovative and nearly inscrutable concept of decreation, which implies an emptying out of self or the created part of the soul that comprises our person. Three subsidiary ideas aid in understanding the two principal concerns: evil caused by harm perpetrated on that which is good, a void created in the soul by affliction and death, and pure good as a means of countering evil and its effects.

The months of friendship and theological discussions between Father Perrin and Simone had inspired a collaboration on composing a collection of works about God that would be in the service of those who

---

[3] Pétrement, *A Life*, 458.

[4] Flannery O'Connor, *The Habit of Being: Letters of Flannery O'Connor*, ed. Sally Fitzgerald (New York: Farrar, Straus & Giroux, 1979), 105.

[5] See footnote 16.

seek. This unique association had a singular and fortuitous nature. André Devaux writes of the profound affinities between them: they had the same care for a life of charity, same desire for a spiritual assimilation into Christ, and same view of contemplation intertwined with action. "Both wished for a true universalization of Christianity, one that would infuse all profane life."[6] Father Perrin was one of only two people in whom she had enough confidence to reveal the mystical contact with Christ that had occurred a few years earlier; even then she could only express it through the discreet distance of a letter. Commensurate with Simone's conviction that God speaks to us in secret, Father Perrin's own spiritual sensitivities were acute, and their relationship was of such an intimacy that he intuitively saw aspects of the "eternal in her message."[7] He dedicated himself to bringing her religious and philosophical ideas to the public by publishing those works she had confided to his care;[8] they comprise a holistic comprehension of reality, an apprehension of a divine order behind reality, and a perception of grace that works silently within the world.

Grace

Following her mystical contact with Christ, the concept of supernatural grace weaves its way throughout Weil's written corpus. She composed no separate essays on grace, nor on evil or decreation, which suggests their elusiveness and ineffability. Flannery O'Connor would have had ample opportunity to perceive the fullness of Weil's understanding of grace through the recurring references in the *Notebooks*. Weil is neither heretical in her concept of grace nor blatantly unorthodox. Nevertheless, her manner of incorporating grace into her writings opens unique insights into an intuitive view of its spiritual value and modes of operation, as well as the many obstacles inherent in human nature that inhibit its full realization.

Sensitive to the aura of meaning conveyed by words, Weil consid-

---

[6] Perrin, *Dialogue.*, 13.
[7] Ibid., 30.
[8] These essays compose *Waiting for God* and *Intimations of Christianity among the Ancient Greeks.*

ered "grace" as among the most beautiful of words. "Grace" in its form and implications has become more multilayered in its evolution from the Greek *charis* to the Latin *gratia* through French *grâce* to English "grace." Its ambiguity and richness gain in its many connotations, such as God's unmerited favor, love, pardon, mercy, elegance, virtue, esteem, gratitude, all of which give an intimation of its expansive layers. Loving certain words that transmit truth, she wrote: "It sometimes happens that a fragment of inexpressible truth is reflected in words which, although they cannot hold the truth that inspired them, have nevertheless so perfect a formal correspondence with it that every mind seeking that truth finds support in them. Whenever this happens a gleam of beauty illumines the words."[9]

Weil considered grace a celestial gift as mysterious as the Incarnation and as unfathomable as the Eucharist. Grace inserts an element of eternity—the realm of the absolute—into time—the realm of the relative. Grace reorients human attention toward the supernatural, making more intimate the relationship between God and human beings. Grace can entice individuals toward the good, diverting attention away from the self with its egoistical desires. As a counterforce to unbridled power, grace, though seemingly far less substantial, can, in truth, be more potent. "That is why the Cross is a balance on which a frail and light body, but which was God himself, was able to lift the weight of the entire world. 'Give me a fulcrum, and I will lift up the world.' This fulcrum is the cross."[10] Weil used illustrations in which something infinitely small prevails: "The grain of mustard seed is the 'least of all seeds'. Persephone ate only one grain of the pomegranate. A pearl buried deep in a field is not visible; neither is the yeast in dough."[11] To reinforce that aspect of grace and to illustrate an additional facet she often referred to the "Valiant Little Tailor" from the Brothers Grimm.

Weil's account of this familiar story reveals her appreciation of met-

---

[9] Simone Weil, *The Simone Weil Reader,* ed. George A. Panichas (New York: David McKay, 1977), 334.
[10] Simone Weil, *The Notebooks of Simone Weil*, vol. 2, trans. Arthur Wills (New York: G. P. Putnam's Sons, 1956), 433 (quoting Archimedes).
[11] Panichas, 337.

aphors of movement or direction to speak about grace. In this folktale, the valiant little tailor, who was a braggart, courted social prestige by boasting of having killed "Seven with one Blow"—the intended allusion is men, but the reality is flies. When challenged by a swaggering giant to throw a stone so high that it takes a very long time to descend, the tailor won the wager by the ruse of releasing a bird from his pocket, which, of course, never comes down. Weil found in this centuries-old story an image of humankind pursuing its mundane ways, when, unexpectedly, a conjuncture of events inspires the descent of grace to help the soul make its own winged ascent. The implicit message is that we are to wait for God to come to us; he never fails to offer salutary grace to each of us, unless we refuse it. She writes:

> Everything without wings always comes down to earth again. People who make athletic leaps towards heaven are too absorbed in the muscular effort to be able to look up to heaven; and in this matter the looking up is the one thing that counts. It is what makes God come down. And when God has come down to us he raises us, he gives us wings. The only effective and legitimate use of our muscular efforts is to keep at bay and suppress whatever may prevent us from looking up; they are negatively useful.[12]

Weil's use of metaphors of direction and movement illustrate the soul's interaction with grace when it comes to lure the soul toward the good. We have generally referred to the vertical movement that comes from the Platonic dialectic process, in which "the soul, at each stage, in order to rise to the sphere above, leans for support on the irreducible contradictions of this sphere wherein it finds itself. At the end of this ascent, the soul is in contact with the absolute good."[13] The image of an ascent and descent movement gives readers an insight into Weil's comment that grace is the law of the descending movement, that is, grace comes down to enter the soul that has made ready a void to receive it. She writes in her aphoristic style: "Creation is made up of the descending

---

[12] Cited in Martin Andic, "Fairy Tales," *Cahiers Simone Weil*, 15.1 (March 1992): 80.

[13] Simone Weil, *Oppression and Liberty*, trans. Arthur Will and John Petrie (Amherst: University of Massachusetts Press, 1973), 190.

movement of gravity, the ascending movement of grace, and the descending movement of grace raised to the second power."[14]

One interpretation of the preceding passage suggests that grace first descended during creation, but then God withdrew in order for his creation to exist apart from him.[15] Human beings were left without grace unless they desired it—explicitly or implicitly; once they desire it, however, grace descends to assist the soul in its ascent. The idea of grace descending evokes the final scene in Flannery O'Connor's short story "The Enduring Chill," in which Asbury, having been stripped of his intellectual and artistic illusions, and even of his patronizing attitudes toward God, imagines that the water-stain image of a fierce bird—"the Holy Ghost"—is descending from the ceiling of his bedroom. As in many of O'Connor's narratives, grace appears to come to the protagonist after some trauma. Whether that character accepts the offering of grace is open to conjecture, as it is in real life.

Weil believed that the essential contradiction in human life is that man, straining after the good, which constitutes his very being, is at the same time subject in his entirety, both in mind and in flesh, to a blind force, that is, necessity, completely indifferent to the good.[16] Contemplating this anomaly in order to find a transcendental unity in good and necessity makes a legitimate use of contradiction, the resolution of which requires faith.

Weil also employs a metaphor of two different realms:[17] the "reality outside the world" and the "reality here below," to show a transversal movement of grace. She makes a distinction of these two realities in her beautifully crafted "Draft for a Statement on Human Obligations,"[18] written as a "Profession of Faith" for would-be leaders in an incarnational society. She advises them that leading their followers well, involves

---

[14] Weil, *Notebooks* 2, 388.

[15] See Rebecca Rozelle-Stone and Lucian Stone, *Simone Weil and Theology* (New York: Bloomsbury, 2013), 165–171.

[16] Weil, *Oppression and Liberty*, 173.

[17] See Bartomeu Estelrich, "Simone Weil's Concept of Grace," *Modern Theology*, 25.2 (April 2009): 239–251.

[18] Simone Weil, *Simone Weil: Selected Writings*, ed. Eric O. Springsted (New York: Orbis Books, 1998), 131–141.

being constantly aware of the true reality that lies beyond the visible surroundings of the material world. Knowing this reality, as the source of all
good, can offer guidelines for living together in the physical world. She
writes: "There is a reality outside the world, that is to say, outside space
and time, outside man's mental universe, outside any sphere whatsoever,
that is accessible to human faculties."[19] In opposition to that reality is the
"terrestrial manifestation of [another] reality, which lies in the absurd
and insoluble contradictions that are always the terminus of human
thought when it moves exclusively in this world."[20] Living with one's perspective limited to the material world intensifies the confusion and chaos
that emanate from the inevitable contradictions.

She underscores the first reality as the "unique source of all the good
that can exist in this world: that is to say, all beauty, all truth, all justice,
all legitimacy, all order and all human behavior that is mindful of obligations." She continues: "at the center of the human heart is the longing for
an absolute good, a longing that is always there and is never appeased by
any object in this world."[21] This unassuageable yearning induces grace to
come to the aid of a soul in need. To mediate between the two realms, a
human being must give attention and love and ardently desire grace as a
transcendent good, although sometimes the desire is veiled even to one's
own consciousness.

Following the descent of grace, the soul's attention shifts from "contemplation of the transcendent good to the active care for the most basic
human needs" of every individual. Grace facilitates the transformation
from the natural human tendency for favoring the ego and seeking personal rights to a supernatural predilection for disavowing the self and
being more focused on the obligations of tending to fundamental needs
of fellow human beings.[22] Evil, on the contrary, inclines one toward ignoring the real existence of others and refusing to acknowledge the
ephemerality of the body and soul, which leads to illusions of self-
sufficiency, dismissing any need for supernatural help.

---

[19] Ibid., 132.
[20] Ibid.
[21] Ibid.
[22] Estelrich, "Weil's Concept of Grace," 245.

Evil

Weil reminds us that the line of the "Our Father," "And lead us not into temptation, but deliver us from evil," reveals the terror of being abandoned to one's own resources in the presence of evil. The whole soul—the ego and the supernatural part—is subject to time and to the vicissitudes of change. "There must be absolute acceptance of the possibility that everything natural in us should be destroyed. But we must simultaneously accept and repudiate the possibility that the supernatural part of the soul should disappear. It must be accepted as an event that would come about only in conformity with the will of God. It must be repudiated as being something utterly horrible" (*WG* 150). God can shield the eternal part of the soul of those who have made real and direct contact with him, but the carnal part of the soul has no such protection.[23] When harm is done to persons, depravity can take hold, along with pain and suffering; it is humankind's duty to limit the effects of evil by helping individual souls prepare for the unexpected advent of contamination and by offering them elements of purity through prayer, the Eucharist, and caritas.

In her religious philosophy, Weil reasons that since evil exists in this world created through God's goodness and love, we must accept it and try to find some use for it, while persistently mitigating to the full extent of our abilities evil's devastating effects. God's intended uses for evil are not always knowable, which gives us the opportunity to trust and obey God and to continue our advance on the path toward perfection. His love does not offer protection from adversity, consequently, the responsibility for countering evil falls directly on the shoulders of human beings; God can only help humankind through the efforts of other human beings who have understood their own nothingness. "To teach us that we are non-beings, God made himself non-being.... God entrusts to evil the work of teaching us that we are not."[24]

She continues on this note of paradox, which is a stumbling block

---

[23] Weil's image of the soul divided into two parts is developed in the "Decreation" section.

[24] Simone Weil, *First and Last Notebooks* (New York: Oxford University Press, 1970), 218.

for many Weil readers: "We must love God through and beyond evil as such; love him through and beyond the evil that we hate, while hating the evil; love him as the author of the evil that we hate."[25] In her Letter I to Father Perrin, Simone writes that everything comes about in accordance with the will of God, without any exception. "Here then we must love absolutely everything, as a whole and in each detail, including evil in all its forms....We must feel the reality and presence of God through all external things."[26] And her commentary on the line "Give us this day our daily bread" in the "Our Father" reads: "when our actions only depend on earthly energies, subject to the necessity of this world, we are incapable of thinking and doing anything but evil" (*WG* 147). In other words, we are nothing without God's help.

The acceptance, however, of a state of "nonbeing" must come from within to be efficacious. When it is imposed from the exterior, such as occurs too often in the penal system, the defilement inflicted is greater in proportion to the innocence of the victim. As Simone observed in the law courts,[27] in which crime is exposed in its horror and nakedness and the contamination of evil is rampant, a legitimate punishment in all cases must come from a just application of the law, in keeping with a true respect for the individual—whether guilty or not. Since only infinite purity is not contaminated by evil and God alone is completely pure, there must be some tie to the supernatural in administering a just punishment to ward off an intensification of evil. Those who judge the accused need to pay attention to him as a person, sacred in the eyes of God; casting him as a vile pariah by treating him with indifference, brutality, and flippancy deepens the guilt, affliction, and fear. These unsettling emotions widen the contagion of evil and lessen the inability of the indicted to consent to a just punishment. Such a consent is vital to the divine part of the soul, which had been usurped by the carnal part. True love of neighbor implies

---

[25] Weil, *Notebooks* 2, 340.

[26] Simone Weil, *Waiting for God*, trans. Emma Craufurd (New York: HarperCollins, 2001), 3. (Hereafter cited as *WG*.)

[27] Simone Weil had the opportunity to observe very closely the workings of the courts of law during her brother's five-month imprisonment in Le Havre and Rouen and during his trial over a question of military conscription.

loving the hardened vicious criminal as one's self.

Due to evil's existence in a cosmos made by God, who is totally good, Weil uses a dialectical style in discussing the mystery of evil, employing a vocabulary suitable to the elusiveness and ambiguity of the topic. Her allusions to the reality of evil, with its heinous effects for the human soul, and to our need to accept the existence of evil, have a salient presence throughout her work. To identify evil, she puts her comments in tandem with reflections on good, such as evil exists in the absence of efficacious good, which is essentially other than evil. She continues in that vein: evil is multifarious and fragmentary, good is one; evil is apparent, good is mysterious; evil consists in actions motivated by selfish wants, good in nonaction that seeks divine wisdom.

Although evil is integral to the nature of the order of the world, humankind is answerable for the flow of evil acts, as well as for the good actions needed to stem the evil. Evil can only violate a degraded good, for pure good is inviolate, hence the need to nurture pure good in our lives and in the lives of those around us. "You shall judge them by their fruits. There is no greater evil than to do evil to men, and no greater good than to do good to men."[28]

While good increases the reality of beings and objects, evil, on the contrary, extracts goodness from them. Evil gives license to destroy tangible things in which there is the real presence of good, and is perpetrated by those who have no knowledge of that real presence. Evil gives a false sense of being limitless, allowing it to perpetrate with impunity endless amounts of harm to others. Such license is the impetus of war and of atrocities that take place daily around the world. Weil wrote: "The relationships of force give Absence the power to destroy Presence.... It is impossible to contemplate without terror the extent of evil that man is capable of causing and undergoing." She then underlines the dilemma of understanding the presence of evil in the world with the question: "How are we to believe that it is possible to find a compensation for this evil, when because of it God suffered crucifixion?"[29]

Evil has the power to destroy souls when persons are not prepared

---

[28] Weil, *First and Last Notebooks*, 144.
[29] Weil, *Notebooks 2*, 564.

to counter its effects. To abolish evil means to de-create;[30] but Weil believed that only God is able to help us de-create when we co-operate. We will look at length in the last section of this chapter on Weil's concept of decreation as a process to diminish evil and to halt its progress by absorbing it within us. The fact that the evil we bear within us is finite inspires hope. By reorienting our will and our attention toward good—though but for an instant—we destroy a bit of evil. She claims: "The purity that is offered to our eyes is infinite. However little evil we were to destroy at each look, by looking often enough, one day we should destroy it all" (*WG* 125).

Since everything in the material world is composed of a mixture of good and evil, finding a pure good with which to confront evil is formidable. For Weil, even here in our material world composed of good and evil, we do have recourse to pure good: in prayer, in the Eucharist, and in the effects of supernatural grace. Grace, with our prayerful consent, opens the possibility to believe in God's love, for he loved us first. Weil cites John 4.19: "We love, because he first loved us." Since supernatural love alone allows us to believe in him, through grace we can love him freely. But grace can only enter into one's soul if there is an empty space to receive it, and very often that empty space, called a "void" by Weil, is created by some violent act—physical or psychological—and this violence would clearly have evil as its source. Trying to reconcile God's goodness with the presence of evil in his created world involves accepting elements of mystery in creation.

FLANNERY O'CONNOR

Flannery O'Connor subtly signals that she will address questions about the dilemma of evil, the goodness of creation, human beings' relation to the created order, and the mystery of grace in the title of her most anthologized short story, "A Good Man Is Hard to Find," which appeared in its first anthology in 1953.[31] Subsequently, her first story collection

---

[30] Weil varied in the spelling between "decreation" and "de-create." We have kept "de-create" for the verb forms.

[31] The title of the anthology was *Modern Writing I*, ed. William Phillips and Philip Rahv (New York: Avon Publications, 1953).

titled *A Good Man Is Hard to Find,* published in June 1955, O'Connor dedicated to Robert and Sally Fitzgerald as nine stories on original sin. Although all of O'Connor's early fiction displays her satiric turn of mind, her sharp eye for human contradictions, and her gift for irony, her maturing work from *Wise Blood* onward combines these fundamental capacities with her deepening interest in perplexing theological and psychological paradoxes such as how evil can exist in a world she believed had been divinely created as good, by and for love.

Even before she began to read about the life and thought of Simone Weil in 1955, O'Connor in rural Georgia, like Weil in Europe, was reflecting on the origins and perpetuation of evil, the relationship of evil to good, and the operations of grace. In addition to Mrs. Shortley's preoccupation with newsreels of bodies in heaps, O'Connor refers to boxcars, trains, and furnaces that bring the European conflagration of evil into her stories. For example, when Asbury in the "The Enduring Chill," returns home, his sister sarcastically remarks "the artist arrives at the gas chamber" (*CW* 553). Mrs. Cope in "A Circle in the Fire" feels thankful that she isn't one of "those poor Europeans ... that they put in boxcars like cattle and rode them to Siberia" (*CW* 234). And Mrs. Turpin dreams repeatedly of social classes "crammed in together in a boxcar, being ridden to be put in a gas oven" (*CW* 636).

In her "A Good Man Is Hard to Find," O'Connor creates a fictional embodiment of these weighty concerns that she soon discovered she shared with Simone Weil. Our interpretation of this story that continues to engage readers with its disquieting mix of captivating humor and shocking violence benefits from Weil's analysis of the existence and varieties of evil, the meaning of death, and the actions and possibility of grace—all concerns that pervade. "A Good Man Is Hard to Find"—and guides our explication.

Parallel Concerns

Despite early charges that O'Connor was Manichean and aligned with the devil because of her presentations of evil,[32] for both Weil and

---

[32] See for example John Hawkes, "Flannery O'Connor's Devil," *Sewanee Review*, 70.3 (Summer 1962): 395–407.

O'Connor the universe is one and divinely created with the possibility for good and evil. There is no separate kingdom of evil. O'Connor thought "good and evil appear to be joined in every culture at the spine...."[33] Evil exists and multiplies due to the ignorance and failure of human beings to honor the reality of the inseparability of the natural and the supernatural. That which gives more reality to beings and objects is good. Evil diminishes or takes away reality with license to destroy tangible things in which there is the real presence of good. Evil can only violate a degraded good. Pure good is inviolate. Weil considers the void as an empty, receptive aspect of the soul in which dependence on God is unbearably present. If that emptiness is borne patiently and with spiritual confidence, the supernatural will fill it. Indeed, emptiness is essential to receive the supernatural filling.

As we saw earlier, Weil regards death as the most precious thing given to human beings, for it is the unadorned stark opportunity to consent to necessity. From the first publication of "A Good Man Is Hard to Find," questions about the actions of grace in the story have confounded readers. Weil's interpretation of grace resembles ideas O'Connor expresses most clearly in *Mystery and Manners* where she repeatedly emphasizes that "the fiction writer presents mystery through manners, grace through nature, but when he finishes there always has to be left over that sense of Mystery which cannot be accounted for by any human formula."[34] For Weil grace is a mysterious gift from God inserted from eternity into time. Grace fills but can only enter where there is an opening waiting to receive it: O'Connor prepares a grandmother, an escaped convict, and readers to confront this reality in an aborted family vacation.

From Comedy through Irony to Tragedy

The metaphor of journey shapes "A Good Man Is Hard to Find" and loosely binds it to the perennial human journey story. Here the jour-

---

[33] Flannery O'Connor, "In the Protestant South," *Mystery and Manners*, ed. Sally and Robert Fitzgerald (New York: Farrar, Straus & Giroux, 1961, 1979), 200.

[34] Flannery O'Connor, "The Church and the Fiction Writer," *Mystery and Manners*, 153.

ney direction is contested, threatened by fear, and radically altered by imagination and nostalgic illusion. O'Connor drops readers into the middle of a family discussion about vacation, immediately engaging them in the comic first part of the story. Through deft humor O'Connor's narrator—familiar with the speech habits of conventionalists, folk Christians, and nihilists—depicts bypassing speech that leaves everyone imprisoned in language. Here the narrator conveys generational differences of opinion and convoluted conversation peppered with clichés about who, how, and where the family should take its vacation. The grandmother, attracted to sensational catastrophes and fearing an escaped convict reported to be headed toward Florida, suggests they head instead to Tennessee. Her son Bailey ignores her, so she turns her prattle to his wife. Only the children John Wesley and June Star, one bearing the name of a Christian evangelist and the other a movie star, lob sarcasm at their grandmother, as O'Connor hints at pervasive twentieth-century spiritual-value tensions their names imply. Comically signaling the grandmother's proclivities for deception and pretense, the narrator reports that the grandmother sneaks her cat into the car by hiding it in a basket and dresses appropriately in hat and gloves—so in case there was an accident, people would know she was a lady. On the road, the grandmother pacifies her spatting grandchildren with anecdotes and stories constructed from nostalgic memories of her Tennessee home embellished with a Civil War legend of silver hidden behind a secret panel of a plantation she visited once.

Throughout the first part of the story, O'Connor slowly builds readers' sympathy for the family and heightens the irony of the second part in two ways: through the grandmother's stories relayed to the grandchildren that eventually alter the journey and through her conversation about the state of the world at the Tower, a filling station and dance hall combination "set in a clearing outside of Timothy" where they stop for lunch.[35] Proprietor Red Sam and the grandmother complain together about the untrustworthiness of people in the world today—"It isn't a soul in this green world of God's that you can trust.... Everything is getting terrible"

---

[35] Flannery O'Connor, *Collected Works* (New York: Library of America, 1988), 140. (Hereafter cited as *CW*.)

(*CW* 142). These laments of the grandmother and Red Sam about the state of the world, combined with locating Red Sammy's near Timothy, Georgia, bring to mind words recorded in Second Timothy about God-lessness in the "last days" where St. Paul describes distressing times when people will love themselves and money; be arrogant, boastful, disobedient, abusive, inhuman, slanderers; lovers of pleasure rather than lovers of God.[36] Hereby O'Connor links one Georgia family story with the human story of Hebrew and Christian biblical history.

As the family journeys through and more deeply into this perilous fallen world in what will shockingly turn out to be their own "last days," comedy gives way to multiplying ironies. For example, the grandmother's stories so excite the imagination of John Wesley that he wants to see the house with the secret panels. Likewise, having boastfully filled her own mind with her story, the grandmother enters a fictive reality, thinking she is in Tennessee instead of Georgia, and directs Bailey where to turn for a house hundreds of miles away that has come alive in her imagination, an overfull imagination that will destroy them all. Lost on a deserted dirt road that only the grandmother suddenly, though privately, recognizes is not in fact in Tennessee, the family has a car accident, turning the car over once. Crashes that usually evoke alarming consternation produce "a frenzy of delight" in the children and, ironically, disappointment that "nobody's killed" for June Star. All wonder if anyone will find them in this desolate wilderness. When the battered black hearse-like car appears on the hill above them, moving with providential slowness, the grandmother waves her arms frantically, anticipating rescue.

In the third part, the arrival of Hiram, Bobby Lee, and the Misfit—three grotesque outsiders, conveyors of death, who will further turn this journey upside down[37]—propels the story toward the complicated con-

---

[36] Second Timothy 3:1–5 (*NRSV*).

[37] Dorothy Tuck McFarland, *Flannery O'Connor* (New York: Frederick Ungar, 1976), 19. McFarland refers to Richard Pearce's *Stages of the Clown* (Carbondale: Southern Illinois University Press, 1970), in which he suggests that O'Connor uses "the grotesque figure, the freak, the madman, the outsider—to turn the world upside down." See also Ruthann Knechel Johansen, *The Narrative Secret of Flannery O'Connor: The Trickster as Interpreter* (Tuscaloosa: University of Alabama Press, 1994) on the trickster figure in O'Connor's fiction.

frontation with evil, the demonic, and tragedy. After the grandmother recognizes the Misfit, his cohort follows his directives for keeping order with aplomb, as they take the family in small groups into the woods to shoot them. While Hiram and Bobby Lee carry out cold-blooded murder, the grandmother pursues the Misfit in a cryptic conversation about goodness, evil, Jesus, and reality, ideas about which O'Connor and Weil both thought intensely.

Evil, Death, and Grace

Against the backdrop of desultory deaths occurring in the woods, the grandmother and the Misfit disclose the causes and ambiguities of evil, as the grandmother, attempting to save her own life and the Misfit's by converting him with fundamentalist religious platitudes and practices, further exposes her own shallowness. As they speak, the grandmother stands over the Misfit who squats on the ground as if in embarrassed contrition, a position that they will exchange by the end of the story. To the grandmother's repeated pronouncements that he is a good man and that Jesus would help him if he would pray, the Misfit announces, "I don't want no hep," says that his daddy called him a questioner, and reveals himself to be a man whose spirit has been displaced by his rational intellect. Although the grandmother's advice to "pray, pray" seems directed simply to the Misfit, the words echo Weil's belief that prayer is a means of purifying the evil within us.

Of the two, both ignoring the inseparability of the natural and the supernatural, the violence-wielding Misfit is more honest than the grandmother wedded to her superficial conventionalisms and shallow pieties. The Misfit confesses that he doesn't know what sent him to the penitentiary; he finds no escape from his confinement whether he looks left, right, up, or down. He accurately sees the injustices of the legal and penal systems, and perceives a lack of order in the universe. In contrast, the grandmother sustains her belief in the ordering power of manners and conventional religion. Her self-preserving directives to pray and repetitions of "Jesus, Jesus," which begin to sound as if she might be cursing, prompt the Misfit's charges against Jesus and his ironic association of himself with Jesus. "Jesus thown everything off balance. It was the same case with Him as with me except He hadn't committed any crime and they could prove I had committed one because they had the papers on me" (*CW* 151).

The Misfit is clear as well about *how* Jesus threw everything off balance: "[He] was the only One that ever raised the dead, and He shouldn't have done it." The Misfit also knows what is required "if He did what He said." What is at stake for both the Misfit and for the grandmother, who cannot apprehend the meaning of their exchange about Jesus, is the reality and the implications of the Incarnation. The Misfit charges, "If He did what He said, then it's nothing for you to do but throw away everything and follow Him, and if He didn't, then it's nothing for you to do but enjoy the few minutes you got left the best way you can—by killing somebody or burning down his house or doing some other meanness to him. No pleasure but meanness" (*CW* 152).

Certainly the most notable religious rebel in O'Connor's fiction, the Misfit is limited and deceived by his commitment to his rational mind and literalism. Whereas the grandmother is comforted by faith without experience and substance, the Misfit cannot trust anything he has not seen or for which he was not present. Weil reminds us that religion as "a source of consolation is a hindrance to true faith" and that "in this sense atheism [can be] a purification."[38] Hence, the central paradox of the spiritual struggle between the Misfit and the grandmother is that the demonic figure "pressures the grandmother with violence and religious vision (perverted as it is) into a higher understanding of Christ's presence in the world."[39] Despite this challenge to the grandmother's religious vision, neither the Misfit nor the grandmother understands the reality of goodness and love announced and embodied in the Incarnation. Both reduce or flatten it to their own limited understandings. For the Misfit, the Incarnation is a lunatic claim. The grandmother uses the name of Jesus as a talisman to offer comfort and protection for her conventional life.

---

[38] Simone Weil, *Gravity and Grace*, trans. Emma Crauford and Mario von der Ruhr (New York: Routledge, 1999), 115.

[39] Robert H. Brinkmeyer, Jr., *The Art and Vision of Flannery O'Connor* (Baton Rouge: Louisiana State University Press, 1989), 187.

Grace a Tricky Mediator

For Weil, grace frequently functions as a counter to brute force, and O'Connor believed that mysterious acts of grace are often preceded by violence or traumatic shock necessary to arouse those oblivious to supernatural reality. Because of their basic assumptions about the mixture of good and evil and that we know the supernatural through the natural or material, Weil and O'Connor consistently discuss and present the interactions of good and evil. In short, grace mediates the *metaxy*,[40] the state of in-betweenness in which human beings exist as participants in both the natural and supernatural realms.

In "A Good Man Is Hard to Find," the operations of grace are especially complex and nuanced first, because the offerings of grace are ambiguous and ambiguously proceed in two directions: grandmother to Misfit and, though less examined, Misfit to grandmother. The grandmother's pronouncement of goodness on the Misfit and her counsel to pray seem on the surface potentially to reach toward his goodness, or as Weil would say, increase his reality, but they are tainted with self-preservation anxiety. The Misfit uses rational explanations to justify his life of meanness, thereby diminishing his own goodness. Second, the offerings of grace are extended by unlikely agents. Throughout the story, the grandmother has revealed herself to be exceedingly self-centered and manipulative, and the Misfit is an escaped convict directing multiple murders of the innocent as he pursues a quasi-theological conversation with the grandmother. Third, the outcomes or opportunity for growth from action that may seem grace-like remain in question. The grandmother appears to have a brief epiphany when, after herself mumbling without understanding that maybe Jesus didn't raise the dead, she acknowledges her doubt and sees herself more honestly. When she reaches out to touch the Misfit saying, "Why you're one of my babies," she unwittingly associates herself with Adam and Eve in Eden and their offspring, Cain and Abel.[41] The Misfit immediately recoils as if bitten by

---

[40] *Metaxu* was defined previously in chapter 3 as a bridge; here *metaxy* refers to a physical state of being, a state of in-betweenness.

[41] Marion Montgomery, *Why Flannery O'Connor Stayed Home* (Lasalle, IL: Sherwood Sugden, 1981), 256–258. Montgomery provocatively links the Misfit

the snake of temptation for knowledge and power from an ancestral garden, and shoots her three times in the chest. In declaring to be himself by himself and to separate himself from the supernatural, Marion Montgomery argues, the Misfit destroys the self: "That is the edge of the abyss upon which [he] stands, looking down at the dead grandmother in the red clay ditch."[42]

The Misfit's closing words, however, over the dead body—"She would of been a good woman if it had been somebody there to shoot her every minute of her life"—intone a haunting benediction of goodness upon her. The violence perpetrated by this demonic agent of the natural world, who intended no good, strips the grandmother's pretenses and brings her to the void of death, that "most precious thing given to human beings." Weil reminds us once again that "Grace fills, but it can only enter where there is a void [an emptiness] waiting to receive it."[43] And the Misfit's final words—"It's no real pleasure in life"—may open a void in him, for even meanness has apparently lost its allure (*CW* 153). Both Weil and O'Connor were clear that although the effectiveness of grace may not be evident immediately or for a long time and certainly not to others, preparation of the souls of characters as well as readers is equally valuable.

Jesus and the Misfit

The Misfit's passing association with Jesus—"It was the same case with Him as with me..."—invites our examination of the Incarnation of God's love in Jesus Christ as the ultimate gift of grace for living in the *metaxy*, between the natural and the supernatural. Although the Misfit suggests a similarity between them, there are disturbing contrasts between the two. Jesus, indeed, did throw everything off balance in the religious community of the Jews and in Roman civil and political society.

---

to Cain, who kills his brother Abel and is destined to be "a fugitive and a vagabond...in the earth," and connects the Misfit's "I don't need no hep" to Cain's "Am I my brother's keeper?"

[42] Ibid., 244.

[43] Simone Weil, *Notebooks*, vol. 1, trans Arthur Wills (New York: G. P. Putnam's Sons, 1956), 198.

Few understood who he was, what his spiritual origin was, what he was teaching, or why he offered redemptive love and grace to outsiders as well as the faithful. He encounters misunderstanding and the brutality of betrayal and violent crucifixion. Because he belongs to a divine order in which the natural and the supernatural are united he absorbs violence without retaliation. By accepting violence into himself, he extends redemptive suffering.

In contrast, the Misfit, ignorant of his own crimes, cannot understand punishment that he thinks doesn't match what he has done. Indeed, Weil's reflections on the penal system shed light on the Misfit's difficulties. Unable to understand the Incarnation of Jesus as pure good and sacrifice or to experience some correspondence between his natural life, which he limits to his rationality, and a transcendent order, he resorts to a life of meanness. In a letter to Cecil Dawkins, O'Connor makes clear the importance of the Incarnation for understanding her work: "It's not a matter in these stories of 'Do Unto Others.' That can be found in any ethical culture series. It is the fact of the Word made flesh.... That is the fulcrum that lifts my particular stories. I'm a Catholic but this is in orthodox Protestantism also, though out of context—which makes it grow into grotesque forms."[44] Without relationship to the Incarnation, all are vulnerable to becoming demonic purveyors of evil, grotesque figures, freaks, madmen, and outsiders vulnerable to distortion and meanness.

Dialogue in the Metaxy

The consequential questions posed about good and evil, the giving or refusal of grace, suffering and violence in "A Good Man Is Hard to Find" and in most of Flannery O'Connor's fiction are ones from which the author herself was not immune. She instinctively knew that these important concerns emerge in the *metaxy*. Not a monologic or didactic writer, O'Connor understood that the problems and conflicts, questions, doubts, temptations, and suffering her characters encounter in her stories require multiple answering voices. She tested her characters as well as

---

[44] O'Connor, Letter to Cecil Dawkins, June 19, 1957, *The Habit of Being*, 227.

herself with different voices and aspects of herself, including fundamentalists, nihilists, farmhands, and Negroes. Brinkmeyer considers that "such dialogic encounters ... helped make her faith deep and rich, and kept her from sliding into the easy going and unquestioned piety that she so deplored."[45]

As discussed in chapter 3, O'Connor employs the *as if* verbal construction as a central dialogic narrative strategy for bridging perception gaps or distances between the factual and the conditional, between concrete reality and mystery. This construction also keeps readers openly uncertain or unsatisfied as if they themselves were on a threshold of meaning. In "A Good Man Is Hard to Find," the attentive reader may observe, as Kessler asserts, that "the significance of a violent physical act can be discovered only in the verbal acts preceding it."[46] Certainly the intense conversation between the grandmother and the Misfit before he shoots her supports Kessler's assertion. In addition, many of the speech acts early in the story referring to last days, the untrustworthiness of people, nobody being killed, and lostness prepare for the violence at the story's end. Words that do not incarnate and communicate a shared reality but rather imprison in isolated perceptions and distortions of reality precipitate violence. O'Connor engages her readers, even those who resist her, through "guile and deceit centering on a violent reversal that subverts almost everything that has come before."[47] With this reversal, the characters confront an emptiness or a void that forces them to consider a new direction. Through such reversals, she draws readers into the *metaxy* within her stories to grapple themselves with the consequential questions she and her characters face.

---

[45] Brinkmeyer, *The Art and Vision of Flannery O'Connor*, 162.

[46] Edward Kessler, *Flannery O'Connor and the Language of Apocalypse* (Princeton, NJ: Princeton University Press, 1986), 63.

[47] Brinkmeyer, *The Art and Vision of Flannery O'Connor*, 192.

SIMONE WEIL

Void

One's full dependency on God is almost unbearably present when a void or an emptiness in the soul is created. The void can be created by an internal willing or an external force; both are tortuous. The immediate protective reaction is to use the illusory imagination to fill up the void,[48] to pretend that one is moving ahead with a project, a need, a participation in something momentous, that one is a person of consequence and in control of one's own situation. Because the concept of a void is a negation—a void is a virtual space in which there is a vacuum, leaving spare energies with no place to expend them—most of Weil's comments about a void refer to the grievous enduring of this moment of vacuous time and space.

Weil makes the point that if a void is sustained patiently, with confident spiritual expectation, the supernatural will fill the void; thus, paradoxically, emptiness becomes plenitude. "In all our acts of willing, whatever they may be, over and beyond the particular object, we must ... gratuitously want the void. For this good that we can neither visualize nor define represents for us a void....If we manage to reach this point, we are out of trouble, for it is God who fills the void."[49] She refers to this humble long-suffering waiting in anticipatory expectancy with the term *hupomone,* a New Testament word in Greek, which implies a patient submission, a sustaining perseverance, and a calm confidence in the face of pain and adversity.

Maintaining a void is contrary to all the laws of nature, as is the beneficial refusal to exercise all the power at one's disposal or to seek vengeance, in even the smallest way, for the most egregious of hurts. Despite the restorative value in manifestly recognizing the reality of the other, that is, his or her good, the effects of moral gravity make such actions bruise our sense of proud self-righteousness. If one truly recognized that other things and beings exist, evil actions that destroy the reality of

---

[48] Weil sees positive and negative applications of the imagination; here, she is referring to its negative aspect.

[49] Weil, *Notebooks* 2, 491.

things and beings would be impossible to commit.[50] But accepting and acting on that knowledge requires supernatural help. Grace is a vital component in facing the real.

Transforming selfish reactions means freely accepting a void, which takes courage and acknowledgment of our wretchedness and nonbeing. The paradox is that grace itself makes this void, and sometimes the fissure through which grace enters only occurs after some violence. The challenge, in the meantime, if one wants to enter the realm of truth, is to keep the imagination from filling the void with lies. She notes: "Continually to suspend in oneself the work of the imagination, filler up of voids and restorer of balances....If we accept any void, whatever it may be, what stroke of fate can prevent us from loving the universe?"[51]

To particularize the ordeal of tolerating a void, she offers as examples the denial of Christ's followers when he needed their support in the Garden of Gethsemane and elsewhere. Their difficulty in remaining openly supportive of Christ came from his being considered a common criminal to be punished by crucifixion. The dissipation of all their prior grand expectations as disciples of Christ left a void that made constancy agonizing. She contrasts the apostles with the soldiers of Napoleon who found it easier to be faithful to their idolized leader, even when he was headed for defeat and ignominy. His soldiers knew they would likely die in his ill-conceived campaigns, but they would die for a glorious cause. She asserts that their vainglorious attitudes facing death were similar to those of the martyrs of the church, who died for an institution already in existence and with a promising future.

With chagrin, she observes: "We die for what is strong, not for what is weak; or at any rate for what, though momentarily weak, retains an aureole of strength. The fact of dying for what is strong robs death of its bitterness—and at the same time of all its value."[52] For Weil, "to love truth signifies to endure the void and, consequently, to accept death. Truth is on the side of death. To love truth with all one's soul is some-

---

[50] Perrin, *Dialogue*, 56.
[51] Weil, *Notebooks* vol. 1, 145.
[52] Ibid., 148.

WHEN FICTION AND PHILOSOPHY MEET

thing that cannot be done without a wrenching."[53]

Death

For Weil, death is the supremely critical time in life; it is when the temporary meets the eternal. The being, totally stripped of any ego, has the stark opportunity to consent to the reign of necessity, which includes annihilation. She considers death as the most precious thing that has been given to man, which is why it is a supreme impiety to make a bad use of it, for oneself or by causing it to happen to others who are unprepared to die. Birth and death are the two major times a person confronts the reality of being created by God with no intervening veils of illusion; these events, in Weil's mind, can be an occasion for purification. Only when newly born or facing death can one adore God in a state of purity without sullying his divinity with base thoughts of self. She entered into her *Notebooks* in memo style: "Death [is an] *Instantaneous state*, without a future or a past—Indispensable for entry into eternity."[54] But bitterness is an important element, for the state of agony constitutes the supreme dark night of the soul, of which even the perfect have need in order to attain to absolute purity. For that purpose, it is just as well that it be bitter.

The rancor comes with the sharp awareness that we are truly nothing.[55] Evil is between God and us; love has to pass across it.[56] This piercing realization comes while we are suffering deep affliction or are at the pivotal moment of death. To keep the purity of the bitterness, there should be no consolation, such as a belief in immortality, which leads beings into thinking that there will be a prolongation of their lives as they knew them, thus robbing death of its purpose. Suppressing the separating distance can put one in the living presence of the Spirit, which brings joy. Weil notes: "If one finds fullness of joy in the thought that God *is*, one must find the same fullness in the knowledge that oneself is not, for it is the same thought. And this knowledge is only bestowed on

---

[53] Ibid., 160–161.

[54] Ibid., 183.

[55] This idea of being nothing is in reference to the divine, not in reference to other human beings.

[56] Weil, *First and Last Notebooks*, 300.

the sensibility through suffering and death."[57] However deep or hidden the love in a soul may be, there is a breaking point when it succumbs; it is this moment that transforms, which wrenches us away from the finite toward the infinite. The soul's love for God then becomes transcendent in the soul, which is the supreme teleological purpose of life.

The soul that, on the verge of death, is not full of love squanders—by clinging to illusory fantasies—an infinitely precious and irrevocable opportunity. It is human nature to design falsehoods to protect all that is unfit in human beings, allowing individuals to continue in circumstances that ordinarily would strip them of prideful conceits. The divine goal is to fill the soul with a supernatural love, but the gravity in our nature contrives to maintain our illusions. To exemplify this dire human struggle when one's death seems pointless, Weil used Arthur Koestler's *Dialogue with Death*,[58] in which he reveals the futility of clinging to the idolatrous idea that power embodies truth. Koestler described with keen sensitivity his own psychological reactions and those of his fellow prisoners as they tried to cope with the anguish of living under capricious and intractable death sentences.

On the point of dying we all will eventually ask: "Why?" "Why me?" For Weil, that question is primordial, but has no answer; one only hears the nonresponse: the essential silence. Dying for an inglorious defeat is indicative of the way the imagination fills an unbearable void. Even though victory brings no personal gain, the thought of losing one's life for a failed cause requires superhuman effort. The advent of death demands a counterweight, and without grace, this counterweight can only be lies. This, she thought, is the rationale behind the exuberant cries of "Vive l'empereur" (Long live the Emperor) by Napoleon's soldiers who were headed for a certain inglorious annihilation.

But, she states categorically, any attempt to fill the void with illusions would block the descent of supernatural grace into our souls. Annihilation is the fount of truth; one needs to remain conscious of the ephemeral quality of human life. Choosing anything less than the entire

---

[57] Weil, *Notebooks* 1, 291.

[58] Arthur Koestler, *Dialogue with Death* (Chicago: University of Chicago Press, 2011).

universe and not consenting to all the necessity contained therein is ignoble. The true aspiration is to craft one's life like a perfect poem or musical composition, to make time into a mobile image of eternity. The value of this ideal comes from the reality that the permanence of the stars and the extreme fragility of flowers equally give the sensation of eternity.

Weil states that, despite gaining nothing by victory, dying for a cause that will triumph is bearable; on the contrary, dying for a cause headed for defeat is unbearable. Her *Notebook* entry marks that giving one's life for something "absolutely deprived of force would be superhuman; Christ's disciples. *The thought of death calls for a counterweight, and this counterweight—apart from grace—cannot be anything but a lie.*"[59]

Decreation

Weil was dedicated to keeping the goal of perfection before herself and before others in this life, and she believed that "the desire to become perfect does make [one] less imperfect."[60] She often referred to Jesus' counsel: "Be perfect, therefore, as our heavenly Father is perfect" (Mt. 5. 48). She called the process for working toward perfection "decreation." Perfection in the love of God requires a renunciation of the inherent belief that we are the center of the universe, which is the source of all error and sin. This concentration on self is conditioned by individual desires and projections, which are not concordant with absolute truth. Weil calls this aspect of the human person the "created" part, and it is this element that needs to be de-created. She writes, "God created me as a non-being that has the appearance of existing, in order that through love I should renounce this apparent existence and be annihilated by the plenitude of being."[61] A premise of her concept of decreation is that the sole purpose of human existence is to love God and his creation by allowing the uncreated part of the soul, although infinitesimally small, to dominate the created part. In this last essay on Simone Weil, we explore her concept of the two parts of the soul, what she means by the decreation of the created part, and how such a process might take place, along with the effects

---

[59] Weil, *Notebooks* 1, 166. Weil's italics.
[60] Weil, *First and Last Notebooks*, 337.
[61] Ibid., 96.

that decreation might have on the individual and collectivity.

"Decreation,"[62] for Weil, signifies a process of uncreating that part of our being that God created to enable us to live in this world, that is, the personal element in us, the part that keeps on crying 'me,' 'me,' 'me,'...in diverse accents of sorrow, exultation, triumph, anxiety, fear, pain. Decreation does not mean destruction; it involves returning the created part into the uncreated state, which is God's. Although this process might seem nihilistic, decreation has the positive effect of leading to a fuller participation in God's joyful act of creation.

To make her concept of created and uncreated parts of the soul clear, Weil presents an image of a soul divided into two variably unequal parts. The one part, considered higher, is that infinitely small part of the soul, which can be called the supernatural or the uncreated part. This part of the soul is the only element in creation that God did not abandon to necessity. An entry in her *Notebooks* reads: "God abandons our whole entire being—flesh, blood, sensibility, intelligence, love—to the pitiless necessity of matter and the cruelty of the devil, except for the eternal and supernatural part of the soul.... God only keeps under his care the part of creation which is Himself—the uncreated part of every creature.... God is absent from the world, except in the existence in this world of those in whom his love is alive."[63] The task of this higher part of the soul is to consent to whatever comes along, that is, to everything that occurs in this world run by the impersonal laws of necessity.

The other part of the soul, or the lower, is the natural part that sets goals, seeks honors, builds up "supplementary" energy for projects, and creates evil, all of which keeps it moving in its own determined direction. When this part of the soul becomes overwhelmed by painful circumstances, it cries for the discomfort to end, and does everything to escape it. As a counterbalance, the task of the higher part of the soul, with its natural relationship to goodness, is to persist in saying, "I accept whatever comes, and I continue to love it because it is of God's making."

---

[62] A neologism first used by Charles Péguy for a different purpose; see Miklos Vetö, *The Religious Metaphysics of Simone Weil*, trans. Joan Dargan (Albany: State University of New York Press, 1994), 11.

[63] Weil, *First and Last Notebooks*, 103.

But maintaining an equilibrium in the soul, so that the uncreated part might consent to God, no matter the pain and affliction imposed by the mechanical laws of necessity, takes training and discipline. These parts of the divided soul may appear stable, but, in Weil's theory, their impacts on the body vary; the overall goal is for the higher part of the soul to play an increasingly potent role in influencing the behavior of the person. The body has several roles to play.

The body serves as a balance, restoring equilibrium between the two contending parts of the soul. Weil reflects on how the body can be trained to be attentive only to the higher part of the soul, considering that sometimes one must do violence to one's thought. The body can be used as a lever, multiplying the force of the part of the soul that desires God's presence over that part that feels horror at it.[64] The controlled body can make the energy of the created part of the soul exhaust itself, and eventually, wear out the autonomous self. Any restoration of their equal roles can only be accomplished with God's goodness.

As we have seen, Weil's intuitive belief is that God's act of creation was by means of his withdrawal.[65] God, through love, withdrew, creating a distance between creatures and God. He added a protective veil of space, time, and matter, to keep the direct radiance of his love from evaporating his creatures like water in the sun. This veil can be pierced to our advantage if we turn toward God only with the part of our soul that is God's; at that point, we could find ourselves on the other side of the veil. "Necessity is the screen placed between God and us so that we can be. It is for us to pierce through the screen so that we cease to be."[66] At that point, we are with God. God's original withdrawal gives humankind an invaluable model of love to imitate in all humility. She believed that humility consists in the knowledge that one is nothing insofar as one is a human being, and, more generally, insofar as one is a creature.

We can discern from Weil's notebook entries and from her essays how basic this idea of decreation is to her religious philosophy. She believes that salvation will only come through the process of decreation.

---

[64] Ibid., 230–231.
[65] See chapter 2.
[66] Weil, *Notebooks* 2, 402.

Although human beings have the responsibility for the process, it remains the work of grace and not the will. Decreation can suppress the distance between God and his creatures, overcoming the freedom of an autonomous "I" granted at birth. Although decreation is contrary to human nature, and appears negative, the diminishment of the autonomous self and the subsequent living presence of the spirit in the regenerated being becomes a source of joy and makes human community more realizable.

FLANNERY O'CONNOR

Flannery O'Connor depicts the consequences of the absence of decreation in her characters, having imbibed in her imagination the legacies of the Civil War from her region. She also lived and portrayed in fiction the displacements effected by World War II and the fragmentation, if not dissolution, of human community. Everywhere in her stories written from the 1950s until her death, she witnesses to the loss or decay of human community through conflicts affecting family, generations, races, cultures, and classes. In so doing, she depicts the consequences of situations where there is an absence of any form of decreation, such as Weil presented. Prophetic artist that she is, O'Connor links her twentieth-century depictions of evil, disintegrations, and death to the fundamental human-divine discord described in scripture, history, and through biblical prophecy. Because O'Connor has dropped shadowy allusions to stories from ancient scripture into "A View of the Woods," perhaps her most gruesome story of family hostility and violence, the Fortune-Pitts story begs to be read on two levels simultaneously. Dimly reflecting the biblical narrative of creation, biblical prophecy, and religious history, and Weil's ideas of evil, death, and decreation, "A View of the Woods" invites intertextual interpretation.

Landscape of Fallen Creation

The story opens with the time-marking phrase "The week before...," raising a question in attentive readers' minds—The week before what?—that is quickly forgotten with the narrator's description of the raptness with which Mr. Fortune and his granddaughter Mary Fortune

Pitts, sitting on the hood of "a battered mulberry-colored Cadillac," watch the "disembodied gullet gorge itself on the clay" to prepare the new lakeside. As the big machine digs, regurgitates, and reshapes the clay of creation from a cow-grazing pasture into a red corrugated lake, a mysterious "black line of woods ... appeared at both ends of the view to walk across the water and continue along the edge of fields" (*CW* 525). Following this unusual, initial appearance, the woods linger throughout the story.

The narrator reveals that damming rivers and creating lakes at the time of this story is encouraging civilizational developments such as making electric power increasingly available in the South, and telephone lines are anticipated.[67] Opportunities to modify human dominion over creation inspired the entrepreneurial spirit of seventy-nine-year-old landowner Mr. Fortune. He rents some of his land to his ne'er-do-well son-in-law Pitts, his daughter, who resents caring for her aging father, and their children. As grandfather and granddaughter day after day watch the machine "systematically [eat] a square red hole in what had once been a cow pasture" (*CW* 525), Mr. Fortune stakes out his position on land use, to his nine-year-old granddaughter, "Any fool that would let a cow pasture interfere with progress is not on my books." By the third paragraph, the narrator has prefigured the lines of intergenerational conflict over landownership and the gift of creation with the description of Mary Fortune Pitts's silence to her grandfather's statement: "Her pale eyes behind her spectacles followed the repeated motion of [the yellow bulldozer] again and again and her face—a small replica of the old man's—never lost its look of complete absorption" (*CW* 525).

Family Lines of Jezebel: Fortune and Pitts

Physical likenesses between parents and children or grandparents and grandchildren appear in several O'Connor stories. In such stories as "Everything That Rises Must Converge," "The Artificial Nigger," and

---

[67] The Tennessee Valley Authority, a federally owned corporation, was approved in May 1933 to provide navigation, flood control, electricity generation, and economic development for Tennessee, Alabama, Mississippi, Kentucky, and small portions of Georgia, North Carolina, and Virginia.

"A View of the Woods," the relationships mirror the central tension of the story, though each with different outcomes. This association of parents and children or grandchildren echoes words from the prophet Malachi, the last prophet in the Hebrew scriptures, when he warns of God's displeasure with the lack of piety in the community around the temple, and promises to send a messenger who will "turn the hearts of parents to their children and the hearts of children to their parents."[68] O'Connor understands from biblical history that such turning of the hearts is not assured, even as Jesus himself—the prophet above all prophets—reveals when he warns his disciples on the Mount of Olives to beware of false prophets who will lead people astray, and the love of many will grow cold.[69]

O'Connor depicts a perverted, even diabolical, turning of the hearts of parents and children in a conflict over land use through the relationship of Mr. Fortune and Mary Fortune Pitts, named for his mother who died giving birth to him. Bearing his physical and temperamental likeness, Mary also carries the burden of her grandfather's desires for companionship, his psychological projections, and his attempts to manipulate her to support his land development plans, with which he infuriates her father, Pitts. In addition, as the youngest of the Pitts children and favored by their grandfather, Mary absorbs the animosity of her father—expressed in the routine beatings at the edge of the woods with Pitts's belt—and of the nuclear family toward the authoritarian control of Mr. Fortune. Stoically enduring the belt lashes yet persistently and vociferously denying that she has ever been beaten, Mary declares each time her grandfather confronts her, "Nobody was here and nobody beat me and if anybody did I'd kill him" (CW 530–531).

Although hinted from the beginning of the story, the rupture in the relationship between grandfather and granddaughter over land use occurs when Mr. Fortune announces that he intends to sell "the lawn" for a gas station–convenience store, thereby removing the place the children play and the cows graze and blocking the view of the woods. Grandfather and

---

[68] Malachi 4:6 (*NRSV*). See Montgomery, *Why Flannery O'Connor Stayed Home,* 222–223, who makes this point as well.

[69] See Matthew 24:3–14 (*NRSV*).

granddaughter fill their angry charges and countercharges with biblical phrases—"He who calls his brother a fool is subject to hell fire," Mary says. "Jedge not," Fortune shouts, "lest ye be not jedged." Interpreting her objections as personal rejection, Mr. Fortune tells Mary to "walk home by yourself. I refuse to ride a Jezebel," to which she retorts, "and I refuse to ride with the Whore of Babylon" (*CW* 533). Ridiculing his granddaughter's lack of knowledge that a whore is a woman, Mr. Fortune reveals his own ignorance that whoredom—faithless, unworthy, prostituting, idolatrous practices or pursuits—can afflict human beings of any gender.

Despite the confused references grandfather and granddaughter make to the ancient Phoenician princess, together they expose the Fortune-Pitts family ties to Jezebel, the wife of Israel's King Ahab. According to that story, Jezebel persecuted the prophets of Yahweh, encouraged worship of Baal, and framed an innocent landowner who refused to sell his property to King Ahab, causing the landowner's death and subsequently her own gruesome death for her transgressions. Mr. Fortune apparently perceives himself ironically as an innocent landowner framed by his nine-year-old granddaughter who refuses to submit to his intentions for his own land.

Idolatrous Power and Punishment

Alongside his special affection for Mary Fortune Pitts and his desire to strengthen her will against her father, Pitts, lie Mr. Fortune's hatred of his son-in-law, who has no first name, his excessive egoism, and his psychological projections foisted on Fortune's granddaughter. Carrying the name of his mother with whom he was deprived relationship at birth, Mary Fortune Pitts offers him connection to the lost past, and through her—whom "he liked to think of … as being thoroughly of his clay"—he projects his wishes for the future (*CW* 528).

Mr. Fortune idolizes power and authority: "When the well had gone dry, [Fortune] had not allowed Pitts to have a deep well drilled but had insisted that they pipe their water from the spring. He did not intend to pay for a drilled well himself and he knew that if he let Pitts pay for it, whenever he had occasion to say to Pitts, 'It's my land you're sitting on,'

Pitts would be able to say to him, 'Well, it's my pump that's pumping the water you're drinking'" (*CW* 526). Knowing that anyone over sixty is in a precarious position "unless he controls the greater interest ... every now and then [Fortune] gave the Pittses a practical lesson by selling off a lot. Nothing infuriated Pitts more than to see him sell off a piece of the property to an outsider..." (*CW* 526). Fortune fills his imagination with schemes to outwit, manipulate, and emasculate his son-in-law in order to secure his control and dominion and advance his vision of material progress.

The mutual hatred in Pitts and Fortune drives the contest over authority, and turns Mary Fortune Pitts, caught in the middle, into both target and pawn. Compounding treachery and the evil of hate, Pitts targets Mary for beatings to express his personal frustration and to anger Fortune. Fortune treats Mary as a pawn to be cajoled or manipulated— with money, with promise of a boat, and by secretly leaving all his assets in a trust for her upon his death—to embrace his vision of progress.

Deceit and Resistance

Beneath this competition of human wills lie differing perceptions of a lawn for play and pasturing, the woods, and the view of them that Mary Fortune Pitts defends against the deceitful wiles of her grandfather. Throughout the story, the description of the woods changes depending on the character of the beholder. Initially, grandfather and granddaughter watch the bulldozer digging out the lake, with the numinous black line of woods in the distance. In repeated exchanges between Mary and Mr. Fortune, Mary associates the lawn with playing and protects the woods for their viewing value.

Nursing his wounded feelings from his granddaughter's resistance to selling the lawn to Tilman, Mr. Fortune takes three looks at the woods: "Every time he saw the same thing: woods—not a mountain, not a waterfall, not any kind of planted bush or flower, just woods. The sunlight was woven through them ... so that every thick pine trunk stood out in all its nakedness," allowing Fortune to conclude, "a pine trunk is a pine trunk." His second look convinces him "of his wisdom in selling the lot. The dissatisfaction it caused Pitts would be permanent, but he could make it up to Mary Fortune by buying her something" (*CW* 538).

His third look at almost six o'clock unsettles him, for "the gaunt trunks appeared to be raised in a pool of red light that gushed from the almost hidden sun setting behind them. The old man stared for some time, as if for a prolonged instant he were caught up out of the rattle of everything that led to the future and were held there in the midst of an uncomfortable mystery that he had not apprehended before" (*CW* 538). Despite this unpleasant vision, Fortune is not deterred from closing the deal with Mr. Tilman the following day, under the only thinly veiled guise of taking Mary Fortune to look for a boat.

Violence, Death, and Decreation

Flannery O'Connor's practice of preparing a character to receive grace through an act of violence raises questions about Mary Fortune Pitts's shocking violent eruption in Tilman's store. Is it an opening for grace from a child who perceives the woods of the world differently than her grandfather? While the hurled bottles may produce a momentary void in Mr. Fortune, he quickly fills it with his conviction that he has not been firm enough with his granddaughter in whose face he sees his own image. He drives to the woods intending to whip her. Before he can begin, however, Mary launches her whole nine-year-old body on him, pummeling him with fists and feet, embodying her denials "Nobody's ever put a hand on me and if anybody did, I'd kill him." In a pause that loosened her grip allowing Mr. Fortune to roll over, reversing their positions, he dashes her head three times on a rock as "pale identical eye looked into pale identical eye."

Grandfather and granddaughter, physical reflections of each other, both die in the woods, one ignoring them and in death trying to escape them because of his willful commitment to his vision of progress, and the other protecting them for the reality they represent. In spite of his earlier, fleeting impression of the woods' mystery—"the gaunt trunks appear[ing] to be raised in a pool of red light that gushed from the almost hidden sun[set]"—Mr. Fortune continues to be so filled with his own egocentric illusions that he kills their innocent defender.

In a letter to Betty Hester as she worked on this story, Flannery

O'Connor explains her own interpretation of the woods: "... the woods, if anything, are the Christ symbol. They walk across the water, they are bathed in a red light, and they in the end escape the old man's vision and march off over the hill."[70] Recalling Simone Weil's conviction that in suffering one is brought to the foot of Christ's cross, in this story, murder and death bring granddaughter and grandfather to the woods, a place suggestive of the cross, if we accept O'Connor's interpretation.

Without grasping that he has killed his granddaughter, Fortune says to her motionless figure, "This ought to teach you a good lesson" (*CW* 546). More importantly, he cannot understand, with Weil, as we noted earlier, that here in the presence of death he encounters one of the two supremely important times in life—birth and death—when a person confronts the reality of being created by God. Falling to the ground from his own enlarged heart, Fortune "look[s] helplessly along the bare trunks into the tops of the pines and his heart expanded ... so fast that [he] felt as if he were running as fast as he could with the ugly pines toward the lake.... He perceived that there would be a little opening there, a little place where he could escape and leave the woods behind him." In his vision, "he look[s] around desperately for someone to help him but the place was deserted except for one huge yellow monster which sat to the side, as stationary as he was, gorging itself on clay" (*CW* 546). According to Weil's description, Fortune appears to be abandoned to his own resources in the presence of evil. Yet the narrator reports that he perceives a little opening through which he might escape. O'Connor leaves readers pondering the ambiguity and mystery of grace: is this an opening of sheer flight, or could it be the small uncreated part of his soul waiting to be reclaimed by God?

With profound disquiet, "A View of the Woods" depicts physical, psychological, and intellectual manifestations of evil evident in the human struggle, since the foundations of the world, to understand what it means for humans to have dominion over the earth.[71] This story, which begins with the enigmatic words "The week before" and concludes with brutal death, offers an inversion of the creation narrative, which ends

---

[70] O'Connor to "A," December 28, 1956, *The Habit of Being*, 190.
[71] See the creation story recorded in Genesis 1:26 (*NRSV*).

with the Creator's pronouncement that it is good. In a world created as good, both O'Connor and Weil acknowledge and wrestle with the tremendous paradoxes evil presents, paradoxes to which prophets are especially attentive.

In "A View of the Woods," O'Connor's characters, contending over land and trees, illustrate the difference between the temporal and the eternal inferred through the beauty and order of the world. When human beings depend simply on temporal or earthly energies subject to the necessities of this world, they are incapable of anything except evil, Weil asserts. Then evil manifests its many forms in egocentrism, willfulness, psychological projection, grandiose illusions, or violence, all of which extract goodness from the reality of nature, objects, and persons.

Perhaps most challenging of Weil's ideas on evil is her conviction that God's love does not protect people from adversity and her certainty that we must love God through and beyond the evil that we hate, while hating the evil. "God entrusts to evil the work of teaching us that we are not. The desire of creatures to be, and their illusion that they are, stirs up evil."[72] When evil gives one a sense of being limitless, as it appears to have done for Mr. Fortune, loving what we hate seems an impossibility. O'Connor's "A View of the Woods" makes visible the power of evil to destroy souls if persons are not prepared to counter its effects. Mary Fortune Pitts and Mr. Fortune in this story are weakly equipped—one by age and the other by willful arrogance—to counter evil. Despite his death ironically from an enlarged heart, Mr. Fortune's inability to see the woods as creation's evidence of the natural and supernatural beauty and order of the world, his relentless, and in the end deadly, efforts to retain his authority and power at the center of the family, and his unfaltering commitment to modify the world in his image of progress obstruct an opening in his soul for God to reclaim, what Weil considers decreation.

Weil suggests that the only way "to abolish evil is to de-create," which requires a human being's cooperation with God. As we discussed earlier, Weil roots her concept of decreation in her understanding of God's withdrawal from the world after creation so that human beings could know freedom and choose relationship and love. Her idea of decre-

[72] Weil, *First and Last Notebooks*, 218.

ation invites human beings to imitate a similar "withdrawal" by renouncing the erroneous and sinful belief that we are the center of the universe. By so doing, according to Weil, we allow the divine to reclaim the eternal and supernatural part of the soul, to participate in the joyful act of creation, and to make a dwelling space for love.

Conclusion

All the concepts introduced in our prior chapters require a poverty of spirit that comes from the act of liberating oneself from the heavy burden of actions that preserve the "precious" ego, which Weil sees as our inherent moral gravity. Attention in all its fullness, love of neighbor with true charity, love of the world with gratitude, affliction endured with the patience of *hupomone*, reading situations and others using a third nonperspective dimension, and creation of a void for grace to enter into the soul, all require a certain effort toward de-creating the created part of the soul. Weil was very interested in the Eastern mystical practices, such as meditation for silencing the disconcerting part of the self.

Weil sees our task as ridding ourselves of pretentious delusions, what she calls a false sense of divinity. She counsels: "He emptied himself of his divinity. We should empty ourselves of the false divinity with which we were born."[73] To sum up Weil's concepts as we have presented them so far: by the kenotic movement of divine descent and crucifixion, God abdicated his omnipotence in order that the universe might be. Christ the Son in his human form allowed himself to be stripped of power and prestige to die on the Cross. So, human beings must reject their affectation of being the center of the world, and admit to the fragility of the human person that causes it to be entirely dependent on external circumstances that have unlimited power to crush it. They must, in consequence, consent to the rule of mechanical necessity in matter, and recognize the existence of free choice within each soul. Giving that consent is an act of love. Turning the face of this love toward thinking persons shows love of our neighbor; the same face of love turned toward matter is love of the order of the world.

---

[73] Weil, *Notebooks* 1, 217.

An essential idea for Weil is that necessity rules the world through obedience not force, for God created the world and then withdrew, leaving its operation to the laws of the cosmos. Weil names this network of laws "necessity," and sees its operation as a model of obedience, for it cannot do otherwise than move according to the laws; this for Weil is perfect obedience. Decreation is in essence putting oneself in a similar state of obedience to the uncreated part of the soul, which is God. "Obedience is the very essence of the brute force inherent in Necessity itself. Everything that hurts me, everything that weighs upon me is obedient to God. Everything that smiles upon me also, such as, the tree that covers itself with blossoms."[74] Father Perrin attests that at the end of her life, she was totally dedicated to her passion for the will of God and her unconditional desire for obedience to his will.

---

[74] Weil, *Notebooks* 2, 600.

Conclusion

The Enduring World

Flannery O'Connor and Simone Weil lived in times of great flux. The American South was coming to terms with major social changes involving the civil rights movement, with its backlash of ugly clashes in the streets and the persistent inhuman cruelty of lynching blacks. In Europe, the massive destruction during the Second World War, increasing in intensity with the development of fighter planes, U-boats, and unmanned bombing missions, caused Weil to despair over what would remain of European civilization. Both women had deep anxieties over the aspects of their worlds that would or would not endure and over whether the commandment to love one's neighbor could ever be a fundamental guide to social behavior. One can imagine that their confidence in divine love and its endurance was profound, but at the same time they saw that humankind's barbarous behavior also seemed without end. In our conclusion, we review what these two writers tried to do with their writing as they headed into a future that would confront serious problems of relationships that still endure today.

These two extraordinary women were seekers and purveyors of truth, products of the same century, but of vastly different milieus. Both were considered to be among the finest writers of the twentieth century. O'Connor's unique narrative fiction conveys her message with humor, violence, and realism aimed toward mystery, while Weil peppers her rational arguments with allegories, metaphors, and literary allusions from folklore through time-honored masterpieces. The brilliant writing gifts of both intellectuals entice readers to enjoy the process of reading them while being reminded of what they saw as humankind's ultimate goal of giving an unquestioning consent to God's love no matter the harshness of the circumstances. Because these questions are perennial, the dialectic and dialogical processes of O'Connor and Weil continue to have relevance for us today. To assist our assessment of their relevance, we consider first their ideas on the ethics of language and literature; second, their practice, as realists of distances, of bringing near realities into relationship with the invisible ineffable; and third, the centrality of the Incarnation to Flannery O'Connor's incarnational art and Simone Weil's invitation for an incarnational world.

Continuing Relevance of Weil and O'Connor

As a Platonist and admirer of the wisdom expressed by ancient Greek philosophers, poets, and playwrights, Simone Weil applies her dialectical[1] philosophical thinking and her acute analytic abilities to social, political, and religious problems for which she seeks resolutions commensurate with the limitations of the human condition. Following her mystical experience, which she integrates through philosophical reflection on the possibilities and implications of religious faith, she expresses a transcendent view of God, who leaves the operations of the created world to Necessity and divine interventions of grace. Having witnessed the blatant atrocities of political totalitarianism, war, and the victimization of marginalized peoples, she strives to make clear that the goal of perfectability for humankind through faith informed by reason can be a guideline for human actions.

Flannery O'Connor, a dialogical[2] storyteller who draws upon biblical story, prophecy, and Protestant folk Christians who hear and speak to God directly or see visions, questions herself, her twentieth-century culture, and disbelieving readers about the lures of nihilism, "the chief moral temptation of the modern world."[3] Her continuing doubts concerning the truth of the human condition led her to value Weil's own philosophical inquiry. In her fiction, O'Connor challenges and tempers her inherited views of God's transcendence derived from Catholic doctrine and the church as the essential, mediating community necessary for faith. She does so by engaging with fundamentalist Christians who sustain a highly

---

[1] *Dialectic* refers to an exchange of logical arguments, often examining a thesis in relation to its antithesis to reach a new conclusion or synthesis.

[2] *Dialogical* is used to indicate participation in dialogue or exploratory conversation.

[3] Ralph Wood, *Flannery O'Connor and the Christ-Haunted South* (Grand Rapids, MI: William B. Eerdmans, 2004), 5.

personal yet communal relationship with God through scripture interpretation, proclamation, and revelation.[4] She admires these fundamentalists for their literal readings of scripture and their radical faith in Christ.
For the folk Christians, as for the early Hebrew people, God, who
formed the world through speech, did not absent himself following creation, but the Word became flesh and continued to dwell among humankind.

Morality and Literature

Literature and art were always a source of truth for Weil; she taught
philosophy through the use of literature in her classes. She believed that
great literature has withstood the test of time because it deals honestly
with eternal questions of good and evil. Fiction of first-rate quality offers
dilemmas that have serious consequences for all involved and, thus, allows the reader to participate vicariously in the actions, as well as in the
aftereffects of bad decisions. Consequently, the reader can understand
the dangers involved without actually suffering the evil effects. Fine art
has an anonymous element stemming from its source in truth, which is
not one with the personality of the artist.

During the last year and a half of her life, Weil was engaged in the
raging controversy over the blame writers deserved for France's dispirit-
ing defeat by the Nazis. Her arguments in the controversy echoed
thoughts expressed in her 1937 essay "The Power of Words."[5] She maintained that since words have an impact on individuals' behavior and since
words are a writers' profession, the moral fiber of a country is nourished

---

[4] Flannery O'Connor reviewed Karl Barth's *Evangelical Theology: An Introduction*, a collection of lectures Barth gave in 1962 at the University of Chicago
and Princeton Theological Seminary, for *Southern Cross* in 1963. In her letters
she commends Barth as one of the best Protestant theologians of the twentieth
century. In her book review she states: "Barth's description of the wonder, concern and commitment of the evangelical theologian could equally well be a description of the wonder, concern and commitment of the ideal Catholic life."
See Leo J. Zuber, *The Presence of Grace and Other Book Reviews by Flannery
O'Connor* (Athens: University of Georgia Press, 1983, 2008), 164.

[5] Simone Weil, *The Simone Weil Reader*, ed. George A. Panichas (New
York: David McKay, 1977), 268–285.

or demoralized by its writers' choice of words that properly express truth or promote self-serving chimeras.

The context of her intellectual life during the first half of the twentieth century had been a time of avant-garde experimentation in art, literature, and mores: Dadaism, Surrealism, *l'acte gratuit* as embodied in the fiction of André Gide,[6] and the movement of "art for art's sake." Weil castigated this vapid communication for its total absence of values, while she prized words that transmit a beneficent aura, as we have seen in chapter 6 with the word "grace." Words such as justice, truth, love, beauty, each has its origin in an absolute value.

At the polar opposite, empty words, such as nation, security, capitalism, authority, democracy, become myths, monsters, isolated abstractions, and cause needless conflicts and loss of life. Such words with little objective meaning can be manipulated to subvert the values that underpin truths of everyday human experience. She writes: "The good is the pole towards which the human spirit is necessarily oriented, not only in action but in every effort, including the effort of pure intelligence."[7] For Weil, writers do not have to be professors of morals, but they do have to be guardians against the harmful subversion of values, and to help their readers be attentive to the fact that every decision holds elements of good and evil. She continued up through her very last works to rail against the exploitative manipulation of language, which misleads people through falsehoods.

Simone Weil's own dedication was to transmitting the truth through words, both spoken and written, based on the purest criterion of values. In her opinion, France's ineffectual reaction to the Nazi invasion had its source in the debasement of language that eroded habits of careful reflection in the silent depths of the human heart. Instead of words transmitting truth, substantive values had been cut adrift from speech and ignored. In this time of chaos, uprooting, and blame tossed about brashly, she composed three brief essays concisely stating the seriousness

---

[6] A disinterested act, pure of any motivation, a term originated by Charles Baudelaire.

[7] Panichas, 288.

of the modern condition: "The Responsibility of Writers,"[8] "Morality and Literature,"[9] and a philosophical exploration on "The Notion of Value."[10] Her thoughts have particular bearing for the contemporary scene with the rapidity of and universal access to disseminating information—true or false—worldwide. Words matter, and the truth of the message is as vital today as it was in Weil's, for lies cause a great deal of harm and lead people's thoughts away from the uphill struggle of seeking truth.

Even in her period of philosophical humanism, Weil believed that the thoughts and actions human beings take always have some perceived good as their goal; this reality is inherent in human nature. Her unfinished essay on the "Notion of Value," which we introduced in chapter 3, was not begun until well after her mystical experience, but it pursues ideas consistent with her past positions, such as how, at every instant, some system of values guides the direction of one's life, for the mind is in constant tension between an egoistic desire and the recognition of a higher truth. Disciplined philosophical reflection results in an entire redirection of the soul toward truth because truth is a value of thought. Since value has a relationship with sensitivity and with action, serious detached reflection during a quiet pause before taking action would generally lead to more persons being able to see others as real persons who suffer and have needs. The problems inherent in philosophical reflection are twofold: pausing to reflect with detachment on the values that underpin one's decisions requires disciplined practice, and sharing another's suffering exacts silence and moral loneliness in the profoundest depths of the human spirit. Generally, persons prefer distraction and illusions to painful loneliness.

Weil was a devotee of authentic genius from the past and believed that contemplation of such works offered an ever-flowing inspiration to guide persons toward the good. Great works of literature give the reader "in the guise of fiction, something equivalent to the actual density of the

---

[8] Ibid., 286–289.

[9] Ibid., 290–295.

[10] Simone Weil, "A Few Reflections on the Notion of Value," trans. Bernard E. and E. Jane Doering, *Cahiers Simone Weil*, 34.4 (December 2011): 455–486.

WHEN FICTION AND PHILOSOPHY MEET

real, that density which life offers us every day but which we are unable to grasp because we are amusing ourselves with lies." The genius of fine works of literature conforms to the true relations of good and evil because the true artist knows that "a necessity as strong as gravity condemns man to evil...except when the supernatural appears on earth, which suspends the operation of terrestrial necessity."[11] The authors of great works are concerned with the moral health of the writers and the public, but are also attentive to the art of literature itself.

Flannery O'Connor was writing finely crafted fiction intended to present the density as well as the mystery of the real. The density and complexity of the intersections of good and evil that O'Connor achieves in her fiction, as a devout Catholic, with the language of Protestant folk Christians and her appropriation of Protestant theology may be underappreciated by literary and theological students and scholars alike. Professor of literature and theology Ralph Wood asserts that "the last century's most eminent theologian, Karl Barth, was relentless in his insistence that preaching is the distinctively Protestant sacrament, the equivalent of the Catholic mass."[12] On suggesting the elevated position of preachers, Barth writes, "[the preachers] place before the I of the hearers a Thou whom they cannot overlook or dissolve or transcend.... Those who speak about God want to set people before God, to claim them for God, to save their souls, to win them."[13] O'Connor's intention to put before her readers a sacred reality largely disregarded by modern and postmodern human beings evokes her kinship with prophets and apostles and preachers—those preachers who put before the I of hearers a divine Thou. When she observes that for those who no longer share the vision of the author the writer has to shout "and for the almost-blind ... draw large and startling figures,"[14] she reflects Barth's insistence that "however apparent its similarity to ordinary discourse, true proclamation of the

---

[11] Panichas, 292.

[12] Wood, *Flannery O'Connor and the Christ-Haunted South*, 162.

[13] Karl Barth, *The Gottingen Dogmatics: Instruction in the Christian Religion*, vol. 1, trans. Geoffrey W. Bromiley, ed. Hannelotte Reiffen (Grand Rapids, MI: William B Eerdmans, 1991), 48–49. Quoted in ibid.

[14] Flannery O'Connor, *Mystery and Manners*, ed. Sally and Robert Fitzgerald (New York: Farrar, Straus & Giroux, 1957, 1979), 34.

Word of God must differ radically from all other forms of address."[15]

Both Weil and O'Connor believe that writers of genius must be anonymous purveyors of words that transmit and are based on the purest values, or in O'Connor's case, on words that point to the redemptive Word, through grace, to truth, love, and beauty. In order to make visible the ways human beings "are amusing themselves with lies," authors of great works—freed from egocentric motivations—concern themselves with the moral health of the public as, at the same time, they are attentive to the art of literature itself. O'Connor is also clear that writers do not need to write uplifting stories, but they do have to express the reality of the human condition, in which every decision holds elements of good and evil.

O'Connor's commitment to fiction grounded in the concrete and that assiduously avoids abstraction reveals her discipline of language congruent with Weil's ideas about the integrity and power of words. As a storyteller, however, O'Connor faced her challenge of combining the concrete with that which is invisible to the naked eye, to mystery. Whereas Weil as a philosopher castigates vapid communication and empty words with little objective meaning—words that she regards as empty and as receptacles for illusions—O'Connor often uses clichés, trite phrases, truisms ironically to expose deception and falsehood. Her narrators and characters often speak ironically in slogans that appear posted on trees or barns along roads across the southern countryside—Jesus saves; the life you save may be your own; repent; the kingdom of heaven is at hand; good country people—some of which may appear as story titles or popular phrases of characters. Paradoxically, O'Connor effectively combines concrete details with the invisible through grotesque characters, often with exaggerated or fantastical speech patterns. In the world of her fiction, her freaks, though comic, are not primarily so; instead "they seem to carry an invisible burden; their fanaticism is a reproach, not merely an eccentricity."[16] O'Connor's grotesque characters expose and reproach human life built on illusions and idolatries. We may laugh at the bizarre behaviors of O'Connor's characters until we recognize that all who de-

---

[15] Wood, *Flannery O'Connor and the Christ-Haunted South*, 162.
[16] O'Connor, *Mystery and Manners*, 44.

fend idolatries constructed on partial realities are amusing themselves with lies and vulnerable to becoming grotesques with vacuous, distorted lives.

Authentic writers of genius, for Weil, provide an inexhaustible source of spiritual inspiration that activates wings against the pull of moral gravity. They recognize that necessity, inseparable from reality, provides the raw material through which writers of genius, oriented toward the good, can offer readers an equivalent of the density of the real. An aspect of the real is the force of gravity that pulls on the soul. A mature writer of the very first order reveals the architecture of that abyss of evil and leads the reader to its virtual edge, in order to peer into its mysterious unity and diversity. The counterforce against plunging into this chasm is the impulse toward the good, which orients the human spirit in action and in intelligence. We have juxtaposed Flannery O'Connor's narrative fiction with Simone Weil's religious and philosophical concepts because O'Connor portrays the human condition in its undisguised mixture of good and evil. Insofar as her first-rate fiction, which portrays the full density of the real with its suffering, relationships, death, and grace, has the potential to legitimately guide human consciences to defy the inherent drag of evil, it illustrates Weil's ideas about the works of literary genius and invites the thoughtful attention of readers.

Realists of Distances

Simone Weil's convictions about the works of writers of authentic genius lead to Flannery O'Connor's process by which she works as a prophetic artist and the ends toward which she is committed. O'Connor explicitly describes this process of bringing the material and supernatural to bear on each other as the work of the prophet or as the prophetic artist's vocation. She names those who can "see near things with their extensions of meaning" realists of distances. Assessing O'Connor's and Weil's individual interpretations of *distance* contributes to our conclusion that as realists of distances their work helps twenty-first-century readers consider the "near things" of today in fuller extensions of meaning.

O'Connor describes her concept of the realist of distances in "The Grotesque in Southern Fiction," an essay on her own writing. She argues that writers must not be determined by what others expect or want from them. "The writer has no rights at all except those he forges for himself inside his own work. We have become so flooded with sorry fiction based on unearned liberties, or on the notion that fiction must represent the typical, that in the public mind the deeper kinds of realism are less and less understandable."[17] Then dismissing superficial interpretations of the labels *grotesque* and *realistic* as applied to southern fiction in particular, O'Connor presents her own description of what she attempts in her stories.

Her work does not imitate and speak with her age, reproducing the things of most immediate concern to readers—the psychic makeup of the characters, the economic situation, or other social ills. Rather she writes against it by seeing through it toward mystery. For the writer who believes "that our life is and will remain essentially mysterious [and that we are] beings existing in a created order to whose laws we freely respond, then what he sees on the surface will be of interest to him only as he can go through it into an experience of mystery itself."[18] Calling herself a realist of distances and trusting her vision of a supernatural, created order, O'Connor descends into herself and into the darkness of the familiar world in order to put her characters' lives and worlds under pressure of the invisible.

As a realist of distances, she affirms the goodness of reality and sees the created world immersed in the transcendent. Her challenge, as illustrated throughout this book, is how to make her vision understandable for an audience that by and large does not share that viewpoint, or how to communicate the reality of Presence in a world preoccupied with the negation of Presence or committed to Absence. She achieves her end of seeing near things in the extensions of their meaning by applying the long tradition of grotesquerie to her southern region and the twentieth-century modern human being.

Bruce Gentry informs his own analysis of the ways O'Connor adapts the tradition of the grotesque with Bakhtin's theories of the dialogical novel, previously discussed in foregoing chapters, and particularly

---

[17] Ibid., 39.
[18] Ibid., 41.

of the medieval and Renaissance form of the grotesque. Before Bakhtin, in the nineteenth century, John Ruskin, art historian and social reformer, describes both ludicrous and terrifying forms of the grotesque found in architectural gargoyles and in fairy tales. What Ruskin calls noble and ignoble grotesque in the third volume of *The Stones of Venice*,[19] Bakhtin would later call positive and negative grotesque in literature. Bakhtin considers the archaic and antique grotesque—linked to the culture of folk humor, the tradition of the fool in drama, and the elf or dwarf in fairy tales—as the positive grotesque, which in the Romantic and modernist periods turned into more negative forms, such as ghosts or monsters. Loss of faith in a moral universe recommended the grotesque as the most genuine style for the twentieth-century world. Combining both elements of the positive and negative grotesque, Gentry identifies several ways in which O'Connor adapts the grotesque tradition to bring the invisible to bear on the visible lives of her characters and their circumstances.[20]

In various forms, O'Connor's grotesque characters unmask the conflict between the grotesque and some ideal; between the fallen nature of human beings and the possibility of redemption; between humorous or ignorant banalities and truth. The foregoing examination of selected stories confirms Gentry's conclusion that O'Connor translated both positive and negative grotesques to serve the redemptive purpose in her fiction. For example, two characters sharing similar self-righteous attitudes, Mrs. Shortley and the grandmother in "A Good Man Is Hard to Find," experience their moments of potential redemptive grace in different ways. Plagued by suspicion, fear, and visions, Mrs. Shortley awakens inwardly in her psyche at the moment of death. The grandmother's transformation is provoked externally by her encounter with the Misfit and her murder.

All of O'Connor's stories are framed or suffused with concrete elements of nature—the sun, the moon, woods, fields, storms—that stand as signs of the beauty and order of creation against the degradations of

---

[19] John Ruskin, *The Stones of Venice*, vol. 3 (London: Smith, Elder, 1851–1853), 112-165, https://hdl.handle.net/2027/yul.11365198_003_00.
[20] Marshall Bruce Gentry, *Flannery O'Connor's Religion of the Grotesque* (Jackson: University Press of Mississippi, 1986), 8–17.

society's ideals. Although she has been frequently criticized for being silent about the racism endemic in U.S. history and particularly during the 1950s and 1960s, O'Connor's presentations of grotesqueries mirror systemic oppressions experienced in the South's economy of tenant farming; in entrenched race and class divisions; in criminality, or physical or mental deformities; in ignorance and arrogance often associated with educational inequalities. Degradations of any form belie the love of neighbor and incur the suffering and affliction graphically depicted by O'Connor. Such degeneracy Simone Weil associated with the suffering and crucifixion of Christ.

Alice Walker, who grew up just a few miles from Flannery O'Connor's home on the Eatonton-Milledgeville Road in Georgia, contributes to the critical debate about O'Connor's racism by appreciating the distance the author retains when creating her black characters. By not entering the "inner workings of her black characters seems to me all to her credit, since, by deliberately limiting her treatment of them to cover their observable demeanor and action, she leaves them free, in the reader's imagination, to inhabit another landscape, another life, than the one she creates for them."[21] Walker understands the near realities—black and white characters, attitudes, social systems—that O'Connor subjects to their extensions in mystery through her prophetic art: "[The] *essential* O'Connor is not about race at all, which is why it is so refreshing, coming, as it does, out of such a *racial* culture. If it can be said to be 'about' anything, then it is 'about' prophets and prophecy, 'about' revelation, and 'about' the impact of supernatural grace on human beings who don't have a chance of spiritual growth without it."[22]

Wood's thorough discussion of race and religion in the South contributes significantly to a fuller understanding of O'Connor's views on race by his inclusion of a quotation from a previously unpublished letter

---

[21] Alice Walker, "Beyond the Peacock," *In Search of Our Mothers' Gardens* (New York: Harcourt Brace Jovanovich, 1976, 1983), 52. See also Wood, *Flannery O'Connor and the Christ-Haunted South*, particularly chapter 3, "The Problem of the Color Line: Race and Religion in Flannery O'Connor's South," 93–119.

[22]Walker, "Beyond the Peacock," 53.

she wrote in 1963: "I feel very good about those changes in the South that have been long overdue—the whole racial picture. I think it is improving by the minute, particularly in Georgia, and I don't see how anybody could feel otherwise than good about that."[23]

The distance or mystery to which Flannery O'Connor refers her characters, or by which she measures them, rests in sacred history and a common human story. She notes that "the Hebrew genius for making the absolute concrete has conditioned the Southerner's way of looking at things." She takes seriously her backwoods prophets and all her characters who exist with the marks of a visible society all around them, believing that "when the poor hold sacred history in common, they have ties to the universal and the holy, which allows the meaning of their every action to be heightened and seen under the aspect of eternity."[24]

Simone Weil was also a prophetic voice, in the sense of being a "divinely inspired interpreter, revealer, or teacher of the will and thought of God."[25] After her mystical experience, all her writings were suffused with biblical allusions. Her confidence in her own abilities to know, at least on the material plane, was always solid enough for her to speak out with authority on social questions. But even in her early adolescence, she sensed that there was a truth beyond the secular knowledge to which she was privy, and she was deeply afraid that she would never gain entry into that realm of truth. Just what that truth was remained uncertain until her mystical experience.

She had always, even in her humanist period, been a realist facing the limitations of human nature. During her early efforts with workers, she had tried hard to convince them that the means of gaining a true recognition of their importance, dignity, and worth in society was within their means. She could not convince them, however, to put aside those aspects inherent in human nature of egoism, pride, and desire for power and prestige, which continually sidetracked their efforts away from the principal goal of a respected place in the social strata. This realism of

---

[23] Wood, *Flannery O'Connor and the Christ-Haunted South*, 103.

[24] O'Connor, "The Catholic Novelist in the Protestant South," *Mystery and Manners*, 203.

[25] Definition from the *Oxford English Dictionary*.

Weil concerning the faults of human nature continued as she later tried to persuade her listeners of the challenge posed by their ultimate supernatural goal and of the seduction in futile entertainments, lies, or material gains.

This divine goal was less visible or tangible than the material goal of being accorded a well-deserved social recognition. For advocating such a seemingly elusive and counterintuitive purpose in life, she was ridiculed, demeaned, and ignored, although her countrymen could neither disregard nor refrain from admiring her gifted intellect. This kind of backhanded adulation irritated her to the extreme, for she considered her message as having supreme importance for everyone. In one of her last letters to her mother, she compares her situation to that of Shakespeare's and Velasquez's fools, who perceive the truth of a situation, but because of their grotesque or abnormal appearance are mocked and scorned. Simone, a wisp of a young woman, with asocial habits of wearing a long black cape and beret, smoking incessantly, ignoring social expectations for feminine appearance, was treated no differently. Even her extraordinary intelligence was off-putting. She writes:

> When I saw *Lear* here, I asked myself how it was possible that the unbearably tragic character of these fools had not been obvious long ago to everyone, including myself…. There is a class of people in this world who have fallen into the lowest degree of humiliation, far below beggary, and who are deprived not only of all social consideration, but also, in everybody's opinion, of the specific human dignity, reason itself—and these are the only people who, in fact are able to tell the truth. All the others lie.[26]

She goes on to suggest that possessing truth contains a bitterness, as seen in the sad eyes of Velasquez's fools; they had gained the power to utter the truth at the price of nameless degradation, and yet were listened to by nobody. She goes on to ask her mother: "Darling M[ime], do you feel the affinity, the essential analogy between these fools and me…? The eulogies of my intelligence are positively intended to evade the question:

---

[26]Simone Weil, *Seventy Letters*, trans. Richard Rhees (London: Oxford University Press, 1965), 200.

'Is what she says true?'"[27]

The truth that she wanted to proclaim to all who would listen was that "the infinite superabundance of the divine mercy is already secretly present here below in its entirety,"[28] and that even in the harshness of affliction, God's love for us is its very substance. The distance of God from us proclaims paradoxically his very nearness to his creation. The challenge that God's total absence from the world poses is that caring for creation is the responsibility of human beings as equal participants in its maintenance. God, as we have seen in the "Implicit Forms of the Love of God," has left signs of his love in the beauty made visible within the or-der of the world, in the purity of liturgical practices, in the caritas that informs the love of neighbor, and in the special circumstances of friend-ship.

Because the supernatural cannot really be described in human lan-guage, God has embedded in the material world his language to us. Weil uses the metaphor of distance to describe the relationship between the natural and the supernatural, even though there is no space or time in the supernatural. This familiar language helps readers to grasp what has hy-pothetically occurred in creation and consequently to deal with it to the best of their ability. She proposes the concept of spatial distance by say-ing that having engendered love in all its forms and created beings capa-ble of love from all possible distances, "God himself went to the greatest possible distance, the infinite distance. This infinite distance between God and God, this supreme tearing apart, this agony beyond all others, this marvel of love is the crucifixion. Nothing can be farther from God than that which has been made accursed" (*WG* 72). She continues that over this tearing apart, supreme love places the bond of supreme union: "God is so essentially love that the unity, which in a sense is his actual definition, is the pure effect of love" (*WG* 74–75). This love triumphs over the infinite separation.

It is the task of human beings to translate God's apparent absence to

---

[27] Ibid., 201.
[28] Simone Weil, *Waiting for God*, trans. Emma Craufurd (New York: HarperCollins, 2001), 44. (Hereafter cited as *WG*.)

others as his secret presence. "It is God within us who loves God."[29] By giving our attention to others' needs of both body and soul we transmit God's presence to them in tangible ways. We are to do the work that he has decreed by eliminating the barriers to our fellow human beings' ability to consent to his love, to accept and to love that infinite distance between God and God, which is the universe. "Even the distress of the abandoned Christ is a good, there cannot be a greater good for us on earth than to share in it. God can never be perfectly present to us here below on account of our flesh. But he can be almost perfectly absent from us in extreme affliction. . . . That is why the Cross is our only hope" (WG 95). We know that Christ, God's only begotten son, on the Cross believed that his father had abandoned him, crying out "My God, why have you abandoned me," yet Christ was taken up into heaven to be with the father.

In her efforts to share her insight that God is infinitely far yet intimately near—just as the abandoned Christ on the Cross was to be joined in the closest possible way to the Father—Weil might also be called a "realist of distances" or perhaps a "realist of the beyond." She wanted to inspire individuals to create a society that would embody an incarnational faith or way of living.

Incarnational Art and Incarnational Life

Despite the similarity of Simone Weil's and Flannery O'Connor's deep religious views, the distinctive ways they expressed their convictions become strikingly clear in their expression of the relationship between art and the Incarnation. Both writers were inspired artists, that is, inspired by something beyond themselves: the truth, the source of which is the supernatural. They loved the beauty of the world, and used their artistic gifts to pierce through the film of unreality that veils this beauty to indicate to their readers the invisible beyond the visible.

Weil believed that the task of an artist is to transport into a limited quantity of matter or words an image of or the promise of the infinite

---

[29] Simone Weil, *First and Last Notebooks*, trans. Richard Rees (New York: Oxford University Press, 1970), 177.

beauty of the entire universe. If the attempt succeeds, this portion of matter would not hide the universe, but, on the contrary, would reveal its reality. When a work of art is perfect, even though created by an author, there is an essence of anonymity, which imitates the anonymity of divine art: the impersonal beauty of all creation. Weil expresses this idea when she states that a "work of the very highest order, true creation, means self-loss" (*WG* 92). Just as God is personal and impersonal at the same time so is an artist who uses personal artistic gifts to express an impersonal truth that has universal application. In writing, O'Connor also believed, "the author has for the most part absented himself from direct participation in the work and has left the reader to make his own way amid experiences dramatically rendered and symbolically ordered."[30] The author does this for at least two reasons: first, to be a channel in which the author's own creative imagination can work, and second, to urge the reader to enter the imaginative space created by the story and let it enlarge his experience. The acts of writing and reading are both creative, requiring attention and patience.

Weil believed that an attitude of patient waiting is the key to writing a beautiful line of poetry or discovering a new scientific truth; this also applies to uncovering a solution for a thorny problem or to perceiving the meaning of a complex situation. Weil's counsel against avid seeking because it leads one astray relates both to the act of forming something beautiful and to the creation of anything that is truly good. Quiet waiting for the inspiration of transcendent goodness and truth, however, is more challenging and intense than searching on one's own. In Weil's religious philosophy, "God has inspired every first-rate work of art, though its subject may be utterly and entirely secular; [consequently] every true artist has had real direct and immediate contact with the beauty of the world, contact that is of the nature of a sacrament" (*WG* 107). True virtue in every domain is, to all appearances, negative, for human beings should do nothing but reject any evil as they wait for the good. This is the concept of action in inaction, that is: not acting for personal gain but for the impersonal good inherent in the situation. This calls to the fore

---

[30] O'Connor, "Total Effect and the Eighth Grade," *Mystery and Manners,* 139.

the practice of *hupomone*, of which we have already spoken.

Literature of the finest kind extends the reader's familiarity with the evil that surrounds us and builds the confidence that grace is never far away; no domain of humankind is purely natural, for the supernatural is secretly present throughout. Authors can and should help readers vicariously experience the opposing good and bad alternatives in every decision. Weil writes: "In the words assembled by genius several slopes are simultaneously visible and perceptible, placed in their true relations, but the listener or reader does not descend any of them. He feels gravity in the way we feel it when we look over a precipice,"[31] and can judge accordingly. Weil and O'Connor recognized that the only true beauty is the real presence of God, and that is the beauty of the universe; nothing less than the universe is beautiful. Each of our authors practiced humility in the use of her extraordinary yet distinctive gifts to bring to the consciousness of their readers the fact that the world's beauty is indistinguishable from the world's reality and that beauty is really an incarnation of God.[32]

Consequently, Weil believed that all art of the first order is, in essence, religious, and that this same high-quality art testifies to the fact of the Incarnation. She writes, "in everything which rouses in us a pure and genuine feeling for beauty, God is really and truly present. There is, as it were, a sort of incarnation of God in the world of which beauty constitutes the sign. The Word as ordering principle."[33] She is awestruck that feelings of what God desires can arise in a human soul. She considers such an event "a marvel as miraculous as the Incarnation. Or rather, it is itself the marvel of Incarnation."[34]

To understand the centrality of the incarnation of God in Christ throughout the interweaving concepts of Simone Weil's religious philosophy, we must return to her focus on God's voluntary renunciation of power out of love for the world he creates. As we have already men-

---

[31] Panichas, 293.

[32] Weil, *First and Last Notebooks*, 341.

[33] Simone Weil, *The Notebooks of Simone Weil*, vol. 2, trans. Arthur Wills (New York: G. P. Putnam's Sons, 1956), 440.

[34] Weil, *First and Last Notebooks*, 150.

tioned, Christ is the Lamb who was sacrificed from the beginning of time, and hence the Creation, Incarnation, and Passion have a simultaneity. "Because he is creator, God is not all powerful. Creation is an abdication. But he is all-powerful in this sense, that his abdication is voluntary. He knows its effects, and wills them.... God has emptied himself. This means that both the Creation and Incarnation are included with the Passion."[35] The Incarnation embodies total obedience to all God's wishes whatever they are. It is through the portrayal of God's action in the Creation, Incarnation, and Passion that Weil elaborates the concepts that we have presented in this book.

As God's creatures, we are all asked to renounce or de-create our personal sense of importance, to give a selfless attention to the beauty of the world and to the affliction of our neighbor, and to further the conditions in which grace is invited to enter where needed, so that people of all faiths will be enabled to serve the needs of others. Weil, who since her birth considered herself as being at the intersection of Christianity and everything that is not Christianity, became deeply engaged in the spiritual practices of non-Christian faiths. She believed that the traditional religions had valid perspectives on the worship and understanding of God, and that humankind can only benefit by being aware of the many ways to love God.

Citing St. Augustine's idea that before Christ, and outside Israel, there were spiritual people to whom the unique Mediator and his future coming were divinely revealed, she asks why believe there were a limited number, suggesting that among them were Buddhists, including members of the Zen school, Taoists, and followers of the Hindu religion. She concludes, "If we admit [this possibility], then those traditions are true, and those who live in them today are in the truth. It is not in virtue of being a historical account that the Good Tidings are important for salvation."[36]

For Flannery O'Connor, the Incarnation is the climactic event of the Christian religion, the "divine intrusion into the drama of temporal

[35] Ibid., 120.
[36] Ibid., 121.

creation."[37] In history it was, and continues to represent, the physical embodiment in Jesus Christ of spiritual existence ordered by love from the beginning of creation. As an artist herself shaped by the spiritual truth of the Incarnation, O'Connor wants readers of her fiction to experience a refocusing of their minds toward the mystery of creation, a reexamination of values, and a reorientation of their lives. The incarnational artist serves that goal in three principal ways: first, by grounding her own reason and imagination in the unity of temporal and spiritual reality; second, by embodying the key values of divine reality made visible in the Incarnation; and third, by offering guidance or resources for awakening to and participating in the divine life that suffuses the material world.

O'Connor knew herself and her location in time and space to be connected to something larger and more transcendent. This perception and faith inform her concern about the great separations that she describes as the burden of human limitation experienced by modern human beings—the breaking apart of nature from grace, reason from imagination, faith and ethics, vision and judgment—because we do not understand the meaning of the Incarnation. These separations, overcome in the Incarnation through love, inspire her efforts to reunite them through her incarnational art. Recognizing the human desire for wholeness that accompanies brokenness, O'Connor makes clear the incarnational artist's role in reconnecting that which has been severed by acknowledging "that no art is sunk in the self, but rather, in art the self becomes self-forgetful in order to meet the demands of the thing seen and the thing being made."[38] Guided by faith in the Incarnation and Christ's example of obedient devotion to God and love for God's creation, the incarnational artist submits her conjoined reason and imagination as an instrument of the transcendent, which is God. For her, St. Thomas Aquinas's view "that the artist is concerned with the good of that which is made"[39] and Maritain's practice of the habit of art support such obedience. For O'Connor this means that "if a writer is any good, what he makes will have its

---

[37] Susan Srigley, *Flannery O'Connor's Sacramental Art* (Notre Dame, IN: University of Notre Dame Press, 2004), 17.

[38] O'Connor, "The Nature and Aim of Fiction," *Mystery and Manners*, 82.

[39] Ibid., 65.

source in a realm much larger than that which his conscious mind can encompass...."[40]

O'Connor points toward that much larger realm of mystery by embodying the values and meaning of the Incarnation, anticipated in Hebrew scriptures and presented in Christian scriptures that were often interpreted literally in the Protestant South. She prefigures the selection of her fictional prophets and their actions in Jesus's calling of disciples, ordinary fishermen without training or credentials, only simple willingness to leave their nets and follow. With creative indirection, by depicting absence rather than presence, through shocking inversions, and through guile and deceit that lead to violent reversals, O'Connor presents the distillation of the love values expressed in the Beatitudes of Jesus and manifested in human lives as poverty of spirit; comfort for mourning; the inheritance of meekness; hunger and thirst for righteousness; purity of heart; peacemaking; and suffering of persecution for righteousness' sake.[41]

O'Connor also incorporates counsel of the apostle Paul to early Christian communities with which twentieth-century Christians wrestled. In I Corinthians 13, St. Paul confesses in verse 12: "For now we see in a mirror, dimly, but then we will see face to face. Now I know only in part; then I will know fully, even as I have been fully known."[42] O'Connor incarnates this verse about mirrors, dimness of sight, and partial knowledge throughout her fiction and with extraordinary perceptiveness in *Wise Blood* through her use of the mirror "as a supplementary field of vision." Here she "sets mysterious images of racial and gender mixing which radically reconstruct Haze's notions of family, community, and selfhood." O'Connor sets up "an analogical or 'mirroring' relationship

---

[40] Ibid., 83.

[41] O'Connor presents inversions or distortion of Beatitude attitudes, for example, in the absence of poverty of spirit in the self-righteous grandmother, Hulga, Julian, or Ruby Turpin. She uses images of hunger and thirst that haunt the rebellious such as Rufus or Rayber, and Tarwater, who envisions the feeding of the five thousand on a Galilean hillside. Divided hearts throughout her stories are more typical than pure hearts, and suffering is more commonly generated by illusions and self-deceit than by persecution for righteousness' sake.

[42] 1 Corinthians 13:12, NRSV translation.

between contemporary history and Christ's Second Coming in order to measure communities of the present day by divine standards."[43] Attentive readers also recall the preponderance of mirrors, windows, reflections in windowpanes, and shifting images of self and other in "The Artificial Nigger," and the way O'Connor uses nature throughout her stories to mirror central story conflicts. All of O'Connor's fiction poses questions for characters and readers about identity, about the singularity of the gospel, and about St. Paul's insistence in Galatians 3:28 on the radical nature, inclusivity, and universal scope of God's grace.

Having reflected throughout this book on Flannery O'Connor's artistic creation of her fiction and the vision that informs her writing, juxtaposed with Simone Weil's religious philosophy, we consider finally the ends for which both writers seek to arouse skeptical or unbelieving audiences and the means they choose to serve those ends. Simone Weil wanted people to reflect on their process of evaluating or reading circumstances based on the sensations they receive from the world around them. To her mind, each situation holds elements of the one and absolute truth, which is discernible only after silent contemplation before action. A true reading, inspired by God's love, creates harmony in human interactions.

Giving attention and learning to read accurately God's language in the beauty and order of the world, through love of the neighbor, by embracing suffering and affliction, and by accepting the divine intrusions of grace that reorient one's life are goals Simone Weil and Flannery O'Connor shared. They committed their gifts for philosophy and fiction writing to the end of awaking audiences—students, workers, readers, citizens—to reality animated by and permeated with divine love from the beginning of creation through the present. In their commitment to this purpose lay the aspiration that such awakening might inspire incarnational living.

Although Flannery O'Connor suggested that readers read her stories with anagogical vision, which enables them to interpret words or passages beyond literal, allegorical, or moral senses to discern a spiritual

---

[43] Susan Edmunds, "Through a Glass Darkly: Visions of Integrated Community in Flannery O'Connor's 'Wise Blood,'" *Contemporary Literature*, 37.4 (Winter 1996): 559–585.

or mystical sense, anagogical reading also relates to Weil's notion of "reading" people and situations in a way that seeks the one true universal meaning. In effect, anagogical reading, whether of written texts or human beings, requires the capacity in the person reading to relinquish narrow self-referential interpretations and to move toward a nonperspective to discover the essential dimensions of persons or situations. The correspondence between Weil's notion of reading and O'Connor's emphasis on the anagogical capacity to identify spiritual meanings in texts or human interactions acknowledges a reciprocal relationship between the temporal-material realm and a supernatural reality in which the temporal abides. Reading the world as sacred text enlarges our ethical obligations toward the natural environment, all creatures, other human beings, and the eternal.

Flannery O'Connor as incarnational artist offers a strategy for developing the capacity to read anagogically and to live incarnationally. As discussed previously, her preference for and regular use of the *as if* linguistic pattern throughout her stories leads readers toward anagogical reading by relating the limits of the actual to conditional possibilities, the real to the imagined, time-bound experiences to the eternal, the visible to invisible. The *as if* construction opens a territory or field of possibility and mystery adjacent to the real and builds a bridge toward incarnational living.

With an intense motivation to promote a society that incarnates the values of Christianity, Simone Weil wrote in 1942 to Father Perrin: "Our obligation for the next two or three years, an obligation so strict that we can scarcely fail in it without treason, is to show the public the possibility of a truly incarnated Christianity. In all the history now known there has never been a period in which souls have been in such peril as they are today in every part of the globe" (WG 32). The widespread destruction of the war and the increasing prevalence of totalitarianism was bringing people's faith to the breaking point. Simone Weil and Father Perrin were composing a collection of essays to share all that they knew about the supernatural. Although she died before they could complete their project, he brought all her contributions together under the title: *Waiting for God*.

Weil dedicated her time and talents to informing her readers about what a society that had incarnated the values of Christianity signified. Despite the destructive chaos that reigned around her, she believed that a society open to grace was eminently possible. It would incarnate perfect obedience to God, equal justice for the lowest in the rungs of power, and compassion driven by selfless love for the persecuted and afflicted. Her last bits of energy were expended on describing her vision in *The Need for Roots*.

While recognizing the great difficulty in obeying the unknown, she strove to obey as Christ did because one cannot know what God's command will be tomorrow. "Obedience to God, that is to say, to nothing, since God is beyond all that we can imagine or conceive ... is at the same time impossible and necessary—in other words it is supernatural."[44] Obedience to God entails reading from a third nonperspective, that is, God's. "Obedience to God is the only motive that is unconditioned and can never disappear. It transports the action into eternity."[45]

Weil believed that a truly Incarnational Christianity should be inclusive, impartial, universal, and thus genuinely catholic. The members of a society that honored justice, equitable actions, and honest treatment for the suffering and marginalized would be motivated by both faith in God and a desire to be his intercessor here on earth: a conduit of his love. Weil writes, "The love of God is only an intermediary between the natural and the supernatural love of creatures.... To die for God is not a proof of faith in God. To die for an unknown and repulsive convict who is a victim of injustice, that is a proof of faith in God."[46] To truly love the least of God's creation, to give that person full attention, one needs to have de-created the part of the soul that seeks recognition and prestige, to have emptied oneself as God did in his act of Creation, Incarnation, and Passion, which involves loving with compassion.

Compassion means to suffer with victims of aggression, bad judgment, dire need, and disease, which have brought affliction. The true measure of one's Christianity implies that through contact with another's affliction one can be a real and effective mediator of divine love and

---

[44] Weil *Notebooks* I, 237.
[45] Weil, *First and Last Notebooks*, 149.
[46] Ibid., 144.

compassion where the Father, withdrawn from the world, is helpless to act. To act in this way is a form of sanctity; Weil writes: "Sanctity is a transmutation like the Eucharist, ... [for] every movement of pure compassion in a soul is a new descent of Christ upon earth."[47]

All the qualities needed for an incarnation of Christianity to be realized take purity of heart and willingness to give up part of oneself, even one's dearest wishes; these qualities are no more widespread today than in Simone Weil's time. On the contrary, our contemporary scene exhibits the polar opposite of an incarnational faith. The behavior that horrified Weil in the first half of the twentieth century seems to take on new life after every small reprieve from chaos. She deplored the destruction—materially and morally—of cities and the exclusion of human beings from livable communities. She condemned harassing certain individuals and groups as social outcasts and severing every bond of poetry and love between human beings and the universe, by plunging them forcibly into the horror of ugliness, as a crime. The degradations that both these writers observed with clear-eyed attention in their contexts present continuing challenges to and need for incarnational life in every location and century.

Simone Weil's and Flannery O'Connor's dedication of their gifts of vision, penetrating thought, and the ability to shape their ideas into translucent philosophical exposition and transformative fiction introduces readers to the kinship of all things. As incarnational artists they invite us into a continuing conversation about our long human story and about the enduring world fraught with affliction caused by illusion, idolatries, wars, and unprecedented human displacement, yet suffused with the beauty and order of divine reality.

---

[47] Weil, *First and Last Notebooks*, 96, 97.

Acknowledgments

We extend our primary gratitude to Simone Weil and Flannery O'Connor who gave to the world their extraordinary intellectual, creative, and spiritual insights in their short lives of a combined seventy-three years. Our experience of the international interest in both writers—the French in O'Connor and North Americans in Weil—confirmed our interest in bringing them together in this conversation. We are indebted to decades of Weil scholars in the American Weil Society and French Association pour l'étude de la pensée de Simone Weil. In particular, we thank Robert Chenavier and Eric O. Springsted for their valuable contributions to Weil studies and to their constant support of Weil scholars. To Larry Schmidt we express sincere thanks for his careful reading of our interpretations of Weil's thought.

Similarly, since her death in 1964, students and scholars have mined the fiction of Flannery O'Connor in classrooms, conference settings, articles, and books, which have informed this study. Rosemary Magee, director of the Stuart A. Rose Manuscript, Archives, and Rare Book Library at Emory University, provided beneficial access to the Flannery O'Connor archives. As the book was imagined, it was enriched by conversations with the late William Sessions. We are particularly grateful to M. Bruce Gentry for his close attention to the O'Connor discussions contained here.

In 2013, a class of graduate students at Bethany Theological Seminary launched this book in a very early stage through discussions in our course Faith, Fiction, and Philosophy. A research grant from the Institute for Scholarship in the Liberal Arts at the University of Notre Dame and interest from colleagues have supported our intention to bring these two writers into conversation. We express special appreciation to Michael Birkel, John Dunaway, Christine Evans, Sonia Gernes, and Valerie Sayers for their attentive readings of the manuscript. During the preparation of the book manuscript, Robert Milks, Jr. and Patrick Jolley provided excellent copyediting expertise for which we express our thanks. We are grateful for Dr. Marc Jolley's interest in publishing *When Fiction and Philosophy Meet* as a Mercer University Press book. Finally, we express abiding gratitude to our spouses, Bernard Doering and Robert Johansen, for loving companionship, intellectual stimulation, models of academic rigor, and our shared valuses.

Bibliography

SIMONE WEIL BIBLIOGRAPHY

Allen, Diogenes. "Natural Evil and the Love of God." *Religious Studies* 16, no. 4 (1980): 439-456.

Andic, Martin. "Fairy Tales." *Cahiers Simone Weil* 15, no. 1 (1992): 61-91.

Birou, Alain. "Introduction à la problématique du mal chez Simone Weil." *Cahiers Simone Weil* 19, no. 2 (1996): 155-76.

———. "LeBeau, 'Présence réelle de Dieu dans la matière.'" *Cahiers Simone Weil* 17, no. 1 (1994): 35-54.

Blumenthal, Gerda. "Simone Weil's Way of the Cross." *Thought* 27 (1952): 225 – 234.

———. "The Cross of Dividedness." *The Third Hour* 5 (1951): 17-24.

Borocco, Claude. "Le Malheur chez Simone Weil." *Cahiers Simone Weil* I, no. 2 (1994): 19-29.

Breton, Stanislas. "Simone Weil l'admirable." *L'esprit* (May 1995): 31-46.

Broc-LaPeyre, Monique. "Simone Weil et Platon: Amour et Beauté." *Cahiers Simone Weil* 8, no. 2 (1985): 128 – 139.

Cabaud, Marie. "Mystique et herméneutique: Simone Weil et sa lecture christologique d'Électre et du Prométhée enchaîné." *Cahiers Simone Weil* 23, no. 1 (2000): 51–78.

Chenavier, Robert. *Simone Weil: Une philosophie du travail.* Paris: Les Éditions du Cerf, 2001.

De Lussy, Florence. "Folklore et Spiritualité." In *Simone Weil: La soif de l'Absolu,* edited by J. P. Little and A. Ughetto. Marseille: SUD Revue Littéraire Bimestrielle, 1990.

Devaux, André. "Le Christ dans la vie et dans l'oeuvre de Simone Weil." *Cahiers Simone Weil* 4, no. 1 (1981): 4 – 15.

———. "Malheur et Compassion chez Simone Weil (Part 2)." *Cahiers Simone Weil* 9, no. 1 (1986): 75–86.

———. "Malheur et Compassion chez Simone Weil." *Cahiers Simone Weil* 8, no. 4 (1985): 386-402.

———. "On the Right Use of Contradiction according to Simone Weil." Translated by J. P. Little. In *Simone Weil's Philosophy of Culture: Readings Toward a Divine Humanity.* Edited by Richard H. Bell. Cambridge, Cambridge University Press, 1993.

————. "Simone Weil et Blaise Pascal." In *Simone Weil: La soif de l'Absolu*, edited by J. P. Little and A. Ughetto. Marseille: SUD Revue Littéraire Bimestrielle, 1990.

Dietz, Mary G. *Between the Human and the Divine: The Political Thought of Simone Weil*. Totowa, New Jersey: Roman and Littlefield, 1988.

Estelrich, Bartomeu. "Simone Weil's Concept of Grace." *Modern Theology* 25, no. 22 (2009): 239-251.

Farron-Landry, Béatrice. "Détachement, renoncement et origine du mal selon Simone Weil." *Cahiers Simone Weil* 2, no. 2 (1979): 71-83.

————. "L'Attente, ou la Porte Conduisant à la Croix-Balance." *Cahiers Simone Weil* 7, no. 4 (1984): 392-402.

Fiedler, Leslie A. "Simone Weil: Prophet Out of Israel: A Saint of the Absurd." *Commentary* (January 1, 1951). https://www.commentarymagazine.com/articles/simone-weil-prophet-out-of-israela-saint-of-the-absurd/.

Frémont, Annette. *"Analyse et Commentaire d'un conte selon l'esprit de Simone Weil." Cahiers Simone Weil* 10, no. 2 (1987): 171-180.

Gabellieri, Emmanuel. "La Psychologie du gros animal et philosophie de la Barbarie chez Simone Weil." *Cahiers Simone Weil* 9, no. 3 (1986): 260-285.

————. *Être et Don: Simone Weil et la Philosophie*. Louvain: Éditions Peeters, 2003.

Heidsieck, François. "Platon, maître et témoin de la connaissance surnaturelle." *Cahiers Simone Weil* 5, no. 4 (1982): 241–149.

Kahn, Gilbert. "Simone Weil et Alain." *Cahiers Simone Weil* 14, no. 3 (1991): 206–212.

————. "Valeur du travail manuel chez Simone Weil." *Cahiers Simone Weil* 1, no. 3 (1978): 51-61.

Kühn, Rolf. "Le monde comme texte perspectives herméneutiques chez Simone Weil." *Revue des Sciences philosophiques et théologiques* 64 (1980): 509–530.

Le Senne, René. "Simone Weil et l'Angoisse de la Révelation." In *Introduction à la Philosophie*. Paris: Presses Universitaires de France, 1970.

Léna, Marguerita. "Deux témoins du Bon Usage des Études Scolaires en vue de l'Amour de Dieu: Simone Weil et Madeliene Daniélou." *Cahiers Simone Weil* 2, no. 2 (1979): 57–70.

Little, J. Patricia. "Action et travail chez Simone Weil." *Cahiers Simone Weil* 2, no. 1 (1979): 4-13.

————. "Le refus de l'idolâtrie dans l'oeuvre de Simone Weil." *Cahiers Simone Weil* 2, no. 4 (1979): 197–213.

Malan, Ivo. "Simone Weil et la responsibilité des écrivains." *Cahiers Simone Weil* 2, no.3 (1979): 161-168.

McCullough, Lisa. *The Religious Philosophy of Simone Weil: An Introduction.* New York: I. B. Tauris, 2014.

Meany, Marie Cabaud. "Le Mal, est-il mystérieux ou banal?" *Cahiers Simone Weil* 36, no. 2 (2012): 255-278.

Miłosz, Czesław. *Emperor of the Earth: Modes of Eccentric Vision.* Berkeley: University of California Press, 1960.

Narcy, Michel. "Ce qu'il y a de platonicien chez Simone Weil." *Cahiers Simone Weil* 7, no. 4 (1985): 365-375.

———. "Le Platon de Simone Weil." *Cahiers Simone Weil* 8, no. 4 (1982): 250–267.

Nava, Alex. "Prophetic Mysticism." The Center for Christian Ethics. 2005. http://www.baylor.edu/ifl/christianreflection/MysticismArticleNava.pdf.

Nava, Alexander. *The Mystical and Prophetic Thought of Simone Weil and Gustavo Gutiérrez: Reflections on the Mystery and Hiddenness of God.* New York: State University of New York Press, 2001.

Oesterreicher, John M. "The Enigma of Simone Weil." *The Bridge A Yearbook Of Judaeo Christian Studies* Vol. I (1955): 118–158. https://archive.org/details/bridgeayearbooko012617mbp.

Perrin, Joseph Marie. *Mon Dialogue avec Simone Weil.* Paris: Nouvelle Cité, 1984.

Pétrement, Simone. "La Vie et la pensée de Simone Weil." *Critique: revue générale des publications françaises et étrangères.* (September 1948): 793–805.

———. "Sur la religion d'Alain, avec quelques remarques concernant celle de Simone Weil." *Revue de métaphysique et de moral* 60 (1955): 306-330.

———. *La vie de Simone Weil,* Vol. 1 & 2. Paris: Fayard, 1973.

———. *Simone Weil: A Life.* Translated by Raymond Rosenthal. New York: Pantheon Books, 1976.

Pirruccello, Ann. "'Gravity' in the Thought of Simone Weil." *Philosophy and Phenomenological Research* 57, no. 1 (1997): 473-493.

———. "Making the World My Body: Simone Weil and Somatic Practice." *Philosophy East & West* 52, no. 4 (2002): 479-497.

———. "Simone Weil's Violent Grace." *Cahiers Simone Weil* 19, no. 4 (1996): 397–411.

Rozelle-Stone, Rebecca and Lucian Stone. *Simone Weil and Theology.* New York: Bloomsbury, 2013.

Ruhr, von der, Mario. *Simone Weil: An Apprenticeship in Attention.* New York:

Continuum, 2006.

Springsted, E. O. "Métaphysique de la transcendence et théorie des 'Metaxu' chez Simone Weil." *Cahiers Simone Weil* 5, no. 4 (1982): 285-306.

———. "Simone Weil and Baptism." http://www.laici.va/content/dam/laici/documenti/donna/culturasocieta/en glish/simone-weil-and-baptism.pdf.

———. *Christus Mediator: Platonic Mediation in the Thought of Simone Weil.* Chico, CA: Scholars Press, 1983.

———. "Beyond the Personal: Weil's Critique of Maritain." *The Harvard Theological Review* 98, no. 2 (2005): 209–218.

———. "Spiritual Apprenticeship." *Cahiers Simone Weil* 25, no. 4 (2002): 325–344.

Springsted, Eric O. and Diogenes Allen. *Spirit, Nature, and Community: Issues in the Thought of Simone Weil.* New York: State University of New York Press: 1994.

Tastard, Terry. "Simone Weil's Last Journey." *America Magazine*, (April 09, 2001). https://www.americamagazine.org/issue/335/article/simone-weils-last-journey.

Tavard, George, H. "The Transfigurations of Thought: Simone Weil's Dialectic." *The Third Hour* (1956): 52-56.

Vetö, Miklos. *The Religious Metaphysics of Simone Weil.* Translated by Joan Dargan. Albany: State University of New York Press, 1994.

Villa-Petit, Maria. "Résister au mal chez Simone Weil et Etty Hillesum." *Cahiers Simone Weil* 6, no. 2 (1983): 173.

Weil, Simone and Joë Bousquet. *Correspondance.* Lausanne: Éditions L'Age d'Homme, 1982.

Weil, Simone, "*The Iliad,* or the Poem of Force," Translated by Mary McCarthy. *Chicago Review* 18, no. 1 (1965): 5-30. https://www.jstor.org/stable/pdf/25294008.pdf.

———. "A Few Reflections on the Notion of Value." Translated by Bernard E. and E. Jane Doering. *Cahiers Simone Weil* 34, no. 4 (2011): 455–486.

———. "Essay on the Notion of Reading." Translated by Rebecca Fine Rose and Timothy Tessin. *Philosophical Investigations* 13, no. 4 (1990): 297-302.

———. *First and Last Notebooks.* Translated by Richard Rees. New York: Oxford University Press, 1970.

———. *Formative Writings.* Translated and edited by Dorothy Tuck McFarland and Wilhelmina Van Ness. Amherst: University of Massachusetts Press, 1987.

———. *Gravity and Grace.* Translated by Emma Crauford & Mario von der Ruhr. New York: Routledge & Co., 1999. http://www.mercaba.org/SANLUIS/Filosofia/autores/Contemporánea/W eil%20%28Simone%29/Gravity%20and%20Grace.pdf?hc_location=ufi).

———. *Intimations of Christianity among the Ancient Greeks.* New York: Routledge, 1998.

———. *Lectures on Philosophy.* Translated by Hugh Price. Cambridge: Cambridge University Press, 1978.

———. *Letter to a Priest.* Translated by Arthur F. Wills. New York: Putnam, 1954.

———. *Need for Roots: Prelude to a Declaration of Duties Toward Mankind.* Translated by Arthur Wills. Boston: Beacon Press, 1952.

———. *Notebooks* Vol 1 & 2. Translated by Arthur Wills. New York: G. P. Putnam's Sons, 1956.

———. *Oppression and Liberty.* Translated by Arthur Will & John Petrie. Amherst: University of Massachusetts Press, 1973.

———. *Seventy Letters.* Translated and edited by Richard Rees. London: Oxford University Press, 1965.

———. *Simone Weil: Oeuvres complètes*, Vol 1, Edited by André Devaux and Florence de Lussy. Paris: Gallimard, 1988.

———. *Oeuvres complètes,* vol. 5, no. 2. Edited by Robert Chenavier, André Devaux, and Florence de Lussy. Paris: Gallimard, 2013.

———. *Simone Weil: Oeuvres complètes,* Vol 6, no. 1. Edited by André Devaux, and Florence de Lussy. Paris: Gallimard, 1994.

———. *Simone Weil: Oeuvres complètes,* Vol 6, no. 3. Edited by André Devaux, and Florence de Lussy. Paris: Gallimard, 2002.

———. *Simone Weil: Oeuvres complètes,* Vol 6, no. 4. Edited by André Devaux, and Florence de Lussy. Paris: Gallimard, 2006.

———. *Simone Weil: Oeuvres complètes,* Vol 7, no. 1. Edited by Robert Chenavier, André Devaux, and Florence de Lussy. Paris: Gallimard, 2013.

———. *Simone Weil: Oeuvres.* Edited by Florence de Lussy. Paris: Quarto Gallimard, 1999.

———. *Simone Weil: Selected Writings.* Edited by Eric O. Springsted. New York: Orbis Books, 1998.

———. *The Simone Weil Reader.* Edited by George A. Panichas. New York: David McKay Co, Inc. 1977.

———. *Waiting for God.* Translated by Emma Craufurd. New York: HarperCollins Publishers, 2000.

Williams, Rowan. *Grace and Necessity: Reflections on Art and Love*. Harrisburg: Morehouse, 2005.

Winch, Peter. *Simone Weil: "The Just Balance."* Cambridge: Cambridge University Press, 1989.

Zambon, Francesco,."La douleur et le mal dans la doctrine cathare et chez Simone Weil." *Cahiers Simone Weil* 19, no. 1 (1996): 1 – 18.

FLANNERY O'CONNOR BIBLIOGRAPHY

Allen, Diogenes and Eric O. Springsted. *Spirit, Nature, and Community*. Albany: State University of New York Press, 1994.

Asals, Frederick. *Flannery O'Connor: The Imagination of Extremity*. Athens: University of Georgia Press, 1982.

Bakhtin, M. M. *Art and Answerability: Early Philosophical Essays*. Edited by Michael Holquist and Vadim Liapunov. Translated by Vadim Liapunov. Austin: University of Texas, Press, 1990.

———. *The Dialogic Imagination*. Edited by Michael Holquist. Translated by Caryl Emerson and Michael Holquist. Austin: University of Texas, Press, 1981.

———. *Toward a Philosophy of the Act*. University of Texas Press Slavic Series 1, Vol. 10. Austin: University of Texas Press, 1993.

Baldwin, James. "Unnameable Objects, Unspeakable Crimes." In *The White Problem in America*. Edited by Ebony Magazine. Chicago: Johnson Publishing Company, Inc, 1966: 173-181.

Blight, David W. *Race and Reunion: The Civil War in American Memory*. Cambridge: Belknap of Harvard University Press, 2001.

Brinkmeyer, Robert H. "A Closer Walk with Thee: Flannery O'Connor and Southern Fundamentalists." *The Southern Literary Journal* 18, no. 2 (Spring 1986): 3-13.

———. *The Art and Vision of Flannery O'Connor*. Baton Rouge: Louisiana State University Press, 1989.

Burns, Stuart L. "Flannery O'Connor's Literary Apprenticeship." *Renascence* 22, no. 1 (1969): 3-16.

Carey, Patrick. *An Immigrant Bishop: John England's Adaptation of Irish Catholicism to American Republicanism*. Yonkers, New York: U.S. Catholic Historical Society, 1982.

Cash, Jean. *Flannery O'Connor: A Life*. Knoxville: University of Tennessee, 2002.

Catherine of Genoa, Saint. *Purgation and Purgatory: the Spiritual Dialogue*.

Translated by Serge Hughes. Mahwah, NJ: Paulist Press, 1979.

Ciuba, Gary M. "Not His Son." In *Dark Faith: New Essays on Flannery O'Connor's the Violent Bear It Away*. Edited by Susan Srigley, 57-86. Notre Dame, IN: University of Notre Dame Press, 2012.

Coles, Robert. *Flannery O'Connor's South*. Baton Rouge: Lousiana State University Press, 1980.

Crawford, Nicholas. "An Africanist Impasse: Race, Return, and Revelation in the Short Fiction of Flannery O'Connor." *South Atlantic Review* 68, no. 2 (Spring 2003): 1-25.

Desmond, John. "The Lost Life of George Rayber." In *Dark Faith: New Essays on Flannery O'Connor's the Violent Bear It Away*. Edited by Susan Srigley, 35-56. Notre Dame, IN: University of Notre Dame Press, 2012.

Desmond, John F. *Risen Sons*. Athens: University of Georgia Press, 1987.

Edmondson, Henry T. *Return to Good and Evil: Flannery O'Connor's Response to Nihilism*. Lanham, MD: Lexington Books, 2002.

Edmunds, Susan. "Through a Glass Darkly: Visions of Integrated Community in Flannery O'Connor's 'Wise Blood'." *Contemporary Literature* 37, no. 4 (Winter 1996): 559-585.

Edwards, Mark J. "Justin's Logos and the Word of God." *Journal of Early Christian Studies* 3, no. 3 (1995): 261-280.

Eliot, T. S. "Little Gidding." In *Four Quartets*. New York: Harcourt Brace Jovanovich, 1971.

Foner, Eric. *The Fiery Trial*. New York: W.W. Norton, 2010.

Fredrickson, George M. *The Inner Civil War: Northern Intellectuals and the Crisis of the Union*. New York: Harper & Row, 1965.

Gallman, J. Matthew. *The Civil War Chronicle*. Edited by David Rubel and Russell Shorto. New York: Crown Publishers, 2000.

Gemes, Ken, "Nihilism and the Affirmation of Life: A Review and Dialogue with Bernard Reginster." *European Journal of Philosophy* 16:3 (2008): 459-466.

Gentry, Marshall Bruce. *Flannery O'Connor's Religion of the Grotesque*. Jackson: University of Mississippi Press, 1986.

Giannone, Richard. "Dark Night, Dark Faith: Hazel Motes, the Misfit, and Francis Marion Tarwater." In *Dark Faith: New Essays on Flannery O'Connor's The Violent Bear It Away*. Edited by Susan Srigley, 7-33. Notre Dame, IN: University of Notre Dame Press, 2012.

Gooch, Brad. *Flannery*. New York: Little, Brown, 2009.

Gordon, Sarah. *Flannery O'Connor: The Obedient Imagination*. Athens: University of Georgia Press, 2000.

Guardini, Romano. *Freedom, Grace, and Destiny: Three Chapters in the Interpretation of Existence.* Translated by John Murray, S. J. New York: Pantheon, 1961.

Guilday, Peter. *The Life and Times of John England 1786-1842*, Vol. 1 & 2. New York: The America Press, 1977.

Hawkes, John. "Flannery O'Connor's Devil." *The Sewanee Review* 70, no. 3 (Summer 1962): 396-407.

Hedda Ben-Bassat. "Flannery O'Connor's Double Vision." *Literature and Theology* 11, no. 2 (June 1, 1997): 185-199.

Hendin, Josephine. *The World of Flannery O'Connor.* Bloomington: Indiana University Press, 1970.

Heschel, Abraham. *The Prophets.* New York: Harper and Row, 1962.

Hudson, Deal W. and Matthew J. Mancini. *Understanding Maritain: Philosopher and Friend.* Macon, GA: Mercer University Press, 1987.

Huelin, Scott. "The Violent Bear it Away as Case Studies in Theological Ethics." In *Dark Faith: New Essays on Flannery O'Connor's the Violent Bear It Away.* Edited by Susan Srigley, 18-135. Notre Dame: University of Notre Dame Press, 2012.

Ingraffia, Brian D. *Postmodern Theory and Biblical Theology: Vanquishing God's Shadow.* Cambridge, GBR: Cambridge University Press, 1995.

Johansen, Ruthann Knechel. *The Narrative Secret of Flannery O'Connor: The Trickster as Interpreter.* Tuscaloosa: University of Alabama Press, 1994.

Jordan, Michael M. "Flannery O'Connor's Writing: A Guide for the Perplexed." *Modern Age* 47, no. 1 (Winter 2005): 48-57.

Jung, C. G. *Modern Man in Search of a Soul.* Translated by W. S. Dell and Cary F. Baynes. New York: Harcourt, Brace, 1957.

Kessler, Edward. *Flannery O'Connor and the Language of Apocalypse.* Princeton: Princeton University Press, 1986.

Kinney, Arthur F. *Flannery O'Connor's Library: Resources of Being.* Athens: University of Georgia Press, 1985.

Lake, Christina Bieber. *The Incarnational Art of Flannery O'Connor.* Macon, Georgia: Mercer University Press, 2005.

Levine, Bruce. *Half Slave and Half Free: The Roots of Civil War.* New York: Hill and Wang, 1992.

Lundin, Roger. *The Culture of Interpretation.* Grand Rapids: William B. Eerdmans, 1993.

Maritain, Jacques. *Art and Scholasticism and the Frontiers of Poetry.* Edited and translated by Joseph W. Evans. 2nd ed. 1974. Notre Dame, IN: University of Notre Dame Press, 1974.

———. *Creative Intuition in Art and Poetry*. New York: Pantheon, 1953.

McFarland, Dorothy Tuck. *Flannery O'Connor*. New York: Frederick Ungar, 1976.

McGurl, Mark. "Understanding Iowa: Flannery O'Connor, B.S., M.F.A." *American Literary History* 19 no. 2 (Summer 2007): 527-545.

McPherson, James M. *Battle Cry of Freedom*. New York: Oxford University Press, 1988.

Montgomery, Marion. *Why Flannery O'Connor Stayed Home*. LaSalle, IL: Sugden, 1981.

O'Connor, Flannery. *Flannery O'Connor: Collected Works*. New York: Library of America, 1988.

———. *Letters of Flannery O'Connor: The Habit of Being*. Edited by Sally Fitzgerald. New York: Vintage, 1979.

———. *Mystery and Manners*. Edited by Sally Fitzgerald and Robert Fitzgerald. New York: Farrar, Straus & Giroux, 1969.

Orvell, Miles. *Invisible Parade: The Fiction of Flannery O'Connor*. Philadelphia: Temple University Press, 1972.

Pegis, Anton C., editor. *Introduction to Saint Thomas Aquinas*. 2nd ed. New York: Modern Library, 1948.

Pfeifer, Michael J. "The Northern United States and the Genesis of Racial Lynching of African Americans in the Civil War." *The Journal of American History* 97, no. 3 (2010): 621-635.

Plato. *The Dialogues of Plato, Vol. II the Symposium*. Translated by R. E. Allen. New Haven: Yale University Press, 1991.

Reginster, Bernard. *The Affirmation of Life: Overcoming Nihilism*. Cambridge: Harvard University Press, 2009.

Ricoeur, Paul. *Figuring the Sacred: Religion, Narrative, and Imagination*. Edited by Mark I. Wallace. Translated by David Pellauer. Minneapolis: Fortress Press, 1995.

Rosen, Stanley. *Plato's Symposium*. 2nd ed. New Haven: Yale University Press, 1987.

Ruskin, John. *The Stones of Venice*. Vol. 3. London: Smith, Elder, 1853. https://hdl.handle.net/2027/yul.11365198_003_00, 112-165.

Scott, R. Neil. *Flannery O'Connor: An Annotated Reference Guide to Criticism*. Milledgeville, GA: Timberlane Books, 2002.

Sessions, William A. *A Prayer Journal*. New York: Farrar, Straus & Giroux,

2013.

Srigley, Susan, editor. *Dark Faith: New Essays on Flannery O'Connor's* The Violent Bear It Away. Notre Dame, IN: University of Notre Dame Press, 2012.

Srigley, Susan. *Flannery O'Connor's Sacramental Art.* Notre Dame, IN: University of Notre Dame Press, 2004.

Underhill, Evelyn. *Mysticism: A Study in the Nature and Development of Man's Spiritual Consciousness.* London: Methuen & Co. Ltd. ed. 1911.

Walker, Alice. "Beyond the Peacock: The Reconstruction of Flannery O'Connor." In *In Search of Our Mothers' Gardens.* New York: Harcourt Brace Jovanovich, 1983.

Wood, Ralph. *Flannery O'Connor and the Christ-Haunted South.* Grand Rapids, MI: William B. Eerdmans, 2004.

Zinn, Howard. *A People's History of the United States.* New York: Harper & Row Perennial, 1980.

Zuber, Leo J. and Carter W. Martin, editors. *The Presence of Grace and Other Book Reviews by Flannery O'Connor.* Athens: University of Georgia Press, 1983.

Index

For works by O'Connor and Weil, see under individual titles.

omnipotence, 34; restraint of, by God, 55
oppression, 9, 10, 36, 38, 76, 100; Weil on resistance to, 146–147
order of the world, 216, 230; and eternal and temporal, 204; as producing beauty, 135; relationships constituting, 147, 179
order of the world, love of. *See* love, of the world
"Our Father." *See* Lord's Prayer
pacifism, 10
pain, infliction of, 2
"Parker's Back," 49
Passion, 39, 55, 57, 127–128, 223, 229
path toward God, 130, 147; unbelief as one, 159
patience in writing and reading, 222
Pearce, Richard, 183n37
Péguy, Charles, 195n62
perception, 3
Percy, Walker, 32
perfection, striving for, 120, 176, 194, 208
Perrin, Father Joseph-Marie, x, xi, 10, 33–34, 40, 51, 69, 107, 138, 139–140, 151, 177, 206, 228; and friendship with Weil, 169–171
personality and impersonality of God, 222
Pétrement, Simone, 29, 69
Plato, 51–54, 62, 102, 107, 113–114
poverty, 109
power, 34, 109, 112, 132; as crushing, 205; countering, 172 ; desire for, 146, 218; as not truth, 193; refusal to exercise, 190, 205, 223–224
"The Power of Words," 209
prayer, 73–74, 86, 176, 179; as purifying evil, 184
pre-Christian faiths, 102–103
presence of God, 69, 70, 101, 103, 215
pressure to conform. *See* coercion, social
prophetic tradition, 49
punishment, legal, 177–78
purgatory, 131–134, 155–156

purity, 71, 72–74, 81, 177; of birth and death, 192; as infinite, 179
pursuit, of humans by God, 110, 112, 135, 142, 144, 157
racism, 100, 109, 119, 134, 217
Ransom, John Crowe, 23, 24, 26
rationality, 3, 33, 71, 78, 112, 113, 162, 184–186
reactions, 83–84
reading, Weil's concept of, 12, 38, 49, 65–66, 72, 77, 81–85, 91, 96, 127; just, 57, 128; misleading, 76–77, 100; situations and others, 205, 227
realists of distances, 208, 214–221
Reality ; divine, 44–47, 171, 186; facing, through grace, 191; mystery of, in O'Connor, 212; opposing form, 175; relationship with ineffable, 208; true, 175; of universe's beauty, in art, 221–222
reason, 59–60, 85
Reconstruction, 16, 17
redemption, 33, 47, 50, 64, 160, 216
"Red Virgin," viii, 7
reflection, 3, 7, 10, 56–57, 68, 76, 84–85, 138, 152, 208, 211, 227
"Reflections concerning the Causes of Liberty and Social Oppression," 9, 113
"Reflections on the Notion of Reading," 12
Reginster, Bernard, 50n37
relationships, human, 101, 204, 207
religious practice, love of, 104, 220
renunciation. *See* emptying
resistance, to aggression, 11
"The Responsibility of Writers," 211
"Revelation," 107, 109–110, 118, 121–122, 123–125, 132, 134
"The Right Use of School Studies for the Love of God," 68, 71, 72–74
"The River," 107, 160
Rousseau, Jean-Jacques, 8
rural to urban movement, 18
Ruskin, John, 216
sacramental order, 109
sacramental vision, 97, 100, 101, 104,